Praise for Th

As someone who has devoted many ye[...] world-view, I am thrilled to see dynamic ar [...] onathan Morrow stepping to the fore. *Think Ch,* [...] ible way, equips Christians young and old to engage the culture winsomely, intelligently, and confidently.

> Chuck Colson, founder of Prison Fellowship and
> the Colson Center for Christian Worldview

Think Christianly is a remarkable and important achievement. Written in an inter-active and accessible style, it covers an exhaustive range of topics. Indeed, I know of no other book like it in this regard, and it is now the first book to turn to for learning the specifics of how to think Christianly.

> J. P. Moreland, distinguished professor of philosophy
> at Talbot School of Theology, Biola University,
> and author of *The God Question*

We Christians love to lob rhetorical grenades at the surrounding culture from the safety of our holy huddle. What's far more difficult—and effective—is to engage the issues of our day with intelligence, moral clarity, and biblical wisdom. That's exactly what Jonathan Morrow does in *Think Christianly*. Morrow has a knack for elucidating complex ideas and applying timeless truth to contemporary topics. And he's done a fine job of gathering top Christian thinkers and presenting their ideas on issues ranging from the role of the Bible to bioethics. *Think Christianly* is a significant addition to the faith and culture conversation and a readable primer for church leaders. It belongs in the library of every thoughtful Christian.

> Drew Dyck, managing editor of *Leadership Journal* and
> author of *Generation Ex-Christian: Why Young Adults
> are Leaving the Faith ... and How to Bring Them Back*

In a time when truth is distorted and biblical teachings are misunderstood, our commitment to engaging culture must not be compromised. If we are to effec-tively stand for Christ, we must be equipped. *Think Christianly* is a much-needed resource as we seek to honor God in both what we believe and how we live.

> Jason Hayes, author, speaker, national young adult
> ministry specialist, LifeWay Christian Resources

In *Future Shock*, Alvin Toffler wrote, "Change is avalanching upon our heads and most people are grotesquely unprepared to cope with it." Toffler wrote in 1970, before personal computers, before the Internet, before 100 cable TV channels! The pace and depth of change has only increased several times over since 1970, and still the evangelical church is unprepared to deal with it. The ideas in Morrow's book offer hope that we can learn how to bring meaning to today's dangerous intersection of gospel and culture and view the intersection more as an opportunity than a threat.

Andy Seidel, executive director of the Howard Hendricks
Center for Christian Leadership at Dallas Theological Seminary

For several years, Jonathan Morrow has helped me see where my faith and what I read on blogs intersect. He has been an enormous help to me personally, and I'm glad to see that a broader audience can have access to his insights. If there is one thing I have learned as a pastor who works with twentysomethings, it's this: If we don't work hard to show how our message intersects with the issues our culture is facing, then they will assume it to be irrelevant. On a large part, that assumption has already been made. Read this book and help reverse that trend.

Jonathan Phipps, equipping pastor at Fellowship
Bible Church, Brentwood, Tennessee

As a pastor, I know my congregation is both beguiled and beleaguered by Western cultural realities. Neither unthinking assimilation nor unsociable rejection is a biblical option for us. The church must engage culture faithfully, but we must also be shown thoughtful ways how. I welcome any book that helps the church do this, and I am confident my friend Jonathan Morrow's will.

Cole Huffman, senior pastor of First Evangelical
Church, Memphis, Tennessee

think CHRISTIANLY

looking at the intersection of FAITH and CULTURE

Jonathan Morrow

ZONDERVAN.com/
AUTHOR**TRACKER**
follow your favorite authors

ZONDERVAN

Think Christianly
Copyright © 2011 by Jonathan Morrow

This title is also available as a Zondervan ebook. Visit www.zondervan.com/ebooks.

Requests for information should be addressed to:

Zondervan, *Grand Rapids, Michigan 49530*

Library of Congress Cataloging-in-Publication Data

Morrow, Jonathan, 1978.
    Think Christianly : looking at the intersection of faith and culture / Jonathan Morrow.
        p. cm.
    Includes bibliographical references.
    ISBN 978-0-310-32865-0 (softcover)
    1. Christianity and culture — Religious aspects — Christianity. I. Title.
BR115.C8M673 2011
261 – dc22   2011017193

Cover design: *Rob Monacelli*
Cover photography: *Gary Black / Masterfile*
Interior design: *Matthew Van Zomeren*

Printed in the United States of America

11 12 13 14 15 16 17 18 /DCI/ 22 21 20 19 18 17 16 15 14 13 12 11 10 9 8 7 6 5 4 3 2 1

For Austin and Sarah Beth.
May you grow to be courageous Christ-followers
who understand the times and take action.

CONTENTS

FOREWORD

THINK CHRISTIANLY is not about withdrawing into the Christian ghetto and escaping from the world around us; it's about discipleship—becoming the very persons God has called us to be and engaging in the mission that he has called us to share with him. And this means engagement with the world, not withdrawal. Engagement necessitates understanding the culture we live in and discerning whether the shaping influence of the culture is *for* or *against* us as we seek to follow Christ.

That is what this book is all about.

Through a fascinating combination of in-depth discussions about our contemporary culture and a series of interviews with major Christian figures, Jonathan Morrow has set the table for a thoughtful reflection about our call to engage the culture as God's people, both individually and collectively. Morrow challenges us to be cautious and avoid being molded by the world around us, but he is not simply advocating a sanctified "great escape" from the world. He is issuing a call to discerning engagement.

The interviews in this book have depth, as does the discussion of culture and its impact on our lives. There are a host of topics to chew on and meditate over: the heart, truth, pluralism, sex (of course!), media, injustice, science, bioethics, and the environment—just to name a few. How would God have us engage wisely, with respect to our calling as believers and those in our world who could benefit from knowing God? This book seeks to thoughtfully answer this question. As Morrow argues, everyone is a theologian. Theology is not only about what I think but about how I live. Since what I *think* impacts how I *live*, what I think and why I think that way really does matter.

Prepare to be challenged, inspired, instructed, and led into a life that honors God and engages the world as you learn to "think Christianly."

> Darrell L. Bock, research professor of New Testament studies and professor of spiritual development and culture at Dallas Theological Seminary, *New York Times* bestselling author, and corresponding editor-at-large for *Christianity Today*

PREFACE

A QUICK GLANCE at the contents pages will reveal that this is an ambitious book—tackling topics ranging from bioethics to spiritual formation, and apologetics to the environment—but don't worry, there is a method to my madness. Everywhere people go and everything they consume shape their beliefs about reality and form their worldview. We live at a time in which Christians are more consumer driven than truth driven. We have unknowingly become apprentices to the blind guides of hedonism, naturalism, and pragmatism, and this is eroding our ability and motivation to communicate and embody the Word of God in this generation.

I deeply believe that to become who God calls us to be, we must move in our thinking from isolation to integration. Christianity, if true, requires this. Our great danger is to so compartmentalize our Christian lives that one area does not impact, influence, or inform another, resulting in the equally tragic outcomes of fragmented lives and diminished impact for the kingdom of God.

Because I believe that God calls *all* of his followers to this kind of integration (Matthew 22:37; 1 Corinthians 10:31), my life's passion is to seek out top-notch Christian thinkers and practitioners from a variety of disciplines and learn from them in order to understand and integrate this knowledge into my own life so that I am prepared to thoughtfully engage today's unique cultural intersection. I am aiming at this—imperfectly, to be sure—and doing my best to pursue this kind of life by God's grace.

Think Christianly is the fruit of my journey so far. And if this book works as I intend, it will serve as a catalyst for your own thinking and creative expression of the principles within it. I do not claim to be or have the final word on such matters, but I do offer another word in the ongoing conversation between Christianity and culture. My prayer is that God will use these pages to refresh your vision for engaging your specific sphere of influence with the good news of the kingdom of God—and that you will be encouraged and equipped to do so.

As any author will tell you, this is probably the most difficult part of the book to write because there are so many people to thank. Let me begin by extending my gratitude to Ryan Pazdur and the whole team at Zondervan for embracing this project and then using their considerable and collective talents to shape it into what you hold in your hands.

Next I would like to thank several Christian leaders and pastors who from afar and in their own unique ways have significantly shaped my approach to ministry along the way — Chuck Swindoll, Tom Nelson, Dallas Willard, Andy Stanley, and John Ortberg. I also want to thank J. P. Moreland, Garry DeWeese, and the other visiting professors in my doctor of ministry program in engaging mind and culture at Talbot School of Theology. Thank you for your instruction, example, and investment in my life.

I have the pleasure of working with a diverse, devoted, and talented staff team at Fellowship Bible Church in Murfreesboro, Tennessee. I am grateful to our teaching pastors and elder team for the opportunity to experiment with unconventional approaches and methods to equip the body of Christ to engage our world and think Christianly about all of life. Thank you for believing in and sharpening me.

Over the years, numerous people have supported, prayed for, and contributed to www.thinkchristianly.org. Thank you, each of you! But I especially thank Austin Henderson, Chris McLaurin, Jeff Tudor, Brian Hogue, Jenny Rone, David Holt, and the Shoemakers for their specific investments.

This year, my wife and I celebrated ten years of marriage, and I am more aware than ever of God's providential hand in knitting our hearts together as partners in life and ministry. Mandi, I love you and am so grateful for your sacrificial love, laughter, and encouragement.

Finally, I am thankful to my Lord and Savior Jesus Christ, who is patiently teaching me how to live. All of our deepest longings, questions, and needs are met in him alone.

At Water's Edge,
Jonathan Morrow

WELCOME TO OUR INTERSECTION

There is no more crucial issue facing us today than the relationship of the church and the gospel to contemporary culture.

Tim Keller

THERE'S NO WAY TO ESCAPE IT; it is simply unavoidable—every generation of Christ-followers lives at the intersection of faith and culture. Here's a snapshot of ours.

- In November 2010, humanists launched a large "godless ad" campaign—especially targeting Christian fundamentalists (defined as "those who read the Bible literally") by contrasting "horrific material" in the Bible that apparently promotes sexism and violence with "more compassionate quotes from humanist thinkers."[1]
- On the two hundredth anniversary of his birth, Charles Darwin's life casts a long shadow of influence as questions of origins, purpose, science, and faith are debated more vigorously than ever. *Are belief in God and Darwin compatible, or are they more like oil and water? Has science made belief in God unnecessary?*
- Islam continues to command a lot of attention in our culture. And while there are many voices claiming to define what Islam is and is not, many wonder who really speaks for Muslims. *And do Muslims and Christians worship the same God?*

- The same-sex marriage debate rages on after Judge Vaughn Walker overturned California's 2008 constitutional ban on gay marriage (Proposition 8). *How can Christians make the case for marriage as between one man and one woman for a lifetime in a culture that thinks Christians are backward, bigoted, and intolerant?*
- Polls indicate a growing undercurrent of unbelief in America and an unprecedented religious mobility. *Newsweek* ran a cover story ("The End of Christian America") that reported, "The number of Americans who claim no religious affiliation has nearly doubled since 1990, rising from 8 to 15 percent."[2] Harvard sociologist Robert Putnam's book *American Grace* reveals that roughly one-third of Americans have switched religions at some point in their lives.[3] *Is it reasonable to believe that Christianity is actually true anymore?*
- David Kinnaman and Gabe Lyons write, "Millions of young outsiders are mentally and emotionally disengaging from Christianity. The nation's population is increasingly resistant to Christianity, especially to the theologically conservative expressions of that faith."[4] *Why is the next generation not embracing the Christianity of their parents?*

Welcome to our intersection. And this is just a sampling of the issues, questions, and challenges we face every day. Are you ready to confidently engage these cultural moments? And if you are a pastor or leader, are the people you serve prepared?

While every generation encounters intersections, every intersection is not the same. In other words, the particular challenges and opportunities that confronted Paul, Tertullian, Augustine, Aquinas, Luther, Wesley, Calvin, G. K. Chesterton, and C. S. Lewis are not the ones you and I face today. And though we can (and should!) be students of how they responded and engaged, we live in different times.

Now we could read these words and think, "Of course we do; isn't that obvious?" And yet we often approach our intersection like we always have, assuming that nothing has really changed. After all, there is nothing new under the sun, right? This isn't good. It is imperative for the health and effectiveness of the church that each generation of Christians — and especially its leaders — understands that we occupy a unique historical moment. Change is difficult to see while you are in the thick of it. So in order to gain some much-needed perspective, sometimes we need to step back and look at the bigger picture. Consider just how profoundly different our world is today from even fifteen years ago (take a minute to read over this chart slowly).

1995	2010
No Google	Google
Marriage = one man and one woman	Gay marriage now legal in six states
Terrorism is what happens somewhere else	A post-9/11 world
Home movies	YouTube (every minute, twenty-plus hours of video are uploaded)
Majority of Americans are pro-choice (56%)	Majority of Americans are pro-life (51%)
Seinfeld is the most popular show on TV	100 million votes—by text/calls in span of four hours—crowned 2009 American Idol
CDs and cell phones	iPods, iPhones, and Droids
Nation still reels from the Rodney King beating / LA race riots	America elects first black president in 2008
Pre-genetic health care	Human genome completely mapped in 2003. Now applied to therapy, treatment, and enhancement
Networking = time + human contact	Are *you* on Facebook?
Traditional news outlets control majority of information (that is, news is centralized)	News is now largely decentralized; blogs drive cultural conversation (for example, the impact on past two presidential elections)

LOCAL INTERSECTIONS ARE A THING OF THE PAST

That list shows just a fraction of the change that has occurred. Who knew that a funny little word like Google would play such a big role in our culture's seismic shift from local to global? Due in large part to the Internet and other media, people have 24/7 access to images, ideas, and information—all of which shape their lives and lead them either toward God and community or self-centeredness and isolation. Let's think about what this new reality means for the people in the church today:

A student can get up from the dinner table and in seconds be face-to-face with all the pain, poverty, and suffering in the world on her laptop and wonder why nothing is ever said about this on a Sunday morning. Does God not care? Does Christianity have nothing to say or offer?

A mom can prop her feet up and watch TV after a long and thankless day of giving her life away to her kids and discover that "the church" (which isn't a big fan of women, it seems from this show) has covered up missing gospels and suppressed "alternative portraits" of who Jesus really is—all in high-definition and presented by impressive Ivy League scholars. She wonders if her pastor knows about this. Has she based her life on a fairy tale?

A dad has real doubts about Christianity. While reading the *New York Times* online, he discovers that "the missing link" has been found. This is yet another scientific discovery that seems to make God irrelevant. He has always considered himself a rational person, but science is a dirty word to most people in his church. Is he just supposed to ignore the evidence and muster up more faith?

A curious, tech-savvy twelve-year-old can find out about any religion in the world from her iPhone. She wonders to herself, "How do I know which one is true? [If any of them are true at all.] If I grew up in India, wouldn't I have been a Hindu?"

A young professional is tired of being a slave to guilt, shame, impression management, and anxiety. Disillusioned by the empty promises of "finding the god within through positive thinking," he wonders if real spiritual transformation and hope are possible. Is there someone with the knowledge and authority to teach us how to live?

A married couple struggles through the pain and confusion of infertility while wrestling with which technologies are permissible to use to have children. Some tell them they shouldn't try to "play God"; others remind them to have more faith. But no one seems to be able to help them navigate these difficult choices from a biblical perspective.

This is where people live. These real-life scenarios need to influence how Christians are encouraged, taught, and equipped in the church today. These examples also remind us that we live in a global society. It no longer matters whether someone lives in small-town America or in New York City; both have equal access to a mind-boggling amount of ideas and information. This is no time for business as usual. These are the kinds of questions that lead to cultural moments, places where faith and culture intersect. That is what this book is all about.

As society strains under the collective weight of pluralism and secularism and is deeply divided along worldview lines (not just political or socioeconomic ones), we need to think Christianly about all of life and seize the opportunities we have as Everyday Ambassadors to speak and embody the eternal kind of life Jesus offers to our culture. Tragically, many of these cultural moments pass us by unclaimed—either because we don't notice them or haven't adequately prepared ourselves to engage them.

So, like the sons of Issachar, who "understood the times and knew what Israel should do" (1 Chronicles 12:32), it is critical for us to understand the state of our culture and of the church at the dawn of the twenty-first century. Gaining clarity on what we face—looking both ways at our intersection—will help us intelligently engage.

OUT THERE IS ALREADY IN HERE

I have thought a lot about this. I've read books, listened to interviews, examined surveys and statistics, and made personal observations in various conversations and ministry settings. The cumulative effect of all this input is leading me to a conclusion that changes the way that I think about ministry in the church today. For a long time, the prevailing wisdom has been that what goes on outside the church is not occurring inside the church. The world is out there, and we are in here. We are in a safe bubble of sorts, insulated from the pagan perceptions and practices of everyone else. In more extreme forms, this line of reasoning explains why some churches have adopted the unbiblical and unhelpful "barricade, and pray for the rapture" approach to ministry.

Here is the conclusion I am more convinced of than ever: Due to the unprecedented influence and availability of constant media (for example, TV, Internet, smart phones, music, movies, news, etc.), the thoughts, attitudes, perceptions, convictions, values, and lifestyles of those inside the church are rapidly growing indistinguishable from the thoughts, attitudes, perceptions, convictions, values, and lifestyles of those outside the church. Or to put it bluntly, "Out there is already in here." If this assessment is accurate, and the data is mounting that it is, then this fact ought to affect how Christian leaders preach, teach, establish programs, and lead. If we assume a certain level of Christian maturity in thinking and spiritual health that simply is not present in our ministry context, then it is time to stop and reevaluate. To be sure, there are pockets of mature Christians within our various ministries who get it, but generally speaking, my conviction is that the worldview out there is the worldview in here. To see this, let's briefly examine three groups: teenagers, emerging adults, and adults.

THE RELIGIOUS LIVES OF AMERICAN TEENAGERS

There are approximately 33 million teenagers in America today. In 2005, the National Study of Youth and Religion undertook the largest and most detailed study of teenagers and religion that has ever been done. The findings of this study were published in *Soul Searching* by Christian Smith and Melinda Denton. Basically, American teenagers break out into thirds: 33 percent are regularly religious, another 33 percent are sporadically religious, and the final 34 percent are religiously disconnected. The spectrum of religions covered the whole gamut.

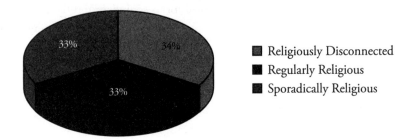

Researchers found that students were remarkably inarticulate about their faith. They could talk with precision and detail about pop culture, social media, and other topics, but when it came to talking about the basic tenets of their faith — what they actually believed — they were not able to say much at all.

One theme, however, did emerge with great clarity. The dominant religion of today's American teenager is Moralistic Therapeutic Deism (MTD), a concept developed by Smith and Denton. Not Protestantism, Catholicism, Islam, Judaism, or Buddhism. Regardless of their *professed* religion, here is what God looks like to the majority of American teenagers (and again this sample includes those in conservative Protestant and evangelical churches):[5]

- A God exists who created and orders the world and watches over human life on earth.
- God wants people to be good, nice, and fair to each other, as taught in the Bible and by most world religions.
- The central goal of life is to be happy and to feel good about oneself.
- God does not need to be particularly involved in one's life, except when God is needed to resolve a problem.
- Good people go to heaven when they die.

God is sort of a nebulous combination of divine butler and cosmic therapist. Smith summarized the approach to life that flows out of this belief system as "be nice and call on God if you need him."[6] It should go without saying that it is impossible to navigate the pressures and challenges of adolescent or adult life with such a feeble worldview. More importantly, this is hardly the vision for life that Jesus offers his would-be followers.

And then there is the growing trend that teenagers seem to be graduating from God. A good number of high school students either will walk away from their Christian faith after high school or simply drift away from a faith they had never actually embraced to begin with.[7] The reasons are always complex and person-specific, but two prominent factors emerge from the research. First, as Chap Clark has documented in *Hurt: Inside the World of Today's Teenagers*, teenagers are relationally hurting and disconnected. They experience isolation and are often quarantined from the adult relationships they so desperately need (his term is "systemic abandonment"). Second, teenagers have not been grounded in a robust Christian worldview and taught *how* to think and arrive at truth. They are also not being given safe opportunities to doubt and honestly explore why they believe what they believe. Smith and Denton document that 32 percent of the teenagers who walked away from God did so because of intellectual skepticism.[8] "University-level questions" are puncturing their "Sunday school-level faith."[9] We will explore how we can reverse this trend in chapter 3.

THE CONFUSING WORLD OF EMERGING ADULTS

Given the rapid changes in the landscape of American industry and life, a new social category now exists: "emerging adults." Just as adolescence came on the scene with modernization and the industrial revolution, so this group of eighteen- to twenty-nine-year-olds is caught in a world of perpetual change. Along with more time for education, better technology, the explosion of social media, and experimentation with various jobs, emerging adults are waiting longer to settle down, get married, have kids, and figure out what they want their lives to really be about and who they want to be when they grow up.

In *Souls in Transition*, Christian Smith applied to the religious lives of this group the same rigorous sociological analysis found in *Soul Searching*. Here is how emerging adults break out into general categories:

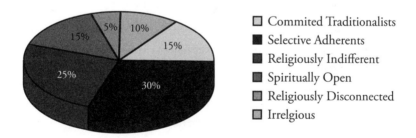

- 15 percent are what Smith calls *committed traditionalists*, those emerging adults who have a strong religious faith that they actively practice and for which they can articulate core beliefs.
- 30 percent are *selective adherents*, those who pick and choose when it comes to certain aspects of their faith.
- 25 percent are *religiously indifferent*, neither practicing nor opposing religion.
- 15 percent are *spiritually open* and have at least a mild interest in religious matters.

- 5 percent, the *religiously disconnected*, aren't really exposed to or connected with religious people, ideas, or organizations.
- 10 percent are *irreligious*, those who are skeptical and critical of religion and who reject and argue against personal faith.[10]

Five years after the *Soul Searching* study, Moralistic Therapeutic Deism is alive and well among emerging adults. Admittedly, there are some differences manifested in increasing diversity of personal expressions, and the irreligious have become more outspoken with age, but the basic vague contours of their worldview—developed as teenagers—still persist.[11] Moreover, a Barna study determined that "young adults rarely possess a biblical worldview" and that "less than one-half of one percent of adults in the Mosaic generation—that is, those aged 18 to 23—have a biblical worldview."[12] Just let the implications of that percentage sink in for a minute.

The Barna Group's assessment is consistent with and corroborated by the conclusions of Christian Smith. Take note of his sobering and heartbreaking conclusion:

> Very many emerging adults simply don't know how to think about things, what is right, what is deserving for them to devote their lives to. On such matters, they are often simply paralyzed, wishing they could be more definite, wanting to move forward, but simply not knowing how they might possibly know anything worthy of conviction and dedication. Instead, very many emerging adults exist in a state of basic indecision, confusion, and fuzziness. The world they have inherited, as best they can make sense of it, has told them that real knowledge is impossible and genuine values are illusions.[13]

A twin riptide of skepticism and relativism exists in American society today that is very difficult to break free from, and many young people have exhausted themselves trying to—usually standing alone. On a personal note, these aren't just statistics to me. Right now, I can picture the face of one emerging adult I know who is on the verge of walking away from God—and everything and everyone he has known and loved—because he no longer believes.

THE CONSUMER-DRIVEN WORLD OF ADULTS

Before we are too hard on the teenagers and emerging adults, we need to take a long, hard look in the mirror. Researchers are concluding that the next generation *becomes* what we are. "In most cases teenage religion and spirituality in the United States are much better understood as largely reflecting the world of adult religion, especially parental religion, and are in strong continuity with it."[14] The simple fact is that core Christian beliefs, that is, a biblical worldview, are not guiding the vast majority of adult Christians. The numbers have not changed over the past thirteen years (for example, four national surveys in 1995, 2000, 2005, 2009). Only

9 percent of all American adults have a biblical worldview. And to be honest, these next six statements, which define a "biblical worldview," are a thin substitute for the robustness of historic Christianity.

1. Absolute moral truth exists.
2. The Bible is totally accurate in all of the principles it teaches.
3. Satan is considered to be a real being or force, not merely symbolic.
4. A person cannot earn his or her way into heaven by trying to be good or do good works.
5. Jesus Christ lived a sinless life on earth.
6. God is the all-knowing, all-powerful creator of the world, and God still rules the universe today.

When narrowing the focus, the news doesn't get much better. Only 19 percent of professing "born again" Christians hold to a biblical worldview (a respondent would have had to agree that "they have made a personal commitment to Jesus Christ that is still important in their life" and that "they believe they will go to heaven when they die because they have confessed their sins and have accepted Jesus Christ as their Savior").[15]

So where on earth, you ask, would teenagers and emerging adults get the idea that God is a cosmic butler and therapist? Well, when we look closely at how approximately 150 million adult "casual Christians" are approaching life, the answer emerges:

> Because they are actively seeking a pleasant and comfortable life, they concentrate on those elements of the Christian faith that fit within those parameters. Rather than allowing the Christian faith to shape their minds and hearts, they have chosen to fit Christianity within the box they have created for it. The outcome is a warm, fuzzy feeling about their faith of choice because it has been redefined according to their desires.[16]

Resonating with the fuzziness that the emerging adults feel, Barna observes, "Although most people own a Bible and know some of its content, our research found that most Americans have little idea how to form a unified and meaningful response to the challenges and opportunities of life."[17]

Perhaps churches need to hit Reset and start at the beginning: What do Christians believe? Why do they believe it? Why does it matter?

BUT AT LEAST CHRISTIANS STILL BELIEVE IN THE EXCLUSIVITY OF JESUS, RIGHT?

Jesus did not shy away from making culturally unpopular statements: "I am the way and the truth and the life. No one comes to the Father except through me"

(John 14:6). Among other things, Christianity teaches the exclusivity and uniqueness of Jesus (cf. Acts 4:12; 1 Timothy 2:5). But according to a Pew Forum on Religion and Public Life study (2009) based on interviews with 35,000 adults and out of a sample size of 9,472 evangelicals, a startling 57 percent of evangelical adults agreed with the statement "Many religions can lead to eternal life." (Interestingly, 56 percent of American Muslims answered the same way, which underscores the powerful undercurrent of religious relativism.) This percentage is also consistent with what emerging unchurched adults believed—58 percent agreed with the statement "The God of the Bible is no different from the gods or spiritual beings depicted by world religions such as Islam, Hinduism, Buddhism, etc."[18]

The Pew study also revealed that 53 percent of evangelicals affirmed the following statement: "There is more than one true way to interpret the teachings of my religion."[19] Notice this doesn't say there are different ways of interpreting various Christian teachings or biblical passages (which is why so many denominations exist) but rather that there is "more than one *true* way to interpret" them. This is a significant difference! It appears that the "true for you but not for me" mentality is alive and well within evangelical churches today.

REJECTING "SUNDAY MORNING ONLY" CHRISTIANITY

As we try to better understand our intersection, what I have labored to show is that we have a systemic problem that cuts across generations. Of course, no survey is perfect, and statistical analysis is certainly not infallible. And the eternal kind of life to which Jesus invites us involves more than just affirming certain propositions on a survey. But it is also true that what people *really* believe determines how they live. These studies provide reasonable and responsibly gathered evidence that we must heed. If these statistics are even in the ballpark, then as Christian leaders we have some serious work ahead of us. In light of this, it would be hard to dispute William Lane Craig's candid assessment that "our churches are filled with people who are spiritually born again but who still think like non-Christians."[20]

But why? How did this happen? I think the short answer is that over time, we have slipped into a "Sunday morning only" Christianity (for a longer answer, see appendix 2). For far too long, we have relegated Christianity to the privatized feeling of faith—not much more than religious wishful thinking—where genuine moral and spiritual knowledge is unimportant and unattainable. Feelings, not truth, reign supreme. In her outstanding book *Total Truth*, Nancy Pearcey makes this penetrating observation:

> Our lives are often fractured and fragmented, with our faith firmly locked into the private realm of the church and family, where it rarely has a chance to inform our life and work in the public realm. The aura of worship dissipates after Sunday, and we unconsciously absorb secular attitudes the rest of the

week. We inhabit two separate "worlds," navigating a sharp divide between our religious life and ordinary life."[21]

A church of "Sunday morning only" Christians will not have the influence that we are called to have and our world desperately needs.

LIVING IN REALITY

Not only do the majority of teenagers, emerging adults, and adult Christians not hold to a biblical worldview, but those outside the church do not think that the majority of Christians live out the supposed virtues of Christianity. As you can see in this chart, Christians have left a pretty bad taste in the mouths of sixteen- to twenty-nine-year-olds not associated or involved with the church (this group will only become *more* influential in American society).[22] Moreover, nearly half of non-churchgoers between the ages of twenty and twenty-nine agreed with the statement "Christians get on my nerves."[23]

Perception of Christianity	Outsiders (16 to 29)
Antihomosexual	91%
Judgmental	87%
Hypocritical	85%
Sheltered	78%
Too political	75%
Proselytizers	70%

So what does this mean? It means we have hard work ahead of us in order to change the way Christians are perceived. It doesn't mean we do this by abandoning truth or ceasing to be distinctively Christian, but it does signal our need to change the tone of the cultural conversation.

We are faced with an uncomfortable truth: the majority of Christians in America are not thinking or living like followers of Jesus Christ ought to. Now I am not an alarmist, and I'm also not trying to heap guilt on anyone; neither approach is helpful. But the one thing we can't do is avoid the implications of this research. Out there is *already* in here. We must live in reality before we can change it. It does no one any good to sanitize these findings, explain away these perceptions, or pretend they are not present in our particular ministry context. *They are.*

Good preaching *alone* will not get the job done (it is necessary for a healthy church, but not sufficient). Our culture is increasingly unwilling to hear anything the church has to say. Engaging our culture will require a change in thinking. We must move beyond Sunday morning Christianity and learn how to speak in a compassionate, winsome, and informed voice to our culture, starting with the questions *they* are asking. As Everyday Ambassadors, we build bridges between cultural moments and the gospel of the kingdom.

Let's be honest; this task is as daunting as it is sobering. But I am optimistic because I am confident that by embracing a mind-set of engagement and doing the hard work necessary, we can make a difference for the kingdom and cooperate with the exciting work God is doing in the world today.

WHAT'S NEXT

In part 1, we will continue to gain understanding of the intersection of Christianity and culture by clearly defining culture and exploring our biblical responsibility to engage it—an essential part of that is equipping the next generation. In part 2, we will unpack the kind of preparation we need to do so that we can engage well. This will involve thinking Christianly—understanding and living *all* of life from God's perspective—so that we can confidently engage from a foundation of knowledge as we are becoming more like the Jesus the world needs.[24] Part 3 will equip us with cutting-edge insight on some of the key issues about which our culture is seeking answers and input. We will look at everything from the historical Jesus and genetic engineering to God's design for sexuality and social justice. Along the way, be sure to check out the insightful interviews with influential Christian leaders and scholars about engaging various aspects of culture. And the "Resources for Engaging Your Intersection" box at the end of each chapter will suggest helpful books, blogs, websites, and DVDs to increase your cultural IQ and guide you as you implement a culture of engagement within your unique ministry context. Half the battle is knowing where to start.

If you are still up for it, let's get to it! Though, to be honest, reading this book (and for me writing it) will be the easy part, because when we put the book down, we still have the challenging task of implementing it *where we live.*

Of course, we could just do nothing, but what fun would that be? God's power and presence are available, and our world is crackling with possibility. Let's *engage.*

RESOURCES FOR ENGAGING YOUR INTERSECTION

Books

- *Soul Searching: The Religious and Spiritual Lives of American Teenagers* by Christian Smith with Melinda Denton
- *Souls in Transition: The Religious and Spiritual Lives of Emerging Adults* by Christian Smith with Patricia Snell
- *Generation Ex-Christian: Why Young Adults Are Leaving the Faith ... and How to Bring Them Back* by Drew Dyck
- *unChristian: What a New Generation Really Thinks about Christianity — and Why It Matters* by David Kinnaman and Gabe Lyons
- *American Grace: How Religion Divides and Unites Us* by Robert Putnam and David Campbell
- *Total Truth: Liberating Christianity from Its Cultural Captivity* by Nancy Pearcey

Websites and DVDs

- www.youthandreligion.org – National Study for Youth and Religion
- www.pewforum.org – The Pew Forum for Religion and Public Life
- www.barna.org – Barna Group
- www.edstetzer.com – LifeWay Research Blog
- *Soul Searching*, DVD
- *They Like Jesus But Not the Church*, DVD

part one

UNDERSTANDING OUR INTERSECTION

chapter one

CULTURE MATTERS

Beyond the pages of the New Testament even a casual history of the church discloses an incredible diversity of situations in which Christians have found themselves: persecuted and reigning, isolated and dominant, ignorant and well educated, highly distinguishable from the culture and virtually indifferentiable from it, impoverished and wealthy, evangelistically zealous and evangelistically dormant, social reformers and supportive of the social status quo, hungry for heaven and hoping it won't arrive too soon. All of these polarized possibilities reflect diverse cultural self-understanding. Inevitably, in most generations Christians have pondered what their attitudes ought to be.

D. A. Carson, *Christ and Culture Revisited*

WHEN SPEAKING ON THE TOPIC of faith and culture, I usually begin with a pop quiz. I ask people to turn to their neighbor and see if they can come up with a definition of culture, and then decide whether Christians should be for or against it. As you can probably guess, the responses are all over the map. (By the way, how would you answer those two questions?)

Why is this? Well, to be honest, *culture* may be one of the hardest words to define in the English language because it is used in many different ways. But if we don't have a clear picture of what culture is, then it becomes extremely difficult to determine what Christianity's relationship to it *ought* to be. In short, we need a robust theology and philosophy of culture that we can understand and then communicate to those we lead. In this chapter, I want to unpack and clarify some concepts that will be essential to our biblical case for engaging culture in the next chapter.

WHAT IS CULTURE?

Culture is as old as humankind is, but the word derives from the Latin *cultura* and *colere*, which describe the tending or cultivating of something, typically soil and livestock. In the eighteenth century, it would come to apply to the cultivation of ideas (education) and customs (manners). Then there are sociological and anthropological definitions, which are helpful in their own way but involve hard-to-remember phrases such as "transmitted and inherited patterns and symbols."

Theologian Kevin Vanhoozer suggests, "Culture is the environment and atmosphere in which we live and breathe with others." That's good. Philosopher Garry DeWeese helpfully unpacks this concept a bit more by defining culture as a "shared system of stories and symbols, beliefs and values, traditions and practices, and the media of communication that unite a people synchronically (at a given time) and diachronically (through history)."[1] The most transferable way I have found to summarize what culture is comes from Andy Crouch: "Culture is what people make of the world." In other words, people interact and organize while taking all the raw materials of planet Earth and doing something with them. This covers everything from microchips to BBQ, computers to cathedrals, music composition to the development of law and government, city planning to education, and entertainment to Facebook. How people communicate, work, travel, order their familial and societal lives, and create technology are all artifacts of culture. And since Christians are people too, they are necessarily involved in the creation of culture. There is no such thing as a culture-free Christianity. So we clearly can't be against culture *in this sense* because Christians, as part of humanity, were given the mandate (in Genesis 1:27 – 28) to make something of the world (more on this later).

WHAT IS THE WORLD?

If we are not to be against culture per se, what are Christians opposed to? The biblical answer is that Christians are to oppose the "world system" and its influence or manifestations in what people make of the world. This is a crucial distinction — especially when it comes to how the church is perceived in the public square. Here are just some of the things we learn about the world in the New Testament:[2]

- The whole world lies in the power of the evil one (1 John 5:19).
- Christians are not to love the world (1 John 2:15).
- Christians are called to be in but not of the world (John 17:11 – 16).
- Those who make themselves friends of the world make themselves enemies of God (James 4:4).
- Christians are not to be conformed to the ideas and patterns generated by the world (Romans 12:2).

Notice the problem that immediately arises if Christians conflate *world* in this biblical-theological sense and *culture.* The unfortunate and unbiblical implication is that you end up with some Christians thinking they are being obedient to God by opposing all of the time what people make of the world. This is not good and not our calling.

World is used a variety of ways in the New Testament and has several different nuances determined by the context.[3] What I want to focus on is its usage in this sense: the realm of sin and hostility toward God and his kingdom — which includes Satan, demons, and principalities and powers — that manifests itself in what people make of the world. But as we dig a little deeper, we learn that inherent within the theological category of *world* are idea systems or worldviews that are raised up against the knowledge of God. In practical terms, the world is manifested in any idea, idea system, or image that leads people away from life with God and toward being consumed with themselves. And it is interaction with these ideas and images that is one of the primary forms of spiritual warfare for the Christ-follower. Paul is clear about this:

> For though we walk in the flesh, we do not war according to the flesh, for the weapons of our warfare are not of the flesh, but divinely powerful for the destruction of fortresses. We are destroying speculations and every lofty thing raised up against the knowledge of God [that is, any ideas, thoughts, arguments, and reasoning hostile to life with God], and we are taking every thought captive to the obedience of Christ.
>
> 2 Corinthians 10:3–5 NASB

In Paul's immediate context, this had to do with certain misconceptions about his apostleship that were undermining his effectiveness in spreading the gospel (notice Paul is trying to change certain ideas people have about him and thus his message). But the pattern of meaning contained in this passage could also be applied and invoked in regard to the naturalism, postmodernism, and hedonism of our day, which I'll consider more carefully shortly.

Elsewhere Paul makes this connection: "For our struggle is not against flesh and blood, but against the rulers, against the powers, *against the world forces* of this darkness, against the spiritual forces of wickedness in the heavenly places" (Ephesians 6:12 NASB, emphasis added). There is an unseen battle raging all around us.

We could go on, but enough has been said to show that culture and world are not the same thing. Culture is simply what people make of the physical stuff on our planet as they relate to one another. The world, on the other hand, is hostile to life with God and his kingdom. So while Christians can't help but be involved in the culture-making process, we must never become friendly toward the world. In the next chapter, I will lay out some principles that will help guide us in the challenging task of discernment, critique, and engagement.

THE POWER OF IDEAS

But here's the rub: the world's leader is very smart. In fact, he has schemes (2 Corinthians 2:11; cf. Ephesians 6:11) and is always looking to steal, kill, and destroy and to lead people away from life with God (John 10:10). He is prowling around like a roaring lion looking for someone to devour (1 Peter 5:8). As I will develop below, Satan embeds "pop culture" with ideas and images that are hostile to the things of God. Interestingly, polls show that many Christians don't even think Satan is real, a belief that gives him quite the strategic advantage. A 2009 Barna poll reveals that "four out of ten Christians (40 percent) strongly agree that Satan 'is not a living being but is a symbol of evil.' An additional two out of ten Christians (19 percent) said they 'agree somewhat' with that perspective."[4]

In his excellent book *Renovation of the Heart*, Dallas Willard offers keen insight: "These higher-level powers and forces are spiritual agencies that work with—constantly try to implement and support—the idea systems of evil. These systems are their main tool for dominating humanity."[5] Let me quickly note that overt and explicit demonic manifestations are real.[6] But which do you think is ultimately more destructive—an insidious idea or a demon manifesting itself? We need only look at the sexual revolution to see what havoc can be caused when people become "liberated" in their understanding and expression of sexuality. Or at the shrapnel that penetrated the souls of parents and children by the idea of "no-fault divorce" in America in 1970.

Ideas have always been and continue to be our Enemy's favorite method of undermining the work of God. Willard observes concerning the garden of Eden: "Ideas and images are ... the primary focus of Satan's efforts to defeat God's purposes with and for humankind. When we are subject to his chosen ideas and images, he can take a nap or a holiday. Thus when he undertook to draw Eve away from God, he did not hit her with a stick, but with an idea. It was with the idea that God could not be trusted and that she must act on her own to secure her own well-being."[7] The battle is for the mind. Unfortunately, many Christians have unknowingly subjected themselves to ideas that lead away from the life with God they so deeply desire.

THE RELATIONSHIP BETWEEN THE WORLD AND POP CULTURE

Now that we have looked at culture and the world, we are ready to see where pop culture fits into our discussion. And there is hardly a more appropriate place to get our definition than from Wikipedia. Pop culture "is the totality of ideas, perspectives, attitudes ... images and other phenomena that are deemed preferred per an informal consensus within the mainstream of a given culture ... Heavily influenced by mass media, this collection of ideas permeates the everyday lives of the society."[8] So if culture is what people make of the world, then pop culture is what people make of the world that *most* people seem to like, resonate with, embrace, and consume.

Technology, media, marketing, and money are the collective engine that drives pop culture, which is then encoded with certain ideas and images (I'll say more about media in chapter 14). It is here that the influence of the world can be seen most vividly. By way of illustration, take Hulu's 2009 Super Bowl commercial. I was floored by how shamelessly direct it was:

> **Alec Baldwin:** Hello, earth. I'm Alec Baldwin, TV star. You know they say TV will rot your brain? That's absurd. TV only softens the brain like a ripe banana. To take it all the way, we've created Hulu. Hulu beams TV directly to your portable computing devices, giving you more of the cerebral, gelatinizing shows you want anytime, anywhere, for free.
> **TV Show:** I only had them because I want you alone.
> **Alec Baldwin:** Mmm. Mushy, mush. And the best part is there is nothing you can do to stop it. I mean what you going to do? Turn off your TV and your computer? Once your brain is reduced to a cottage cheese-like mush, we'll scoop them out with a melon baller and gobble them right on up. Oooops, I think I'm drooling a little. Because we're aliens, and that's how we roll.
> **Narrator:** Hulu, an evil plot to destroy the world. Enjoy.[9]

I laughed too. But this really isn't funny when you consider that most Americans and most born-again Christians do not hold to even a basic Christian worldview. Yes, universities still teach students. But they are not really the primary professors anymore. The news media, Facebook, YouTube, iTunes, blogs, TV shows, satirical news (for example, *The Daily Show* and *The Colbert Report*), and movies are the most influential professors. Embedded in all of these are images and ideas. Images are extremely powerful because they bypass rational thought and make direct impressions on the mind. And they are what drive culture today. Moreover, consumption of media is virtually the same inside and outside the church. This consumption then leads to the formation of certain universal background beliefs, or what sociologists call "plausibility structures." In other words, people's mental defaults are set regarding truth, Jesus, the Bible, religion, ethics, and knowledge (just to name a few) — and they don't even know it.

Unfortunately, many of the ideas and images we encounter today are in direct opposition to the eternal kind of life that God offers. In fact, they make life in God's reality difficult indeed, and we need to factor this in as we think about cultural engagement and equipping people within the church. Pop culture often reinforces false worldviews, thus making it harder for people to escape from them. It would be hard to refute religion editor Phyllis Tickle's observation that "more theology is conveyed in and retained from one hour of popular television than from all the sermons that are also delivered on any given weekend in America's synagogues, churches, and mosques."[10] And when you consider that the average American watches about 1,812 hours (75.5 days!) of television each year, that is a lot of influence.[11] This observation also underscores our earlier conclusion that out there is already in here.

RESISTING THE SPIRIT OF THE WORLD AT OUR INTERSECTION

Paul wrote to the Colossians, "See to it that no one takes you captive through hollow and deceptive philosophy, which depends on human tradition and the elemental spiritual forces of this world rather than on Christ" (Colossians 2:8). This is not a blanket condemnation of philosophy, but rather philosophy based on human reason alone. Ideas can captivate and capture us if we are not careful. Furthermore, we must "no longer be infants, tossed back and forth by the waves, and blown here and there by every wind of teaching and by the cunning and craftiness of people in their deceitful scheming" (Ephesians 4:14). Our adversary is clever, and he brings the battle to us in different ways in different generations. As Francis Schaefer prophetically reminds us, "The Christian must resist the spirit of the world *in the form it takes in his own generation*."[12]

There are idea systems today that are neutralizing the effectiveness of the church. Two of the most corrosive idea systems being perpetuated by the world system are naturalism and hedonism. If the physical universe is all there is, there is no room for God. Christianity is then false by definition. If humans exist only to satisfy their desires and live only for their own pleasure, then life with God becomes practically impossible. Who will passionately engage with the gospel if we are conditioned to think that the supernatural is for fairy tales and that all of our time, energy, money, and resources are devoted to the pursuit of more stuff? Our cultural intersection requires a specific response, and Christians need to be equipped to resist the spirit of the world system as we engage the world God loves. We will explore the biblical basis for this high calling in the next chapter.

RESOURCES FOR ENGAGING YOUR INTERSECTION

Books

- *Christ and Culture Revisited* by D. A. Carson
- *The Culturally Savvy Christian: A Manifesto for Deepening Faith and Enriching Popular Culture in an Age of Christianity-Lite* by Dick Staub
- *Kingdom Triangle: Recover the Christian Mind, Renovate the Soul, Restore the Spirit's Power* by J. P. Moreland
- "What is Everyday Theology? How and Why Christians Should Read Culture" by Kevin Vanhoozer in *Everyday Theology: How to Read Cultural Texts and Interpret Trends*
- *Renovation of the Heart: Putting on the Character of Christ* by Dallas Willard
- *Margin: Restoring Emotional, Physical, Financial, and Time Reserves to Overloaded Lives* by Richard Swenson
- *Thrilled to Death: How the Endless Pursuit of Pleasure Is Leaving Us Numb* by Archibald D. Hart

Websites and DVDs

- www.thinkchristianly.org – Think Christianly
- www.thepointradio.org – The Point with John Stonestreett
- www.thegospelcoalition.org – The Gospel Coalition
- www.qideas.org – Q: Ideas That Create a Better World
- www.albertmohler.com – Thinking in Public with Albert Mohler
- *The Faith* by Chuck Colson with Gabe Lyons, DVD

LEVERAGING THE INTERNET TO MAKE GOD KNOWN

AN INTERVIEW WITH RANDALL NILES

Jonathan Morrow: You have called the Internet the mission field of the twenty-first century. Could you expand on what you mean in light of the work you are doing online and also share how Christians can more strategically leverage the Internet as we engage our culture?

Randall Niles: Our team is nearing a decade of ministry on the Web. Between the strategic networks of AllAboutGOD.com and GotQuestions.org, we're now blessed with over 5.5 million visitors each month. It's absolutely surreal to read the thousands of e-mail testimonies that demonstrate how God is using the Internet to proclaim the gospel in the twenty-first century.

Over 1.8 billion people are now on the Internet. Many of these people use search engines such as Google, Yahoo, and Bing as their primary source for online information. In recent years, the Internet has moved beyond mere information to social interaction, with hundreds of millions immersing themselves in Web 2.0 tools such as Facebook, YouTube, and Twitter.

Indeed, people still have spiritual questions. It's just that most of them aren't walking through the front doors of local churches to seek their answers anymore. The research shows that an increasing number of people are seeking their spiritual and religious answers on the Internet. The key to our strategy is to meet these people right where they are. They type a specific question into a search engine, and we're there with a relevant answer at the top of their search results. Our initial goal is to establish credibility and authenticity. We then use a relational foundation to share God's truth and love.

So how can we ensure that truth is available to our target audience? Keyword research is the key! In traditional marketing, it's simply discovering what a potential customer is typing into a search engine that could lead to a potential "conversion" (sale of a product, registration for a service). Keyword research for successful Internet evangelism is no different.

For example, if a seeker named Sara wants basic information about Jesus, she goes to Google, Yahoo, or Bing and types, "Who is Jesus?" The search results can lead Sara to the gospel or lead her astray. In marketing lingo, Sara is a "hot lead," not a "cold call." We can assume that Sara is spiritually interested in the message of Jesus Christ because she "prequalified" herself by the nature of her search query.

When it comes to Internet evangelism, the primary question is, "What do all the Saras on the Internet type into search engines that would cause them to come to sound, biblical presentations of the gospel?"

Using a free resource such as the Google Keyword Tool, anyone can get a meaningful snapshot of the spiritual questions and real-life concerns showing up in search engines. Get creative! You may be surprised to discover how many thousands of hurting people type phrases like "God, help me," "I hate my life," and "Why me, God?" into Google each month.

Once we know our "market" through keyword research, we can produce compelling content (text, audio, video, and images) to target that market through the search engines. Search Engine Optimization (SEO) is a method of designing, writing, coding, and structuring links to our web content to improve the likelihood that it will appear near the top of the search results. The goal of SEO is positioning high in the natural search results (as opposed to paid advertising). Since very few users ever go past page 2 of their search results, the importance of SEO for Internet evangelism is obvious.

In recent years, hundreds of millions of Internet seekers have added interactive, relational components to their information gathering by immersing themselves in Web 2.0 tools such as Facebook, MySpace, and Twitter.

Similar to SEO, Social Media Optimization (SMO) is a way to structure content so it can be weaved into these community-based websites and social media networks. Examples of SMO include social bookmarking, Share buttons, networked blogs, RSS feeds, video embeds from YouTube, and slide shows from Flickr.

It's clear that the search-engine landscape is now fully leveraging social media. Therefore, the more we link, loop, and leverage our content among various websites, network profiles, and social media tools, the more opportunities we will have for effective Internet evangelism.

I encourage the body of Christ to engage the huge number of spiritual seekers on the Internet. You don't have to establish a ministry or develop a website. Just use the tools that already exist and join the communities that resonate with your interests. Spiritual confusion is now online and available for the world to see. By positioning content in the search engines and engaging the dialogue in the social networks, we are creating a new, authentic voice for the church.

Randall Niles is an attorney, educator, and writer who spends most of his time on the Internet, serving as a director at www.AllAboutGOD.com and www.GotQuestions.org.

chapter two

CALLED TO ENGAGE

Everyone with the experience of cross-cultural mission knows that there are always two opposite dangers, the Scylla and Charybdis, between which one must steer. On the one side there is the danger that one finds no point of contact for the message as the missionary preaches it; to the people of the local culture the message appears irrelevant and meaningless. On the other side is the danger that the point of contact determines entirely the way that the message is received, and the result is syncretism. Every missionary path has to find the way between these two dangers: irrelevance and syncretism. And if one is more afraid of one danger than the other, one will certainly fall into the opposite.

Lesslie Newbigin, *A Word in Season*

IN THE LAST CENTURY, there have been two general responses to the challenges that culture raises. The first option was to withdraw and attack. Christians isolate and insulate, hoist the drawbridge, batten down the hatches, and fix bayonets. The culture may be going to hell in a handbasket, but we aren't going to go down without a fight. Many of the culture wars in the last forty years, though well intended, have not been redemptive or beneficial and have put too much hope in the ability of politics to bring about transformation.[1] Moreover, it has generated an "us versus them" mentality. This response is typically associated with the Religious Right.[2]

The other response has been to imitate and assimilate. The understandable desire to be relevant and fit in has caused those opting for this approach to lose much of their saltiness. Christians in this category are hard to distinguish from the culture they are trying to reach. This posture is typically associated with the Secular Left.

But there is a better, more biblically faithful way. It flows out of Paul's teaching to the church at Colossae: "Be wise in the way you act toward outsiders; make the most of every opportunity. Let your conversation be always full of grace, seasoned with salt, so that you may know how to answer everyone" (Colossians 4:5–6). It sees each intersection as an opportunity. I suggest the Bible teaches that Christians are to *engage* in and with culture. The *Oxford Dictionary* further clarifies what this engagement looks like: "to participate or become involved in" and "to establish a meaningful contact or connection with." Jesus reminds believers that they are still to be in the world even though they are not of the world (John 17:11, 16). But we need to be wise, in the words of Paul, and shrewd as snakes, according to Jesus (Matthew 10:16).

A THEOLOGY OF ENGAGEMENT

Our biblical calling and responsibility for cultural engagement can be expressed in four theological principles: (1) Kingdom Citizens, (2) Everyday Ambassadors, (3) Creative Image Bearers, and (4) A Community of Radical Love.

Kingdom Citizens

Our fundamental identity is that we are Kingdom Citizens. The apostle Paul is clear that "our citizenship is in heaven" (Philippians 3:20). While we have obligations as earthly citizens, what defines us is our status before God because he has "rescued us from the domain of darkness, and transferred us to the kingdom of His beloved Son" (Colossians 1:13 NASB). We are under a new ruler because the kingdom is all about the comprehensive reign of God. He alone defines reality.

In the parable of the sower, Jesus referred to the "good seed" as "the people of the kingdom" (Matthew 13:38) and calls his followers to seek first God's kingdom and his righteousness (Matthew 6:33). We are to make it our highest priority. Furthermore, training our minds on and by this new "life with God" from above informs our lives with distinctively kingdom priorities. Paul reminds believers, "Since, then, you have been raised with Christ, set your hearts on things above, where Christ is, seated at the right hand of God. Set your minds on things above, not on earthly things. For you died, and your life is now hidden with Christ in God" (Colossians 3:1–3). The author of Hebrews reminds us that we are to follow the example of those who have gone before us. These faithful saints and "fellow citizens" (Ephesians 2:19) allowed God's revealed truth and promises to define their lives, even as they lived as "foreigners and strangers on earth" (Hebrews 11:13). Peter reinforces this imagery by also using the language of "foreigners and exiles" who are to abstain from the sinful desires of this world, which wage war against our souls (1 Peter 2:11–13).

The bottom line is that we are to be different, but for kingdom reasons (not just for silly legalistic or Christian subculture reasons). As Kingdom Citizens, we should have a worldview that reflects the revealed truth of our eternal God and King (1 Timothy 1:17). Followers of Jesus should live differently and think differently than those around them. It is this principle that keeps us from becoming indistinguishable from the culture around us, which in general marches to the beat of priorities calibrated to "the pattern of this world" (Romans 12:2).

We set our minds on kingdom realities, and our values and priorities are set by God in what he has revealed in creation, in Scripture, and finally in the life of Jesus Christ (Hebrews 1:1–4). This is where growing in the knowledge of God in community produces a biblical worldview. To sum up, Kingdom Citizens are to think Christianly about all of life. We are to live in reality as God defines it and come to see reality as God sees it. Unfortunately, at today's intersection Christians who know what they believe, why they believe it, and why it matters are the exception, not the rule—a reality at odds with the vision of life recorded in the New Testament.

Everyday Ambassadors

If recovering our identity as Kingdom Citizens offers the necessary corrective for the general lack of worldview training, then our calling as Everyday Ambassadors addresses the "Sunday morning only Christianity" so prevalent in American churches today. Paul lays out the vision for this in 2 Corinthians 5:20: "We are therefore Christ's ambassadors, as though God were making his appeal through us. We implore you on Christ's behalf: Be reconciled to God."

The play on words here is intentional because there is a false but widespread belief that only "superspiritual" people or paid professionals are to do the work of the ministry. Not according to the New Testament. Everyday Christians are to be equipped for the works of ministry (Ephesians 4:12). *Everyone* is a minister of the gospel. We certainly all have different spiritual gifts, life experiences, opportunities, and roles to play, but we are to all employ these as Christ's ambassadors according to kingdom priorities.[3]

Notice too that there are no days off from being an ambassador. We see this principle embodied by parents in the Old Testament: "These commandments that I give you today are to be on your hearts. Impress them on your children. Talk about them when you sit at home and when you walk along the road, when you lie down and when you get up. Tie them as symbols on your hands and bind them on your foreheads. Write them on the doorframes of your houses and on your gates" (Deuteronomy 6:6–9). Paul wants to make sure we see our calling as a comprehensive way of life, and he removes any room for misunderstanding: "Whatever you do, whether in word or deed, do it all in the name of the Lord Jesus, giving thanks to God the Father through him" (Colossians 3:17).

Paul's use of the word *ambassador* is instructive as well. Professor of Bible exposition Tom Constable writes, "Ambassadors authoritatively announce messages for others and request, not demand, acceptance. The Christian ambassador, moreover, announces and appeals for God."[4] We represent the King of kings and his kingdom agenda to the world that Christ died to redeem. We proclaim his message that reconciliation is now available in Christ. If you name the name of Christ, then you are an Everyday Ambassador.

The Bible gives us a front row seat to watch Paul live out this mind-set in an unchristian environment:

> While Paul was … in Athens, he was greatly distressed to see that the city was full of idols. So he reasoned in the synagogue with both Jews and God-fearing Greeks, as well as in the marketplace day by day with those who happened to be there. A group of Epicurean and Stoic philosophers began to debate with him … Paul then stood up in the meeting of the Areopagus and said: "People of Athens! I see that in every way you are very religious. For as I walked around and looked carefully at your objects of worship, I even found an altar with this inscription: TO AN UNKNOWN GOD. So you are ignorant of the very thing you worship—and this is what I am going to proclaim to you."
>
> Acts 17:16–23

First, did you notice that he is *reasoning* with people about Christianity, not just appealing to blind faith, emotions, and felt needs? He is "contend[ing] for the faith that was once for all entrusted to God's holy people" (Jude 3). The book of Acts repeatedly records Paul doing this (Acts 14:15–17; 17:2, 4, 17–31; 18:4; 19:8).

Second, Paul is greatly distressed by the idolatry in Athens, but he didn't preach hellfire and brimstone. Rather, modeling the wise engagement he commands believers to employ (Colossians 4:5–6), he compliments their religiosity. Paul translates the right response of sadness and channels it into connection with his audience. His tone is instructive here.

Finally, notice that Paul finds connecting point after connecting point with his audience. He understands the times (1 Chronicles 12:32). He has studied their works and ideas, quotes their poets, and is familiar with Stoic and Epicurean philosophy. He is a student of their culture, not merely an observer (Acts 17:23). He studies it so he can find connections between the true story of Christianity and their cultural story. And then at the end, he subverts their story by naming the unknown God as the Jesus who was resurrected.[5]

Here is what this means for us at our intersection. We have to know our story well—the kingdom story—and we also need to know the major cultural stories at our intersection. This will take effort, study, and intentionality and is part of what it means to always be prepared to give a defense of the hope within us (cf. 1 Peter 3:15).[6]

The primary responsibility of the Everyday Ambassador is not the response of the person we give the message to; it is our faithfulness to engage them with the message of the kingdom and give them, with the aid of the Holy Spirit, the best connecting points we can so that they can hear and connect. We take their stories and help them see that they are not big or compelling enough to answer all the questions they are asking. We help them find their place in the larger kingdom story.

Everyday Ambassadors discover and create connecting points between kingdom and culture. This activity, which Dick Staub calls "dual listening," requires that we know the kingdom story, the biblical worldview, well enough to creatively translate and correlate and even subvert the story being told in our culture so that people can become Kingdom Citizens as well.[7] Christians need to be trained in how to do this, and it begins as our leaders model a thoughtful faith.

Creative Image Bearers

Most Christians are familiar with the Great Commission: "Therefore go and make disciples of all nations, baptizing them in the name of the Father and of the Son and of the Holy Spirit, and teaching them to obey everything I have commanded you. And surely I am with you always, to the very end of the age" (Matthew 28:19 – 20). These are the marching orders of Christ's church.

But what many of us don't often think about is the fact that before Jesus ever spoke those words, or even needed to become incarnate to redeem us and entrust us with this global calling, we *already* had a Great Commission. This mandate was rooted in God's original intent for humanity and was given before we fell into sinful rebellion against our creator: "So God created mankind in his own image, in the image of God he created them; male and female he created them. God blessed them and said to them, '*Be fruitful and increase in number; fill the earth* and *subdue it.* Rule over the fish in the sea and the birds in the sky and over every living creature that moves on the ground'" (Genesis 1:27 – 28, emphasis added). Notice the social and natural dimensions of this statement.

As we read the opening chapters of Genesis, we see that both creation and the fall were comprehensive (1:1; 3:14 – 21). So why would we think that redemption would be limited just to the individual? As Nancy Pearcey observes, "Redemption is not just about being saved *from* sin; it is also about being saved *to* something — to resume the task for which we were originally created."[8] Our job from the beginning was to develop the powers and potentials that God had originally built into creation. As human beings, we were created to represent our creator God and reflect his image as we cultivate the earth (2:15). This rightly has been called the cultural commission.

So in light of this, and supplementing our earlier definition of culture, Christians are commanded *to make something of the world for the glory of God.* In short, we are called to be Creative Image Bearers. The task is more difficult now because of sin, but "in cultivating creation, we not only recover our original purpose but also bring a redemptive force to reverse the evil and corruption introduced by the fall. We offer our gifts to God to participate in making his kingdom come, his will be done. With hearts and minds renewed, our work can now be inspired by love for God and delight in his service."[9]

Even as we face a broken world stained by evil, we have hope. Andy Crouch reminds us, "In the kingdom of God a new kind of life and a new kind of culture become possible — not by abandoning the old but by transforming it. Even the cross, the worst that culture could do, is transformed into a sign of the kingdom of God — the realm of forgiveness, mercy, love and indestructible life."[10]

However, it is critical for us to remember for whose glory we are engaging in culture making — God's. Genesis 11 is the tragic story of the garden of Eden 2.0. Humans were making something of the world, all right, but not for the glory of God. They were seeking to exalt themselves and live in direct opposition to the kingdom of God. This is a textbook example of "the world system" at work, fueled by Satan. And this will always be our temptation this side of the new heaven and the new earth. We must be ever vigilant as we engage as Creative Image Bearers.

A Community of Radical Love

When God created a new community in Christ Jesus (Ephesians 2:14–22), by the power of the Holy Spirit he built into the DNA of this new community the capacity and calling of radical love. The pages of the New Testament are saturated with this vision:

> By this everyone will know that you are my disciples, if you love one another.
> John 13:35

> And this is my prayer: that your love may abound more and more in knowledge and depth of insight.   Philippians 1:9

> May the Lord make your love increase and overflow for each other and for everyone else.   1 Thessalonians 3:12

> We love because he first loved us. Whoever claims to love God yet hates a brother or sister is a liar. For whoever does not love their brother and sister, whom they have seen, cannot love God, whom they have not seen. And he has given us this command: Anyone who loves God must also love their brother and sister.   1 John 4:19–21

> "Hear, O Israel: The Lord our God, the Lord is one. Love the Lord your God with all your heart and with all your soul and with all your mind and with all your strength." The second is this: "Love your neighbor as yourself." There is no commandment greater than these.   Mark 12:29–31

We are to engage in our culture as a community of radical love. *Love* is one of those words, like *faith*, that means everything and nothing. We love pizza, cars, video games, golf, and computers. This is not the love we are called to embody and demonstrate (I will develop this in chapter 15). Christians must not embrace the facile "new tolerance" that accepts anything and everything as equally good and conducive to human flourishing; rather, loving well means seeking another's highest good. First Corinthians 13:4–8 is not meant to be just a sentimental add-on to wedding ceremonies; it offers us knowledge of what real love is. And as we love well—as Kingdom Citizens, Everyday Ambassadors, and Creative Image Bearers—the world will take notice, and we will be coworkers in God's redemptive plan for creation.

THE ULTIMATE MEASURE OF SUCCESSFUL ENGAGEMENT

If we live out all we have talked about above, will we change the world? Will everyone become a Christian? Not ultimately. Jesus taught that the wheat and the weeds will grow together until they are sorted out in the end (Matthew 13:24–30). So how will we know if we are being successful in our engagement? Since the fullness of the kingdom of God awaits the second coming and ultimate reign of the Messiah, how we measure successful engagement in this present age is faithfulness, not utopia. We faithfully engage in the spheres of influence that God has providentially placed us within and leave the results to God.[11]

Transformation in any given generation may or may not occur—the results are up to God—so our call is to be faithful to a theology of engagement as we make disciples of all the nations. God's providential and redemptive plan marches onward, and we play a part in that. And as leaders, we need to cast this vision and equip the church to engage well, always mindful of Paul's words: "Whatever you do, do your work heartily, as for the Lord rather than for men, knowing that from the Lord you will receive the reward of the inheritance. It is the Lord Christ whom you serve" (Colossians 3:23–24 NASB).

POSTSCRIPT: GETTING BETTER AT *HOW* WE SAY WHAT WE SAY

The church has an image problem, and some of this is a product of our own doing. One reason is that we often don't say things very well. Christians can come across as hateful, ignorant, or arrogant (or some unfortunate combination of the three!). We must cultivate a winsome and thoughtful voice in our churches and our culture, or people will tune us out before hearing anything we have to say (see Colossians 4:5–6). If people are going to stumble, we want them to stumble over Christ, not us. The gospel is offensive enough. Remember Paul's words to Timothy: "The Lord's servant must not be quarrelsome but must be kind to everyone, able to teach, not resentful. Opponents must be gently instructed, in the hope that God will grant them repentance leading them to a knowledge of the truth" (2 Timothy 2:24–25).

Here are two suggestions. First, we need to stop being against everything — especially the media. While our viewpoints may not be fairly represented all the time, grumbling and complaining about it on camera will not change anything. Most Americans can tell you what Christians are against — usually homosexuals — but few could tell you what Christians are actually for, namely, truth, redemption, justice, and human flourishing.

Second, as Christians we need to understand those we disagree with (and why), be fair in representing their positions (especially from the pulpit), and do our homework on the issues of our day (part 3 of this book will help). People may still disagree, but they will notice that our carefully considered convictions are based on clear thinking — which will help them see that Christianity is a thoughtful faith.

Finally, our distinctions of culture, pop culture, and the world help us shape the appropriate response, given the particular cultural moment we find ourselves in. What we are against is the influence of the world system on culture. We need to abandon the sledgehammer mentality, which often causes collateral damage and unintended consequences, and instead adopt a surgical and tactical approach.

How Is Your Church's Body Language?

Have you ever been misunderstood because your tone of voice or body language didn't coincide with the words coming out of your mouth? Me too. There is what we say, and then there is what people hear. Unfortunately, others don't always experience us in the way we intend. Well, the same thing happens to the church. Therefore it is worth taking a closer look at our "church body language."

In *Culture Making*, Andy Crouch offers a helpful distinction between postures and gestures. A posture is "our learned but unconscious default position, our natural stance. It is the position our body assumes when we aren't paying attention."[12] The dictionary defines *gesture*, on the other hand, as "a movement of part of the body, esp. a hand or the head, to express an idea or meaning." Crouch explains:

> Appropriate gestures toward particular cultural goods can become, over time, part of the posture Christians unconsciously adopt toward every cultural situation and setting. Indeed, the appeal of the various postures of condemning, critiquing, copying, and consuming — the reason that all of them are still very much with us — is that each of these responses to culture is, at certain times and with specific cultural goods, a necessary gesture.[13]

Let's look at some appropriate gestures Christians can make toward particular cultural situations.

- *Condemning culture.* Pornography in all its forms, the global slave trade, the fact that our nation permits the murder of vulnerable unborn children through elective abortion, unnecessary pollution of the environment, exploitation and abuse of the poor and underprivileged, and people at risk are all issues that ought to be opposed because God loves and values *all* of life. But how we voice our opposition requires careful discernment and prudence. We must speak in such a way as to be heard. If we are only a shrill voice of condemnation, we will be ignored. If our goal is redemption or change, then we must be shrewd with what we say and how we say it. The danger here is that Christians take on a posture of being against everything.

- *Critiquing culture.* The most obvious category is the arts, which deals with ideas, images, and values. To critique is to offer a detailed analysis, evaluation, and assessment of something. Blanket condemnation is unhelpful and counterproductive. Crouch writes, "It is difficult to think of a single instance where condemnation of a work of art has produced any result other than heightened notoriety for the work and the artist."[14] The possible liability is that Christians have not developed the sophistication in the relevant areas to have something meaningful to say.

- *Consuming culture.* Examples of normal and appropriate cultural consumption are eating various kinds of foods and using basic technology (talking on a cell phone, for example). There is nothing worldly about them; they just are part of our existence. However, according to most polls, the overwhelming majority of self-described evangelicals consume the very same kinds and amounts of media as everyone else. *Not good.* We need to have a more discerning palate than that. The danger is in drifting with those around us down the river of mindless consumption.

- *Copying culture.* There is nothing wrong with using a good idea for the kingdom because "even the practice of copying cultural goods, borrowing them from mainstream culture and infusing them with Christian content, has its place."[15] Examples are communication, technology, architecture, infrastructure, social media, and the Internet. The danger is that Christians will fail to see that not every technological advance leads to human flourishing.

The church gets in trouble when appropriate responses to specific cultural goods, situations, or questions become rigid postures. Our goal, according to the biblical framework spelled out above, is to develop engagement toward culture in order to establish a meaningful connection with our world as we create redemptive cultural goods. If we take to heart this way of thinking, we will get better at how we say what we say.

RESOURCES FOR ENGAGING YOUR INTERSECTION

Books

- *Culture Making: Recovering Our Creative Calling* by Andy Crouch
- *The Culturally Savvy Christian: A Manifesto for Deepening Faith and Enriching Popular Culture in an Age of Christianity-Lite* by Dick Staub
- *Total Truth: Liberating Christianity from Its Cultural Captivity* by Nancy Pearcey
- *Apologetics for a New Generation: A Biblical and Culturally Relevant Approach to Talking about God* edited by Sean McDowell
- *A Faith and Culture Devotional: Daily Readings in Art, Science, and Life* by Kelly Monroe Kullberg and Lael Arrington
- *The Case for Civility: And Why Our Future Depends on It* by Os Guinness

Websites and DVDs

- www.thinkchristianly.org – Think Christianly
- www.culture-making.com – Culture Making
- *Gospel in Life: Grace Changes Everything* by Tim Keller, DVD
- *Where Faith and Culture Meet*, DVD

TRUTH, SECULARISM, AND THE MODERN UNIVERSITY

AN INTERVIEW WITH KELLY MONROE KULLBERG

Jonathan Morrow: As the founder of The Veritas Forum, you are obviously passionate about the pursuit of truth, and your organization exists to provide students venues in which they can seek it. Why is truth so valuable?

Kelly Monroe Kullberg: Truth yields life. If we are sailors lost at sea, we need true north. If we're branches on tree hoping to bear fruit, which we are, we need connection to a true vine. Truth tells us where we are, who we are, to whom we belong, and the real story in which we can fully live. It seems to me that our American culture, in its present condition, is both lost and starving for truth, and therefore vulnerable to the deception of power politics, marketing schemes, and politically correct slogans of professors, politicians, and media that often lead to the death of the soul and the body. Lies lead to death and a culture of death, but the truth sets people free for life.

Jonathan: Why is cultivating a whole-life, integrated vision of Christianity so important for both student and adult Christ-followers?

Kelly: Again, students come to the university wanting to find a story big enough for thoughtful human beings to live in — to flourish and thrive. A story that makes sense of our past, animates our present, and yields hope for the future. They want to change the world, even if it means conquering the forces of darkness, fear, and doubt to do so. Being made in the image of God, they want to build in the ruins of our world and to advance the kingdom of love, life, and beauty. But they are either subtly or openly indoctrinated to believe that no grand story, no metanarrative, is true. Of course, the claim that no grand story exists is its own grand story.

Jonathan: Why is it important for churches to care about and be involved in what is happening on university campuses across America?

Kelly: American universities are now mission fields of those in confusion, pain, pride, cultural privilege, and spiritual poverty. From these fields will emerge the next generation of American leadership. This should both concern and inspire us to great creativity and hospitality. Bridges between churches and universities must be built—primarily by churches. It's exciting to see lives change and brighten, as students and professors awaken to the light of the gospel.

Churches interested in foreign missions should also consider prioritizing work in American universities. The foreign missions field has come to us, with students from hundreds of countries in our nearby universities. They are Muslims, Buddhists, Hindus, secularists, and while they are here, they have a chance to meet Christ and then go home to positions of leadership as Christians who care about the poor, justice, righteousness, evangelism—God's kingdom. Hospitality is a great spiritual gift that opens hearts and minds. Once trusting relationships are built, Americans are often invited to visit internationals in their home countries, and real relationships are nurtured. This strikes me as an organic, cost-efficient, and effective approach to world missions.

Jonathan: At our cultural intersection, what do you think is the most significant challenge or opportunity that we as Christians must engage? Why?

Kelly: The current radical attempt to redefine America as a secular nation feels like a dark cloud that by requiring conformity to or "tolerance" of its secular worldview could destroy our actual cultural diversity at the deepest levels (intellectual, spiritual, moral, and aesthetic). This top-down "tolerance" stifles the freedom, beauty, and vitality of the Christian tradition and other faith traditions as well.

Secularism is flat, gray, and boring. It is not neutral, but rather a religion of its own, a story that tells us there is no God, or that if God is real, he, our Creator and Redeemer, doesn't matter. This is absurd, but real and dangerous. This story will yield a world of technique, but not joy and not love. Pastors and laypeople need to wake up—and stand up—to forces that will remove religious liberties and freedom of conscience and tradition.

> **Kelly Monroe Kullberg** is the founder and director of project development of The Veritas Forum, which she organized at Harvard in 1992 (www.veritas.org). She edited and coauthored the best-selling *Finding God at Harvard: Spiritual Journeys of Christian Thinkers* (1996). A decade later, she wrote *Finding God Beyond Harvard* (2006) and in 2008 coauthored *A Faith and Culture Devotional*. Kelly lives in Ohio with her husband, David, and their children.

chapter three

EQUIPPING THE NEXT GENERATION

As Christian parents, pastors, teachers, and youth group leaders, we constantly see young people pulled down by the undertow of powerful cultural trends. If all we give them is a "heart" religion, it will not be strong enough to counter the lure of attractive but dangerous ideas. Young believers also need a "brain" religion—training in worldview and apologetics—to equip them to analyze and critique the competing worldviews they will encounter when they leave home. If forewarned and forearmed, young people at least have a fighting chance when they find themselves a minority of one among their classmates or work colleagues. Training young people to develop a Christian mind is no longer an option; it is part of their necessary survival equipment.

Nancy Pearcey, *Total Truth*

WHAT CONSTITUTES A GOOD LIFE? What kind of life do you want to lead? What values do you hope to live by? What kind of community or society do you want to live in? How should you reconcile the claims of family and community with your individual desires? These are questions that Yale University president Richard Levin asked the class of 2011. "An important component of your undergraduate experience," he told them, "should be seeking answers to the questions that matter."[1] These are worldview questions. But as a society that operates at a frantic pace with little reflection on these questions, either personally or culturally (a habit the next generation is picking up on), we have great skepticism that *anyone* can guide us to true and fruitful answers.

In centuries past, the university was a place to explore and answer these questions. Today, with rare exceptions, university life has become a mixed bag of hedonism and the exaltation of personal autonomy. This occurs in a context in which education is increasingly perceived as having value only insofar as it makes you more money or translates to a better job rather than leading toward flourishing as a human being. Consequently, they learn that the highest value in their worldview needs to be the passionate pursuit of their own self-interest. And yet the assumption President Levin admits is that the best Yale can offer to students is the ability to ask good questions amid world-class resources: "It is true that your professors are unlikely to give you the answers to questions about what you should value and how you should live. *We leave the answers up to you.*"[2]

I am all for good questions, but how does one find good answers? And more importantly, what constitutes a good answer? On this, students are left adrift. Moreover, as the pressures and responsibilities of life increase, the time to contemplate the questions becomes spoken for very quickly.

To make matters worse, a recent study conducted by Harvard and George Mason University professors found that 52 percent of college professors regard the Bible as "an ancient book of fables, legends, history, and moral precepts." This number increased to 73 percent when professors at elite universities were surveyed. Moreover, the percentage of atheist and agnostic professors in America is three times greater than that of the general population (with numbers higher in fields such as biology and psychology).[3] Listen to the candid admission of Richard Rorty, professor of comparative literature at Stanford University, concerning his approach to students whom he calls Christian fundamentalists (that is, people who actually believe the Bible is true):

> We try to arrange things so that students who enter as bigoted, homophobic, religious fundamentalists will leave college with views more like our own ... When we American college teachers encounter religious fundamentalists, we do not consider the possibility of reformulating our own practices of justification so as to give more weight to the authority of the Christian scriptures. Instead, we do our best to convince these students of the benefits of secularization ... So we are going to go right on trying to discredit you in the eyes of your children, trying to strip your fundamentalist religious community of dignity, trying to make your views seem silly rather than discussable.[4]

College is not always faith friendly—especially if you happen to be a Christian. In short, it is much more likely that students will encounter someone who will not be sympathetic to a Christian worldview as they process life's biggest questions. I don't cite this as a scare tactic, but this thought should sober us.

Sociologists Christian Smith and Patricia Snell, after conducting a rigorous survey of over 2,500 emerging adults, provide an assessment that should serve as a wake-up call to the church:

Very many emerging adults simply don't know how to think about things, what is right, what is deserving for them to devote their lives to. On such matters, they are often simply paralyzed, wishing they could be more definite, wanting to move forward, but simply not knowing how they might possibly know anything worthy of conviction and dedication. Instead, very many emerging adults exist in a state of basic indecision, confusion, and fuzziness. The world they have inherited, as best they can make sense of it, has told them that real knowledge is impossible and genuine values are illusions.[5]

This excerpt indicates the crisis of knowledge in our generation. Odds are that many of the students who pass through our ministries have this trajectory as well. Where will they find answers? Who will reliably guide them into the knowledge of God?

Our responsibility as parents and Christian leaders is made clear by Asaph in the Psalms:

> He decreed statutes for Jacob
>   and established the law in Israel,
> which he commanded our ancestors
>   to teach their children,
> *so the next generation would know them,*
>   even the children yet to be born,
>   and they in turn would tell their children.
> Then they would put their trust in God
>   and would not forget his deeds
>   but would keep his commands.
>
> Psalm 78:5–7, emphasis added

Every one of us is called to equip the next generation to know and follow God. Now, how exactly do we go about doing this in today's world? First I need to highlight three specific challenges, and then I'll suggest some proven ways for helping students develop a lasting faith.

THREE CHALLENGES WE MUST ADDRESS

Boredom and Apathy

Most teenagers today are overstimulated, perpetually connected to technology, and bored. These aren't unrelated. They have learned well from their parents — the baby boomer generation — that happiness is bound up in seeking pleasure. Well, we reap what we sow. Students are becoming numb to life and suffer from an overstimulation-induced, low-grade depression — even amid activities that used to bring them pleasure. In his provocative book *Thrilled to Death*, Dr. Archibald Hart describes the effect this is having on our brains and our ability to enjoy pleasure at all.[6] The clinical diagnosis is *anhedonia*—the inability to experience pleasure in the little things of life. In our culture of entertainment, we must help students set boundaries for their own good and for the future that God wants for them. We must help them strategically unplug and use technology wisely. In short, we must redefine the good life for them and cast a compelling vision for it (more on this below).

Relational Disconnection

In 2003, Dartmouth Medical School, in conjunction with the YMCA and the Institute for American Values, commissioned a study on youth. They analyzed 260 current studies on youth development. Why? In the committee's own words, the study was prompted by "the deteriorating mental and behavioral health of U.S. children. We are witnessing high and rising rates of depression, anxiety, attention deficit, conduct disorders, thoughts of suicide, and other serious mental, emotional, and behavioral problems among U.S. children and adolescents." Furthermore, they note that this is being "treated" with medication, psychotherapy, and "at risk" programs. Each of these is sometimes necessary and can help, but they wanted to probe deeper to get at the root *environmental* causes of this crisis rather than just perpetually treating symptoms.

They continue, "In large measure, what's causing this crisis of American childhood is a lack of connectedness ... close connections to other people, and deep connections to moral and spiritual meaning ... the human child is 'hardwired to connect.' We are hardwired for other people and for moral meaning and openness to the transcendent. Meeting these basic needs for connection is essential to health and to human flourishing."[7]

Chap and Dee Clark make the case that our society has created an environment that leads to the systemic abandonment of our young people at the very time they need connection the most—adolescence. In adolescence, students do not have the connection with the older adults and parents they desperately need, which explains something of why they go underground into social networking or groups they would not normally pursue to find acceptance. Nor are they receiving the vision and nourishment these pivotal relationships provide. In the words of the rock band Linkin Park, this generation is looking for "somewhere I belong."

Intellectual Disengagement

It is not that students can't think or won't think; it's just that they have not been taught *how* to think. According to the National Study of Youth and Religion, the top reason formerly religious young people cite for leaving their faith is intellectual skepticism (32 percent). Here are some of the responses to the open-ended survey question of why they no longer believe: "I think scientifically and there is no proof," "It didn't make any sense anymore," and "Too many questions that can't be answered."[8] Sadly, they have not been exposed to the powerful scientific, philosophical, and historical evidence for belief in God in general and specifically in Jesus of Nazareth. This really must change.

In their provocative book *unChristian*, David Kinnaman and Gabe Lyons observe that a primary reason ministry to teenagers fails to produce a lasting faith is that "they are not being taught to think."[9] Life cannot be lived only from the emotions or our moment-to-moment feelings. We must base our lives on true knowledge of reality. God designed us as rational beings to think and reason and to love him with all of our being—including our minds (Matthew 22:37). And the primary way to become more like Jesus Christ and grow spiritually is by the renewing of our minds (Romans 12:2).

HOW TO EQUIP THE NEXT GENERATION TO KNOW AND LOVE GOD FOR A LIFETIME

While these are significant challenges, they can be overcome. We can prepare the next generation to follow God for a lifetime. In his monumental study on the spiritual lives of emerging adults, sociologist Christian Smith lists the most common factors leading a young person to grow up to be highly religious. These include having highly committed parents (or other influential adults), considering one's religious faith to be of high importance, practicing spiritual disciplines, having few doubts, and believing in divine miracles as a teenager. Notice that last one—beliefs about the supernatural in the teenage years are deeply important for lasting faith. Smith concludes, "By taking a cognitive stand on miracles during the teenage years, youth who do so solidify a certain intellectual and affective structure that is more likely to resist the authority claims of secular modernity than those who do not."[10] Teaching students to defend their faith is critical during the years when it will be under the most direct assault (1 Peter 3:15; 2 Corinthians 10:3–5).

Steve Wilkins and Mark Sanford offer a helpful analysis as to why some Christians leave Christianity five or ten years after college and others continue on in the faith:

> Without exception, those who successfully integrated faith with life followed three practices. They developed a relationship with a mentor who practiced an active Christian life. Second, they met regularly with peers who were deeply committed to living out Christianity. Finally, they had developed a Christian worldview sufficient to meet the challenges of the competing worldviews they encountered after leaving college.[11]

Let's look at each of these.

First, we see that *mentors* are crucial to spiritual development. This was certainly the case in my own faith journey. I had three significant mentors in high school and college and as a newlywed—and these relationships profoundly shaped me. I felt prepared to face the challenges and uncertainties of life because they modeled the Christian life for me. Mentoring was the key in Jesus' ministry with the twelve disciples. Paul reminds Timothy, "The things you have heard me say in the presence of many witnesses entrust to reliable people who will also be qualified to teach others" (2 Timothy 2:2; cf. 1 Thessalonians 2:8).

We all need people to learn from and imitate in the faith (1 Corinthians 4:16; 11:1; Philippians 3:17). We need youth leaders, adult volunteers, and parents to engage. Youth specialist Chap Clark observes:

> For a long time the church has been using the ratio of 5:1—five kids to one adult. We have felt that if you get that, you are doing well. I think it needs to be reversed: one kid to five adults. We need to develop a strategy of ministry across the developmental span, childhood through high school, so that by the time they graduate every kid has five adult 'fans'—five adults who know their name, pray for them regularly, and talk to them often.[12]

Imagine the difference this would make! Josh McDowell, who has spoken to millions of young people and adults over the years, concludes:

> Do you want to pass your values on to young people? Do you want your children to come to know your Savior? Do you want the next generation to grasp and live biblical truth? If so scientific research says you must do two things: (1) build loving, intimate connections, relationships with your children, or they will almost certainly reject the truth you care about, and (2) model the very value or truth in the presence of those young people.[13]

Second, *peers* are critical to developing a lasting faith. We need people to run the race with and to spur us on. There are many challenges in life, and it's easy to cave in or give up. Again, listen to Paul's admonition to young Timothy: "Flee the evil desires of youth, and pursue righteousness, faith, love and peace, *along with those* who call on the Lord out of a pure heart" (2 Timothy 2:22, emphasis added). We pursue God *together*! Solomon highlighted the strength found in community: "Two are better than one, because they have a good return for their labor: If either of them falls down, one can help the other up. But pity anyone who falls and has no one to help them up… Though one may be overpowered, two can defend themselves. A cord of three strands is not quickly broken" (Ecclesiastes 4:9–10, 12). We not only need friends we can run with but ones who are committed to following Christ. "Walk with the wise and become wise, for a companion of fools suffers harm" (Proverbs 13:20). The principle is clear: "Your friends will determine the direction and quality of your life."[14] None of us outgrows this principle, so choose wisely!

Third, a robust *Christian worldview*—the answers to the questions we asked at the beginning of this chapter—allowed the students analyzed by Steve Wilkins and Mark Sanford to navigate life. Students need to be challenged to explore what they believe, why they believe it, and why it matters. Merely professing an unexamined or ungrounded belief will be easily swamped by the emotional, intellectual, and social challenges of college life and beyond. And given the fact that the dominant religion of the American teenager is Moralistic Therapeutic Deism, we need to spend some time on what makes us distinctively Christian.[15] Christian educator Sean McDowell observes, "Much ministry today is focused on meeting a felt need, but the real difficulty is to take a genuine need and make it felt."[16] That is especially true when it comes to this area. Here are some essential issues students need to explore:

- Does truth exist?
- Is it reasonable to believe in the existence of God?
- Can we know who Jesus was and claimed to be?
- Can you trust the Bible?
- Are science and faith enemies?
- Is Darwinian evolution true?
- Am I more than my brain?
- What does it mean to be human?
- How can Jesus be the only way to God?
- If God is good, then why is there evil?

These are all key apologetics issues that every student needs to be grounded in by the time they leave for college. They need room to doubt and discover. And they need to hear the tough questions from us first—in a safe context where we can wrestle with the answers together.

Furthermore, we must provide creative training in doctrine and help students connect truth to life. For example, the truth that all humans are made in the image of God and are inherently valuable means they are not to be used. Pornography is using another person for your own pleasure, and thus it dehumanizes both the person being used and the user.

In addition, students need training in how to grow spiritually. In chapters 7 and 8 we will explore what it means to learn from Jesus how to live—the "Vision, Intention, Means" pattern—developing faith skills, spiritual practices, and habits as we train wisely, not just try harder, to become more like Jesus. Another element of worldview formation is imparting wisdom to face the moral challenges that are so common today. Young people need a compelling vision of dating, sexuality, and marriage. To say yes to this will make sense of all of the noes they will need to say along the way. And they need to be prepared to engage in discussion of controversial issues like abortion and homosexuality.

Finally, we need to engage students with a compelling vision of the Christian life. Life is not just about getting a good job and satisfying desires and pursuing pleasure (the world's definition of happiness); it is about serving and following God and his kingdom agenda (Matthew 6:33). We need to help students discover God's unique calling on their lives—what part will they come to play as God's kingdom story unfolds? We need to connect them to God's mission. Help them dream. Provide opportunities to serve locally, nationally, and internationally. As Greg Ogden reminds us, "At the core of our being, there is also a particular heart call that defines the unique purpose for our existence. It is like a golden thread that runs through the fabric of our lives. It is the story line of our life that provides a sense of continuity and coherence in an otherwise fragmented and confusing world."[17] We all require something larger than ourselves to live for. From a very early age, students need a vision of God and his mission that is large enough to give their lives to. Life with God may be many things, but boring is not one of them!

WHY ORANGE SHOULD BECOME YOUR CHURCH'S FAVORITE COLOR

As a wrap-up, I highlight two critical findings from the survey on emerging adults mentioned above and look at what this means for the church. First, as we think about our calling to train up the next generation to know and love God, we need to recognize the compelling evidence that "individual family households" and "individual religious congregations" are the two most significant socializing factors. Christian Smith concludes, "What the findings of this book clearly show is that for better or worse, these are the two crucial contexts for youth religious formation in the United States. If formation in faith does not happen there, it will—with rare exceptions—not happen anywhere."[18] Should this really surprise us (see Deuteronomy 6:4–9)?

The other important sociological factor is this: "Of the approximately 70 percent of youth who at some time or other before mid-emerging adulthood commit to live their lives for God, the vast majority appear to do so early in life, apparently before the age of 14."[19]

While I don't want to restrict God or make too much of this number, it does point to the need to begin earlier rather than later. High school youth groups should be places that are beginning to put the finishing touches on a Christian worldview, not beginning to lay the foundation. We need to start early. Kids are smart and will respond to the challenge. I think we tend to underestimate what they can and will learn. My experience has been that if you ask open-ended questions and cover provocative and culturally relevant issues, students will engage. For example, I teach a class at our church on Sunday mornings exploring the question: Is Christianity true? There are middle school, high school, and college students in there, and they are learning and being challenged by their peers (it also helps that a generous family in our church cooks a big pancake breakfast for them every week right after class so we are feeding both stomachs and minds!).

To sum up, the earlier the better. And the faith (or lack thereof) of parents is the most significant indicator of students who will follow God later in life. Coming in a close second are other older adults in a faith community. In light of the biblical mandate to pass on our faith, both in the home and the church, how can your church partner with and equip parents to engage their children with the Christian worldview? In short, *think orange.*

Here's what I mean. Big church, kids' church, and youth group are often islands within the very same church. There is not much integration. On another island is the family, leaving the church and the family with segregated activity instead of integrated strategy.[20] But what if they began partnering in the same things? As founder of the reThink group, Reggie Joiner says, "When you think orange, you see how two combined influences make a greater impact than just two influences."[21] What if we integrated the family (red) and the church (yellow)? That's thinking orange and is exactly what we need to be doing to equip the next generation. To catch a vision for what this could look like in your church, read the interview with Reggie Joiner at the end of this chapter.

I KNOW IT WORKS, BECAUSE IT HAPPENED TO ME

In my college years, I didn't know about all of the sociological data I included in this chapter, but I did experience it firsthand. I became a follower of Jesus at seventeen, and as a college freshman I was involved with Campus Crusade for Christ. During these formative years, all four of the elements mentioned above converged in my life: (1) mentors, (2) peers, (3) Christian worldview formation, and (4) vision.

I had mentors who invested in my life. I saw them live out their faith. I had peers — friends and roommates — who were actively seeking to follow Christ during college and with whom I could run. I had access to biblical truth as my worldview was being formed. I was owning my faith and exploring the whys and whats of Christianity. And finally, I was being given a compelling vision for what my life in Christ *could* be.

This vision manifested itself in two primary ways. First, I was able to wait for the person I would date and marry, and second, I determined to give my life to helping others grow up in Christ. This happened on a weekly basis, on occasional fall and winter retreats, and during three summer projects. In this relational context, God shaped me to walk with him for a lifetime. I know it can be done, and one of my great passions is helping the next generation come to know and love God and give themselves to his mission.

In light of all that we have discussed, what role may God be calling you to play in equipping the next generation? May we be like the psalmist who prayed:

> O God, You have taught me from my youth,
> and I still declare Your wondrous deeds.
> And even when I am old and gray, O God, do not forsake me,
> until I declare Your strength to this generation,
> Your power to all who are to come.
>
> Psalm 71:17–18 NASB

RESOURCES FOR ENGAGING
YOUR INTERSECTION

Books

- *Welcome to College: A Christ-Follower's Guide for the Journey* by Jonathan Morrow
- *Souls in Transition: The Religious and Spiritual Lives of Emerging Adults* by Christian Smith with Patricia Snell
- *Think Orange: Imagine the Impact When Church and Family Collide . . .* by Reggie Joiner
- *Disconnected: Parenting Teens in a MySpace World* by Chap and Dee Clark
- *Do Hard Things: A Teenage Rebellion against Low Expectations* by Alex and Brett Harris
- *Parenting beyond Your Capacity: Connect Your Family to a Wider Community* by Reggie Joiner and Carey Nieuwhof
- *The Unshakable Truth: How You Can Experience the 12 Essentials of a Relevant Faith* by Josh and Sean McDowell
- *The Apologetics Study Bible for Students* edited by Sean McDowell

Websites and DVDs

- www.cpyu.org – The Center for Parent Youth Understanding
- www.whatisorange.org – The Orange website for church/ family integration
- www.fulleryouthinstitute.org – The Fuller Youth Institute
- www.summit.org – Summit Ministries Worldview Training Camps
- www.wheatstoneacademy.com – Wheatstone Academy Summer Conferences
- www.familylife.com – Family Life (see especially "Passport 2 Purity")
- *Parental Guidance Required* by Andy Stanley and Reggie Joiner, DVD
- *TrueU Series*, Focus on the Family, DVD

CHURCH, FAMILY, AND THE NEXT GENERATION

AN INTERVIEW WITH REGGIE JOINER

Jonathan Morrow: You are the author of the brightly colored book *Think Orange*. Could you explain what Orange is and why you wrote the book?

Reggie Joiner: We believe that churches and families are both trying to do their best to impact the next generation, but neither alone is as strong as both are together. For too long, parents have turned their kids over to children's and student ministries and expected them to do the spiritual work in a young person's life. Or they didn't expect anything more than a drop-off babysitting service. It works the other way too. Too many churches look at parents as add-ons or obstacles, not partners in a child's spiritual formation. But Orange says that if we combine the light of the church (yellow) with the heart of the home (red), we get something stronger and more powerful: Orange. Two combined influences have more impact than either influence alone.

Jonathan: One of the biggest challenges facing students today is that they are disconnected. What can be done to help reverse this trend?

Reggie: We're all familiar with the numbers that say most college-aged students drop out of church between the ages of eighteen and twenty-five. Now the newest study shows that in the past ten years, the dropout age is even younger: sixteen. We think there are a few ways to counter this trend. First, we need to challenge students to *be* the church, not just go to church. At North Point Community Church, where I served as executive director of family ministries, we decided not to do Sunday morning small groups for high school students because we wanted to get them involved in serving and being the church. (We had their small groups on Sunday afternoon.) That's just one way to give them the tools to make faith real. If it's their own faith, they'll likely stay involved longer. If we spent three more years teaching a high schooler how to read the driver's manual, he'd get pretty bored. But if we give him the keys to the car, he'll make it his own. We're also talking about the difference that adult leaders can have by staying connected with those who are college-aged. We know some high school leaders who are "graduating" with their seniors and walking them spiritually through the first year of college. We've seen a few churches designed completely around helping a student make a spiritual transition into the college years, with leaders who aren't in the church for themselves but for the college kids in their city.

Jonathan: Church ministry is a challenge. Can you offer some advice and encouragement to Christian leaders for how to begin integrating family and church ministry?

Reggie: Here's something I wrote for *Think Orange* that sums up what we think can happen if churches and families decide to think Orange together:

- There are two powerful influences on the planet—the church and the home. They both exist because God initiated them.
- They both exist because God desires to use them to demonstrate his plan of redemption and restoration.
- If they work together, they can potentially make a greater impact than if they work alone.
- They need each other. Too much is at stake for either one to fail.
- Their primary task is to build God's kingdom in the hearts of men and women, sons and daughters.

Orange is a strategy, not a method or a model. The five Orange essentials are easily accessible for every leader, no matter the size or style of church:

1. *Integrate strategy.* Synchronize leaders and parents to build an authentic faith in children and teenagers.
2. *Refine the message.* Refine your message so it clearly communicates God's story of restoration.
3. *Reactivate the family.* Help parents be more intentional about nurturing an everyday faith in their kids' lives.
4. *Elevate community.* Give every child and teenager a spiritual coach or leader who can reinforce what a Christian parent would say.
5. *Leverage influence.* Fuel passion in the hearts of this next generation to be a demonstration of God's love to a broken world.

Jonathan: Parents can get overwhelmed very quickly. What have you found that encourages them? What kind of help are they asking for?

Reggie: We always remind church leaders of the 40/3000 principle. Once you take away vacations and holidays and other reasons a kid misses a Sunday, churches get about forty hours a year with children and students. But parents get way more than that—about three thousand hours a year. So doesn't it make sense that we as church leaders would want to help parents maximize this time?

We suggest five family values that every mom and dad can embrace to encourage the spiritual development of their children:

1. *Imagine the end.* Understand what you'd like your young person to be, and know that there's a strategy to guide this process.
2. *Fight for the heart.* Decide in advance never to give up. Be compelled by a love that crosses boundaries and takes risks.
3. *Make it personal.* Prioritize your own spiritual life first. Be real in the good times and difficult times. It has to be in you before it can be in them.
4. *Create a rhythm.* Be attentive to times that lend to spiritual conversations. We call them morning time, drive time, meal time, and bed time.
5. *Widen the circle.* Parents shouldn't try to do this alone. Bring together a community of other trusted adults and leaders, including the church, to impact your kids.

> **Reggie Joiner** is the founder of the reThink Group and Orange; a nonprofit organization that helps churches and parents maximize their influence on the spiritual growth of the next generation. Orange is known for its innovative curriculum, resources, and training that equip leaders with relevant strategies for impacting preschoolers, elementary children, teenagers, college students, and families. Reggie is the author of *Think Orange* and *The Orange Leader Handbook*, and the coauthor of *7 Practices of Effective Ministry* and *Parenting beyond Your Capacity*. You can visit him at www.whatisorange.org.

part two

PREPARING TO ENGAGE

chapter four

THINKING CHRISTIANLY ABOUT ALL OF LIFE

> The whole point of Christianity is that it offers a story which is the story of the whole world. It is public truth.
>
> N. T. Wright, *The New Testament and the People of God*

EVERYONE HAS A WORLDVIEW – IT'S UNAVOIDABLE. Now whether or not people are aware of it, and whether this worldview adequately explains reality, is another story altogether. Briefly put, a worldview is simply the total set of beliefs that a person has about the biggest questions in life. Here is the longer but more precise definition, offered by Christian thinker James Sire:

> A commitment, a fundamental orientation of the heart, that can be expressed as a story or in a set of presuppositions (assumptions which may be true, partially true, or entirely false) which we hold (consciously or subconsciously, consistently or inconsistently) about the basic construction of reality, and that provides the foundation on which we live and move and have our being.[1]

This additional insight is important because 99.9 percent of people didn't form their worldview by reading a textbook. Furthermore, in a fallen world system that tilts away from life with God, all of us have been shaped by various cultural stories—many of them hidden to us.[2] As the old saying goes, worldviews are often caught rather than taught.

Worldviews function much like eyeglasses or contact lenses that either bring the world into focus or make things harder to see. Or we could think about a worldview as a mental map or GPS of the way things are. If you have a reliable map, then you will arrive at your intended destination. While it is the case that all of us are habituated to see the world in certain ways over time by the particular culture we live in, this does not condemn us to a life of hopeless relativism. Despite the claims of postmodernism (which I'll examine below), we can examine our glasses and maps *alongside* what we experience and critically evaluate them. Scripture assumes this is possible, for as the apostle Paul reminds us, "See to it that no one takes you captive through hollow and deceptive philosophy, which depends on human tradition and the elemental spiritual forces of this world rather than on Christ" (Colossians 2:8). We can correct our worldview if we take the time and effort to think carefully about life.[3]

While it is certainly true that worldview formation is a holistic process in that it affects our thoughts, feelings, actions, commitments, relationships, and overall identity, it is also true that the transformation of a worldview is the primary task of our thought life (Romans 12:2). Moreover, to affirm this does not "intellectualize" Christianity; thinking well is indispensable to living well. We serve an eminently rational God, and sound reason is the friend of Christians (Isaiah 1:18; Romans 11:33 – 36). Where modernism went wrong was the exaltation of reason — almost deifying it — while rejecting revelation and authority as legitimate sources of knowledge. The corrective is right reason, not the abolition of reason (for example, postmodernism).

LIFE'S ULTIMATE QUESTIONS

Life is full of questions: where to eat dinner, who will win the Super Bowl, and the suspense of who the next American Idol will be. And then there are the questions that *really* matter, the ones that keep us awake at night and get us out of bed in the morning. We usually entertain these questions only after we've finally unplugged from our entertainment- and technology-induced slumber or when a painful event happens to us. The big questions of life fall into five basic categories:

1. **God** (Theology) — Does God exist? What is God like? Can this God be known? Has this God spoken?
2. **Ultimate reality** (Metaphysics) — Has the universe always existed or did it have a beginning? Is the natural world all there is? Are miracles or the supernatural possible?
3. **Knowledge** (Epistemology) — What is knowledge? Can we know anything at all? Does objective truth exist? Can we trust our senses? What are the proper roles of faith, reason, and sense experience in knowledge? Can we have knowledge of God?
4. **Ethics** (Axiology) — Are there objective moral values and duties that

govern human conduct? What are they? Or is morality relative to individuals, cultures, or historical periods? What is the good life? Who is
really well off? How do I become a good person? What is beautiful?

5. **Human nature** (Anthropology) — What does it mean to be human?
Where did humans come from? Do we possess inherent dignity and
value? What is our purpose and destiny in life? Do humans possess free
will? Is there life after death?

To be sure, we don't ask all of these questions at once or even necessarily in
this order; but what is undeniable is that people and cultures are operating with
convictions concerning these ultimate questions. And at the end of the day, we all
desperately want solid and authoritative answers to these questions. A great snapshot into what these convictions are can be found by examining how the popular
movies, media, and music of a given generation answer the basic worldview questions listed above.

WHEN WORLDVIEWS COLLIDE

Images and information constantly wash over us via high-definition TVs, high-
speed Internet, 4G smartphone networks, and Facebook updates. All of these are
mediums for constant messages, which necessarily flow out of different worldviews that, for good or ill, have a huge influence on us individually and culturally. Every person filters the information that enters their minds and their daily
experiences through their worldview. They then make sense of this information
and their experiences based on their worldview. This process is automatic, and
over time the filtered information shapes their beliefs and influences how they
function in society, including the smallest decisions they make. One critical problem we face is that too much information removes our ability to discern good
from bad answers. In our age of relativism, we are simply left with answers and
preferences.

People behave as they really believe. But our actions are only the tip of the ice-
berg. What really drives us is our invisible worldview that lives beneath the surface.
Our worldview is shaped by a complex collection of broken relationships (with
God, parents, and others), a mixture of true and false beliefs about reality, and values that are primarily directed toward the self. Embracing a Christian worldview —
thinking Christianly — means growing in our ability to understand and live *all* of
life from God's perspective.[4] This becomes possible as our relationship with God
is restored in the gospel (and this serves as the basis for restoration of relationships
with others), we replace false beliefs with truth as our minds are renewed (Romans
12:2), and we give priority to God over self and come to increasingly love what God
loves by the constant enablement of the Holy Spirit.

Plato rightly said, "Those who tell the stories rule society." Currently the three dominant stories (or worldviews) contending for the hearts and minds of people today are scientific naturalism, postmodernism, and Christian theism.[5] If you pay attention, you can see this struggle play out in the media, at the movies, and in the classroom. The language of conflict and struggle is no overstatement. For as sociologist James Hunter points out, the ideas that shape the cultural elites shape the next generation: "The struggle over the ivory tower is significant for the contemporary culture war for the simple reason that its outcome will ultimately shape the ideals and values as well as the categories of analysis and understanding that will guide the next generation of American leaders."[6]

As Christians we are commanded to love God with all our heart, soul, mind, and strength and to think Christianly about all of life (Luke 10:27; Colossians 3:17). Since all truth is God's truth, there is no sacred/secular split. As Kingdom Citizens, we are to understand the Christian worldview and be prepared to engage others at such a cultural moment as this. Charles Colson and Nancy Pearcey write:

> Christians must understand the clash of worldviews that is changing the face of American society. And we must stand ready to respond as people grow disillusioned with false beliefs and values and as they begin to seek real answers. We must know not only what our worldview is and why we believe it but also how to defend it. We must also have some understanding of the opposing worldviews and why people believe them. Only then can we present the gospel in language that can be understood. Only then can we defend truth in a way that is winsome and persuasive.[7]

Naturalism

Scientific naturalism is the view that the physical universe is all there is, was, and ever will be. Only material stuff exists, and science is the only source of reliable knowledge concerning the world; everything else is mere conjecture. Physics, chemistry, biology, and genetics are the naturalist's only explanatory tools. One obvious implication of this worldview is that there can be no human soul or immaterial persons like angels or God because, by definition, the supernatural is excluded. Furthermore, there is no spiritual reality in this world or the next; religious faith is delusional; objective moral duties and values are illusory; the grave is all there is. Consider this candid summary of naturalism by the famous twentieth-century atheist Bertrand Russell:

> That man is the product of causes which had no prevision of the end they were achieving; that his origin, his growth, his hopes and fears, his loves and his beliefs, are but the outcome of accidental collocation of atoms; that no fire, no heroism, no intensity of thought and feeling, can preserve an individual life beyond the grave; that all the labors of the age, all the devotion, all the inspira-

tion, all the noonday brightness of human genius, are destined to extinction in the vast death of the solar system, and that the whole temple of man's achievement must inevitably be buried beneath the debris of a universe in ruins — all these things, if not quite beyond dispute, are yet so nearly certain that no philosophy which rejects them can hope to stand ...

Brief and powerless is man's life; on him and all his race the slow, sure doom falls pitiless and dark. Blind to good and evil, reckless of destruction, omnipotent matter rolls on its relentless way; for man, condemned today to lose his dearest, tomorrow himself to pass through the gate of darkness, it remains only to cherish, ere yet the blow falls, the lofty thoughts that ennoble his little day.[8]

Wow, that's depressing. Twenty-first-century atheist Richard Dawkins adds more naturalistic cheer by explaining what you can expect from evolutionary and naturalistic accounts of reality:

In a universe of blind physical forces and genetic replication some people are going to get hurt, other people are going to get lucky, and you won't find any rhyme or reason in it, nor any justice. The universe we observe has precisely the properties we should expect if there is, at the bottom, no design, no purpose, no evil and no other good. Nothing but blind pitiless indifference. DNA neither knows nor cares. DNA just is. And we dance to its music.[9]

If the universe is all there is, was, and ever will be — then the gospel of Russell and Dawkins is all one can expect. The rest of life amounts to nothing more than a trivial illusion of your own creation. (I will say more about naturalism in chapter 18.)

Postmodernism

Postmodernism is an elusive worldview that by its nature resists a definition. But philosopher J. P. Moreland offers a helpful general description: "We may safely say that postmodernism is a form of cultural relativism. According to postmodernism, truth/falsehood, real/unreal, right/wrong, rational/irrational, good/bad are dichotomies relative to different linguistic communities. What is true, real and so forth, for one community may not be so for another."[10] Postmodernism says there can be no "one way" to view the world because reality is constructed through my community's perspective and linguistic practices. In other words, reality is something I create based on the way I view things (this would make religion a social construction as well). Popular postmodern slogans are "Everything is interpretation" (reality is how I interpret it to be) and "Incredulity toward metanarratives" (being unwilling to believe a universal story, explanation, or belief).

Francis Beckwith vividly illustrates one of the absurd implications of a consistently applied postmodern worldview:

To deny the existence of universally objective moral distinctions, one must admit that Mother Teresa was no more or less moral than Adolf Hitler, that torturing three-year-olds for fun is neither good nor evil, that giving 10 percent of one's financial surplus to an invalid is neither praiseworthy nor condemnable, that raping a woman is neither right or wrong, and that providing food and shelter for one's spouse and children is neither a good thing or a bad thing.[11]

Postmodernism is a fundamental redefinition of truth, language, and reality. Mainly because of the diversity of views under this umbrella, defining postmodernism is not easy.[12] (I will explore some of its pluralistic expressions in chapter 11.)

Christian Theism

In stark contrast to both scientific naturalism and postmodernism, Christian theism maintains that God is a trinity, meaning there is only one God who eternally exists as three distinct persons (Father, Son, and Holy Spirit). He is infinite, omnipotent, omniscient, omnipresent, self-existent, holy, loving, just, and good. Since God is personal, humanity can have a relationship with him. Everything that exists, God created out of nothing, and everything is contingent on God to sustain it. Christian theism values both the physical and nonphysical components of reality.

Furthermore, the laws of logic and rationality are grounded in the nature of God himself. Truth is knowable and transcends culture and language. Objective morals and values exist. Humans have inherent dignity as creatures made in the image of God. There is a spiritual reality of our world that is able to be discovered and interacted with through rational investigation, sense experience, and direct acquaintance. The grave is *not* all there is.

Christian theism teaches that evil is real and a fundamental departure from the way things ought to be (that is, God's intended design for humanity). Our world and all who inhabit it are broken, fallen, and in desperate need of redemption. The true story of Christianity can be captured in three universal acts: creation, fall, and redemption (we need to resist the temptation to understand redemption as applying only to individual souls rather than to all of creation, including the cultural commission).[13]

CHRISTIANITY OUTSHINES THE COMPETITION

C. S. Lewis once wrote, "I believe in Christianity as I believe the sun has risen, not only because I see it but because by it I see everything else."[14] What a profound insight! Not only is there substantial independent evidence for the truthfulness of Christianity; Christianity best explains the ultimate worldview questions we all ask. When people set out to test various worldviews, I suggest three questions to help evaluate them: (1) Is it rational? (2) Is it livable? (3) Who says so?[15]

First, it must be *rational.* Is it logically coherent? Do its teachings fit together into a unified picture of reality? Is it logically contradictory? (Postmodernism fails on this regard.) Does it provide satisfactory answers to *all* of the ultimate questions of life?

Second, it must be *livable.* Can we put it into practice? When we follow it like a map, does it lead to successful interactions with reality? Do we get where we want to go? Does it fit with what we know about the world out there? And does it fit with our internal world of desires, hopes, dreams, experiences, and values? I couldn't agree more with Nancy Pearcey when she writes, "When Christianity is tested, we discover that it alone explains and makes sense of the most basic and universal human experiences."[16]

Third, it must originate from an *authoritative source.* Who says so? This question cuts through a lot of the noise and slogans in our spiritual but not religious culture. Here are some inadequate authorities on life's biggest questions: celebrities, friends, emotions, movies, songs, and polls. The founder of Christianity is Jesus of Nazareth. And if it is really true that he rose from the dead and is who he claimed to be, then he has the authority to answer life's biggest questions.

CULTIVATING A WELL-TRAINED MIND

There is much more I could say about worldviews, how to evaluate them, and how they get expressed in pop culture, but I want to wrap up this chapter with three suggestions for cultivating a well-trained mind. First, read good and challenging books (I have included plenty of helpful options at the end of each chapter). Become a lifelong learner. This will enable you to navigate and interact with the ideas of the day and hold fast to what is true and good. (My first recommendation would be *Total Truth* by Nancy Pearcey.)

Second, learn and practice the basic rules of reasoning, critical thinking, and logic.[17] Ours is an experience-based society that runs on slogans and sound bites. We need Christians who know how to think. Invest the necessary time so that you will be able to help others understand and distinguish between fundamental concepts like truth, faith, knowledge, and worldview.

Finally, seek integration in your knowledge. Ask where what you are encountering and learning each day fits and how it impacts other areas of the Christian worldview. The more you do this, the more it will become second nature. As I shared in the preface, this book is really an expression of my own attempt at integration.

If all truth really is God's truth, then we must not live fragmented lives leading to Christian schizophrenia. We cannot mindlessly absorb the hidden worldviews of our culture and still expect to have the courage and conviction to fulfill our mission as the people of God. God has already defined reality; it is our job to respond thoughtfully and engage it appropriately. Many have bought into the lie that you need to keep your Christian faith to yourself. Christianity is deeply personal but certainly *not* private. We have the exciting opportunity and challenge to greet each new day thinking Christianly.

RESOURCES FOR ENGAGING YOUR INTERSECTION

Books

- *Why You Think the Way You Do: The Story of Western Worldviews from Rome to Home* by Glenn Sunshine
- *Total Truth: Liberating Christianity from Its Cultural Captivity* by Nancy Pearcey
- *The Divine Conspiracy: Rediscovering Our Hidden Life in God* by Dallas Willard
- *A World of Difference: Putting Christian Truth-Claims to the Worldview Test* by Kenneth Samples
- *The Drama of Scripture: Finding Our Place in the Biblical Story* by Craig Bartholomew and Michael Goheen
- *Life's Biggest Questions: What the Bible Says about the Things That Matter Most* by Erik Thoennes
- *The God Who Is There: Finding Your Place in God's Story* by D. A. Carson

Websites and DVDs

- www.thinkchristianly.org – Think Christianly
- www.probe.org – Probe Ministries
- www.thepointradio.org – The Point with John Stonestreet
- *The Truth Project*, DVD

WORLDVIEW, CULTURE, AND THE INFORMATION AGE

AN INTERVIEW WITH JOHN STONESTREET

Jonathan Morrow: You spend a lot of time studying our culture. What are some of the most important themes or trends that Christian leaders need to be aware of?

John Stonestreet: In general, I think Os Guinness articulated it well when he suggested that a big failure of Christians has been our lack in understanding the sociology of knowledge. This is just a complicated way of saying that we need to look at what in our culture makes things believable or unbelievable. Our interaction with culture has tended to be much shallower in recent decades. Either we've committed ourselves to being "relevant" at all costs, or we've become alarmists who panic at anything and everything new. Both of these approaches just show how poorly we understand what culture is and how it really influences us.

In particular, I think the most significant aspect of our culture is that it is being created across the board from a fundamental misunderstanding of human beings. Secularism has won the day in the sense that while most people believe in God, they actually live and move and have their being as if God is actually irrelevant to most of life. But secularism always dehumanizes. We see this in politics, fashion, technology, medicine, and even what passes as ministry methods. So a major task for those of us who wish to take the gospel and its cultural implications seriously is to re-humanize culture. If we don't know what human is, we won't know what Christian is.

There is much to be said about what comes with "the Age of Information." Some prophetic thinkers such as Neil Postman, Jacques Ellul, and T. S. Eliot predicted that too much information, especially if it is without context, will quickly lead to foolishness. So we can know a little about everything but a lot about nothing. Trivia replaces wisdom, and noise replaces real conversation and wrestling with ideas. Some have suggested that we have created a generation in perpetual adolescence. For Christians, there is a real danger of the truth being lost amid all the noise and triviality. We must find ways of teaching truth not merely as an end to itself but as a lens for seeing all of reality.

Jonathan: How can Christians do a better job of redemptively engaging our culture in the areas of media and technology?

John: One of the signs that secularism has triumphed is the prevalence of the pragmatic. Today, most of us approach media and technology with an "ends justify the means" mentality. In other words, current thinking suggests, "If it sells, it must be good." Or "If we *can* do it, we *should* do it." The Christian version of this thinking has been to "Christianize" whatever is popular as long as it "works." The problem is that the Christian worldview does not present a vision of reality that is pragmatic. Easier isn't always better. This leads Christians away from their God-given call to lead in the creation of culture (Genesis 2).

Christians can do better with media and technology. First, it's not so much what we are taking in but *how* we are taking it in. How much of our time, resources, and energy are being wasted in trying to be entertained or in entertaining others? It's a tough issue, but each of us needs to address it.

Second, we need to expand the analysis and application of a biblical worldview to the areas of the arts and technology. What is art for, as image bearers? Does current Christian "art" meet these ends? What is technology for, in the biblical worldview? Is there a time where ease and efficiency is actually a bad thing and not a good thing for humans? T. S. Eliot suggested that before we ask, "What can something do?" we should ask, "What is that something for?"

Third, we need to invest in training a new generation of culture makers in the areas of media and technology. What a mission field this is! What a difference it would make if our discipleship efforts included producing a new generation of wise *consumers* and *producers* of media and technology. Journalists, especially in the new media formats, exert enormous influence today. The power of the arts and technology to shape the individuals of a particular culture should not be underestimated.

Jonathan: You work with thousands of students each year at Summit's Worldview conferences. Could you talk about the unique challenges they face as well as the unique opportunities they have for influence?

John: Let me start with the opportunities. I am very, very encouraged by this generation. While there are some real problems, the potential they wield is significant. First, they tend to care more about injustice and suffering. I think this results directly from a fatigue of too much stuff. They've been sold everything, so all that is left is cynicism or compassion. Many have chosen compassion. This means they have a greater resistance to apathy than we Gen Xers did.

Second, they are open to spirituality and big questions. This also comes from a fatigue of having too much stuff—they realize there has to be more to life than what they've been sold. Of course, each of these things is a potential disaster if we as leaders and mentors don't deepen our understanding of real discipleship. The fact that they care about the poor is terrific, but because they don't know *how* to care about the poor, many are being attracted to wrong (very wrong) solutions. Their openness to spiritual things can also lead them to embrace anything spiritual with no discernment (many of them already have).

The bottom line is that this generation is full of stories, but they lack a "big story" in which they can find themselves and their place in the world. They therefore lack a reference point to handle the significant challenges that come at them.

Frankly, we make things worse when we reduce Christianity and discipleship to "you and Jesus and a Bible verse at a quiet time." This is a truncated view of Christianity, a neutered view of the gospel, and it will largely be ineffective in creating long-term commitments to the faith. The gospel is, first and foremost, a unique, compelling, and all-encompassing story of God and his world. Discipleship must include placing students in this story without apology. Worldview, apologetics, culture analysis, and especially training in reading the Scriptures well must be included in the equation.

> **John Stonestreet** is the executive director of Summit Ministries (www. summit.org) a Wilberforce Fellow of the Colson Center, and the host of The Point, a nationally aired one-minute commentary on worldview and culture. A popular speaker at camps, conventions, and conferences, he works annually with thousands of parents, teachers, and students on developing a biblical worldview, understanding comparative worldviews, defending the Christian faith, applying a biblical worldview to education, and engaging important cultural issues. He holds an MA in Christian thought from Trinity Evangelical Divinity School and is the coauthor with W. Gary Phillips and William E. Brown of *Making Sense of Your World: A Biblical Worldview*.

chapter five

CULTIVATING A THOUGHTFUL FAITH

Our current times require us to know what people are saying and how to fully and lovingly explain our beliefs.

Dan Kimball, "You're Not a Fundamentalist If ..."

WHY DO *YOU* THINK CHRISTIANITY IS TRUE? How do you know God isn't just a figment of your imagination? If you grew up in India, wouldn't you be a Hindu? You talk about God's goodness and love—then why is there evil? What makes you think Jesus is unique from other figures in pagan mythology? How can you trust a document like the Bible, which has been corrupted and changed by power-hungry church leaders? Hasn't science made God irrelevant?

You don't have to try hard to come face-to-face with questions like these. If you're being honest, you've probably had them yourself. And if you're a student, they find *you*—kind of like Facebook ads.

Every time I speak on issues of apologetics inside or outside the church, Christians come up to me afterward and thank me for talking about that issue. Usually, they have been wondering about it for a while or had a friend who had questions about it, and they had no idea what to say. Sadly, why we believe what we believe is seldom talked about in our churches or youth groups. That is, it's seldom talked about until someone's son or daughter or spouse or friend is about to walk away from the faith. Then people become all too aware of how relevant reasons for our faith are, and they ask for help. And we try to help, but how much better would it have been to have had those conversations all along the way?

The way in which people form beliefs is complex, and there are more than just intellectual factors at work. Social, personal, and moral factors are three biggies. But logic, reason, and publicly available evidence play a central role in our making the case for the truthfulness of Christianity.[1]

WHY CHRISTIANS NEED APOLOGETICS

Apologetics is a funny word, isn't it? While it has nothing to do with being sorry, it can sound pretty intimidating. I have defined it as simply "learning what Christians believe and why they believe it, and then being able to tell others about it." There are both rational and relational components to it, but it always points ultimately to the hope of Christ.[2] This flows right out of the New Testament: "In your hearts revere Christ as Lord. Always be prepared to give an answer to everyone who asks you to give the reason for the hope that you have. But do this with gentleness and respect" (1 Peter 3:15). The half brother of Jesus put it this way: "But now I find that I must write about something else, urging you to defend the faith that God has entrusted once for all time to his holy people."[3] In this chapter, I want to convince you that apologetics is important for the overall health of the local church and then highlight one prominent cultural example we need to engage today—the new atheism.

ONLY FOR ACADEMICS?

I want to first respond to a common objection you may have encountered: Isn't apologetics only for academics and intellectuals? The short answer is no. Here's why. Everyone has questions—you do, your kids do, your friends and neighbors do, your family does, and our culture certainly does. It's that simple. We will either think carefully or poorly about these questions, but the questions themselves cannot be avoided.

A MATTER OF OBEDIENCE

First and foremost, learning why we believe what we believe is a matter of personal obedience and discipleship to Jesus Christ (1 Peter 3:15) and part of how we love God with all of our minds (Matthew 22:37). Now, that doesn't mean everyone needs to get a PhD. Loving God with our minds will look differently for everyone because of their unique blend of personality, experience, education, and sphere of influence. But the New Testament doesn't view defending the faith as optional. In fact, notice how the gospel is proclaimed and defended in the book of Acts: the apostles are constantly reasoning and making their case for the resurrection as an event in history. Herbert Schlossberg summarizes it this way: "Christians must avoid the intellectual flabbiness of the larger society. They must rally against the prevailing distrust of reason and the exaltation of the irrational. Emotional self-indulgence and irrationalities have always been the enemies of the gospel, and the apostles warned their followers against them."[4] Cultivating a mature faith means understanding what we believe, why we believe it, and why it matters.

BELIEVERS ARE STRENGTHENED

Next, the study of apologetics strengthens believers. Here are two examples. First, it gives Christians confidence in sharing the gospel with others. Who hasn't wrestled with the fear that we will be asked something we won't know—and we will!—but just because we don't know everything doesn't mean we can't know *something* about the most important areas of our faith (for example, historical evidence for the resurrection of Jesus). And the more we have thought about these matters, the more confidence we will have in our conversations. For example, there was a student who was attending a class I was teaching on the evidence for Christianity. After three weeks, he came back and told me he shared his faith with two lifeguards at work. Why? Because he now had some reasons to share why God exists! Imagine what it would look like for all of our students to have this confidence.

Apologetics helps believers overcome tough questions and feelings/seasons of doubt. There are times when we don't feel our faith. But our faith does not ultimately rest on what we feel; it rests on truth because truth is what sets us free. As Os Guinness eloquently puts it, "If you have never been given a reason why for faith, there won't be a reason why not for doubt."[5]

IT REMOVES BARRIERS

Third, awareness of Christian evidences and arguments prepares us to help remove the barriers that often keep people from seriously considering the life and good news that Jesus offers. Granted, everything is not a rational issue. But if we can help someone resolve one of their questions, then it helps them see that there are answers for their other questions too. So by God's grace, we have cooperated with the work of the Holy Spirit to move them a step closer to understanding and hopefully embracing the gospel.

THE GOSPEL IS *ALWAYS* HEARD IN A CULTURAL CONTEXT

Finally, the gospel is never heard in isolation; there is always a cultural backdrop.[6] The penetrating words of twentieth-century Princeton theologian J. Gresham Machen are helpful:

> False ideas are the greatest obstacles to the reception of the gospel. We may preach with all the fervor of a Reformer and yet succeed only in winning a straggler here

and there, if we permit the whole collective thought of a nation or of the world to be controlled by ideas which, by the resistless force of logic, prevent Christianity from being regarded as anything more than a harmless delusion.[7]

Lebanese philosopher and diplomat Charles Malik observes, "The problem is not only to win souls but to save minds. If you win the whole world and lose the mind of the world, you will soon discover you have not won the world."[8] Every culture has a plausibility structure, which simply means there are background beliefs that every person has that inform what they will rationally entertain or not. So, for example, if people think the claim "God exists" is on par with "Santa Claus exists," then they are going to stumble long before they have a chance to consider Jesus. If it is largely believed that science has disproven God—or at least made him irrelevant—then miracles and God's action in time and space are out the window. If history is not knowable and truth is relative, then the Jesus who stepped into history claiming to be God's unique Messiah and the only way to restore humanity's relationship to God will not be seriously considered.

People don't choose their plausibility structure; rather, it is formed over time. The good news is that people's plausibility structures can be shaped over time by regularly talking about reasons for faith in the local church context. This is another reason that worldview formation is crucial.

Of course, Machen's observation resonates with the apostle Paul's conclusion nearly two thousand years earlier: "For the weapons of our warfare are not of the flesh, but divinely powerful for the destruction of fortresses. We are destroying speculations and every lofty thing raised up against the knowledge of God, and we are taking every thought captive to the obedience of Christ" (2 Corinthians 10:4–5 NASB; cf. Colossians 2:8). Knowledge of the truth sets people free from lies. Just think of the power that Darwinian evolution (that is, natural selection acting on random mutation can account for the origin and complexity of all life) and naturalism (only what physics, chemistry, and biology can tell us is real) has had in our culture. Do you think these ideas have made it easier or more difficult for people to believe in God?

Notice, too, that Christians are called to destroy arguments and ideas, not people. (Be sure to reread this.) We are to defeat and refute bad ideas because people's lives are at stake—and ideas *always* have consequences. But we *always* treat people with patience and respect. The Bible is clear about this: "The Lord's servant must not be quarrelsome but kind to everyone, able to teach, not resentful. Opponents must be gently instructed, in the hope that God will grant them repentance leading them to a knowledge of the truth" (2 Timothy 2:24–25). Apologetics sometimes has the unfortunate effect of making some believers arrogant and abrasive. But what this indicates is a need for humility, graciousness, and spiritual formation, not an abandonment of the study of apologetics.

LEARNING TO ASK GOOD QUESTIONS

As we cultivate a thoughtful faith, we will have more confidence to talk to others about what we believe, why we believe it, and why it matters. The next step is growing in our ability to have productive spiritual conversations. Paul put it this way: "Be wise in the way you act toward outsiders; make the most of every opportunity. Let your conversation be always full of grace, seasoned with salt, so that you may know how to answer everyone" (Colossians 4:5–6). One of the best skills Christians can acquire to effectively and confidently share their faith, as well as deal with those who challenge their faith, is to learn to ask good questions. Sometimes we feel as if we need to do all the talking. Not true. A strategically placed question can be far more powerful than a thirty-minute lecture (see Jesus' use of questions in Matthew 17:25; 21:28–32; Luke 20:1–4, 22–26; all in all, he asked 288 of them!).

The best way to learn how to do this is described in *Tactics: A Game Plan for Discussing Your Christian Convictions* by Greg Koukl, president of Stand to Reason. He has developed an approach called "the Columbo tactic" in which a person can go on the offensive in a disarming way. Lieutenant Columbo, the bumbling TV detective whom everyone thought was harmless, had the annoying habit of discovering the truth through asking a series of innocuous questions. The following are two basic questions, with an optional follow-up question:

- *What do you mean by that?* This is an information-gathering question that clarifies what the other person is saying. For example, if someone says, "There is no God," you could respond, "What do you mean by 'God'?" This question is important because it engages the other person and challenges them to think more deeply about what they are saying (maybe they don't know what they mean by "God" because no one has ever asked them).

- *How did you come to that conclusion?* The first question helps you know what they think; this question explores why they think this way. Of course, this assumes they have thought through why they believe something. Suppose this person says, "God is everything and everywhere." Rather than saying, "No he isn't, God is omnipresent yet distinct from creation," you could ask, "How did you come to believe that?" This can be much more effective.

- *Have you ever considered . . . ?* If you are comfortable with the conversation and would like to press a point further, ask this third question. After listening to what a person believes and why, you may discover a weak point to expose. Continuing from our conversation about God being everything, do this with a question: "It seems that you are saying that you and I are 'God,' but also that the waste flowing through a sewer pipe is 'God' too. Is that correct?" By asking questions, you have exposed an absurd claim. Perhaps they will abandon it and be more open to what you have to say about the reasonableness of Christianity.

Memorize these questions and start working them into your conversations. Employing this approach will allow you to guide most of your spiritual conversations in a productive direction. Remember, you don't have to have all the answers; you just need to learn how to ask good questions.

THE APOLOGETICS PYRAMID

Where do you start when it comes to defending the faith? Chad Miester has developed the apologetics pyramid to explore six central issues in a clear, logical progression. While it's never this neat, tidy, and logical in real-life conversations, if you are looking for an approach to strengthen your own faith, or if you are teaching on the reasons for faith in a Sunday school class or from the pulpit, this is a great way to do it:

1. Does truth exist? (truth)
2. Which worldview makes the best sense of the biggest questions in life? (worldviews)
3. Does God exist? (theism)
4. Has God spoken? (revelation)
5. Who is Jesus and did God raise him from the dead? (resurrection)
6. What was the good news of Jesus, his message? (gospel)

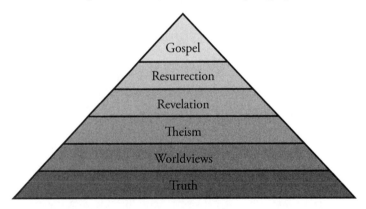

THE RISE OF THE NEW ATHEISTS

Atheism is not new, and the arguments aren't necessarily new either. But what is new is the powerful rhetoric combined with a post-9/11 and increasingly post-Christian culture. Their battle cry is clear: Christianity is not just false; it's dangerous. If you browse some of their writings, you'll come across quotes like, "Religion has run out of justifications. Thanks to the telescope and the microscope, it no longer offers an explanation of anything important."[9] And from Richard Dawkins, author of *The God Delusion*: "When one person suffers from a delusion, it is called insanity. When many people suffer from a delusion, it is called Religion."[10] Another interesting feature of the new atheists is that they are evangelistically spreading the good news of atheism. Note the zeal with which Dawkins addresses his reader: "If this book works as I intend, religious readers who open it will be atheists when they put it down."[11] Sean McDowell and I address these and other challenges in *Is God Just a Human Invention? And Seventeen Other Questions Raised by the New Atheists*.

But the new atheists present us with both an opportunity and a challenge. There is an opportunity for engagement because people are talking about God, which allows Christians to share why they believe what they believe about God. But the challenge is that since most churches talk so little about why we believe what we believe, students and parents are simply unprepared to engage in this area. Unfortunately, students are being persuaded by the emotional rhetoric of the new atheists on the Internet mainly because it's the only voice they encounter. "The first to speak seems right, until someone comes forward and cross-examines him" (Proverbs 18:17). It's quite easy to argue someone out of a belief they've never been argued into.

FOR PASTORS ONLY

As Christian leaders and pastors, we need to take seriously our charge to watch over the souls of those in our spiritual care and to prepare them for what they will face from Monday morning through Saturday night (cf. Hebrews 13:17). If we don't teach them, who will? C. S. Lewis famously remarked that "good philosophy must exist, if for no other reason, because bad philosophy needs to be answered."[12] We can no longer just relegate apologetics to the small group that 5 percent of the people in our churches will participate in. We need to creatively include it in our sermons where appropriate and in church life regularly.

Pastor Tim Keller, author of *The Reason for God*, shared the following regarding apologetics and his ministry: "Over the last twenty years my preaching and teaching has profited a great deal from doing the hard work of reading philosophy, especially the work of older Christian philosophers and scholars (Plantinga, Wolterstorff, Mavrodes, Alston) and the younger ones. Ministers need to be able to glean and put their arguments into easy to understand form, both in speaking and in evangelism."[13] Furthermore, "If pastors fail to do their homework in these areas [science, biblical criticism, philosophy], then there will remain a substantial portion of the population — unfortunately, the most intelligent and therefore most influential people in society, such as doctors, educators, journalists, lawyers, business executives, and so forth — who will remain untouched by their ministry."[14]

On a personal note, the best-attended equipping seminar we've offered at our church was a streaming broadcast of the *Does God Exist?* debate between Christian philosopher William Lane Craig and new atheist Christopher Hitchens. Afterward, I facilitated a Q&A time. It was a wonderful evening. People were given an environment in which to consider the evidence for God that didn't come across heavy-handed. I was reminded that people are hungry to understand why they believe what they believe. And I am more convinced than ever that Christianity is true and that our faith is well placed. But we need to do the hard work to make these good reasons available in an accessible way to everyday Christians.

RESOURCES FOR ENGAGING YOUR INTERSECTION

Books

- *Is God Just a Human Invention? And Seventeen Other Questions Raised by the New Atheists* by Sean McDowell and Jonathan Morrow
- *On Guard: Defending Your Faith with Reason and Precision* by William Lane Craig
- *Apologetics for a New Generation* edited by Sean McDowell
- *Tactics: A Game Plan for Discussing Your Christian Convictions* by Greg Koukl

Websites and DVDs

- www.thinkchristianly.org – Think Christianly
- www.str.org – Stand to Reason
- www.rzim.org – Ravi Zacharias International Ministries
- www.reasonablefaith.org – Reasonable Faith, William Lane Craig
- www.leestrobel.com – Lee Strobel, Investigating Faith
- *Tactics* by Greg Koukl, DVD
- *The Reason for God* by Tim Keller, DVD
- *The Case for Christ* by Lee Strobel, DVD
- *The Case for Faith* by Lee Strobel, DVD
- *The Case for the Creator* by Lee Strobel, DVD

CHRISTIAN INTELLECTUALS SERVING THE CHURCH

AN INTERVIEW WITH PAUL COPAN

Jonathan Morrow: As the current president of the Evangelical Philosophical Society (EPS), can you talk about the revolution that has been taking place in Christian philosophy over the past fifty years?

Paul Copan: It's hard to improve on atheist philosopher Quentin Smith's description in the journal *Philo* several years back. He describes the academy's desecularization that came in 1967 with the publication of Christian philosopher Alvin Plantinga's *God and Other Minds*. (Being a "realist theist" wasn't intellectually respectable back then.) Suddenly, "the secularization of mainstream academia began to quickly unravel." Realist theists "were not outmatched" in their rigor, precision, and erudition. "Naturalists passively watched as realist versions of theism, most influenced by Plantinga's writings, began to sweep through the philosophical community, until today perhaps one-quarter or one-third of philosophy professors are theists, with most being orthodox Christians."

Thus, "almost overnight" it became academically respectable "to argue for theism, making philosophy a favored field of entry for the most intelligent and talented theists entering academia today." Philosophy of religion journals like *Philosophia Christi* (from the Evangelical Philosophical Society) and *Faith and Philosophy* (from the Society of Christian Philosophers) are truly reshaping the philosophical landscape. Smith laments, "God is not 'dead' in academia; he returned to life in the late 1960s and is now alive and well in his last academic stronghold, philosophy departments."[15]

It's an exciting time to be a Christian philosopher, and the EPS is seeking to make an impact in the academy, the local church, and the general culture's marketplace of ideas for the sake of God's kingdom. Members of the EPS are writing and editing scholarly books, presenting papers at conferences, and participating in important philosophical debates and colloquia. And Biola/Talbot School of Theology has set the gold standard for training the next generation of Christian philosophers and apologists.

Jonathan: How can Christian philosophers and the work they are doing help Christian leaders and the local church?

Paul: By God's grace, the EPS is strategically positioned to encourage a thoughtful Christian faith here and throughout the world. Believers around the world are looking to the EPS for guidance and encouragement. EPS members engage in discussion, outreach, and training in different parts of the world, and here at home we put on a well-attended apologetics conference for lay Christians each November. Presentations from this conference have been published in *Passionate Conviction* and *Contending with Christianity's Critics* (Broadman) — part of an ongoing series. Rather than keeping to the ivory tower, many of us EPS philosophers publish apologetics and Christian philosophy books at a popular level to equip believers. (For example, I've written books like *True for You, But Not for Me* and *When God Goes to Starbucks*.) We blog, make resources available at our websites, and speak at conferences and on university campuses.

Jonathan: Ideas discussed in the academy today show up in the public square tomorrow. As you look at the current academic climate, what are some of the most important ideas or trends that pastors need to be prepared to engage?

Paul: Christians need to learn to wisely respond to common objections to the Christian faith (for example, the problem of evil, Old Testament ethics, the uniqueness of Christ in the face of the world's religions) as well as challenging cultural and ethical issues (for example, homosexuality, gay marriage, church-state issues, moral relativism). Church leaders can offer training in apologetics, engage university and international student ministries, and hold discussion groups (for example, Skeptics Anonymous) and book studies.

We must speak the *truth* in *love*. Christian leaders (John Stott and Tim Keller come to mind as models) must preach and teach thoughtfully and reflectively so that Christians will not be misled by intellectual fads like *The Da Vinci Code*, Bart Ehrman's *Misquoting Jesus*, or the new atheism; further, Christians should be helped to winsomely defend their faith in the marketplace of ideas. But truth without love and grace will create suspicion and resentment. David Kinnaman's book *unChristian* is a powerful reminder that pastors must equip Christians to live lives of love, grace, and integrity before a watching world.

> **Paul Copan** is professor and Pledger family chair of philosophy and ethics at Palm Beach Atlantic University. He is the author of *True for You, But Not for Me* (Bethany House), *That's Just Your Interpretation*, *How Do You Know You're Not Wrong?*, *When God Goes to Starbucks: A Guide to Everyday Apologetics* (all with Baker), and *Loving Wisdom: Christian Philosophy of Religion* (Chalice). These books seek to make available accessible answers to the toughest questions asked of Christians. His website is www.paulcopan.com.

chapter six

CONFIDENT ENGAGEMENT FLOWS FROM KNOWLEDGE

Are the central teachings of the Christian tradition things that can be known to be true if appropriately examined? Are they possible subjects of knowledge? Are there people who actually know them to be true? Or are they things you can only believe or choose to commit yourself to, perhaps only profess? And does it really matter one way or the other?

Dallas Willard, *Knowing Christ Today*

AS CHRISTIANS TRY TO FOLLOW JESUS' COMMAND to share his good news, they find they are ignored and not taken seriously. The very things they consider most important are relegated by non-Christians to categories such as *sincere opinion, emotion, blind commitment,* or *tradition.* In other words, Christians are said to cling to nothing more than religious wishful thinking for weak-minded people who need that sort of thing.

But the discerning person will see that these descriptors fall far short of what we usually refer to as *knowledge.* With knowledge, people skillfully and successfully navigate reality and instruct others how to do the same. And if you haven't noticed, reality does not adjust itself to our ignorance in a particular area. When we slam into it, we "get educated."

We want our dentists, mechanics, and doctors to act based on knowledge, not merely on good intentions or vague feelings of faith. Shouldn't we expect the same when it comes to the spiritual life? But what is knowledge and how do we get it? These questions are typically the arena of philosophers, but one of the themes of this book is how important the way we think is to how we live. This is not abstract. I assure you that we all operate according to a theory of knowledge. The question we all must answer is whether our understanding of knowledge is consistent with the reality of the kingdom of God. Remember that part of our calling as we engage our culture is to be Kingdom Citizens who are confident in what we believe and why we believe it.

KNOWLEDGE OF GOD MATTERS

Which do you think shows up more in the Bible—faith or knowledge? If you do a concordance search, you will find something surprising. Knowledge (including *knowing, know,* etc.) shows up far more than faith does. Of course, without faith it is impossible to please God, but knowledge is far more important to God than people realize. Listen to the words of the Lord as recorded by the prophet Jeremiah—words reminding us that knowledge of God is to be prized above all else:

> "Let not the wise boast of their wisdom
> or the strong boast of their strength
> or the rich boast of their riches,
> but let the one who boasts boast about this:
> that they have the understanding *to know me,*
> that I am the Lord, who exercises kindness,
> justice and righteousness on earth,
> for in these I delight."
>
> Jeremiah 9:23–24, emphasis added

Or pay attention to the indictment of the Israelites by the prophet Hosea:

> Listen to the word of the Lord, O sons of Israel,
> For the Lord has a case against the inhabitants of the land,
> Because there is no faithfulness or kindness
> Or knowledge of God in the land ...
> My people are destroyed for lack of knowledge.
> Because you have rejected knowledge,
> I also will reject you from being My priest.
> Since you have forgotten the law of your God,
> I also will forget your children.
>
> Hosea 4:1, 6 NASB

People are destroyed for the lack of the knowledge of God. God has revealed himself so that he could be known and we could know how to live—and we can offer this knowledge to others. In our day, how do we perish for lack of knowledge? In his classic work *Knowing God,* J. I. Packer reminds us:

We are cruel to ourselves if we try to live in this world without knowing about the God whose world it is and who runs it. The world becomes a strange, mad, painful place, and life in it a disappointing and unpleasant business, for those who do not know about God. Disregard the study of God, and you sentence yourself to stumble and blunder through life, blindfold[ed], as it were, with no sense of direction and no understanding of what surrounds you.[1]

In stark contrast to Hosea's audience, and relevant to our calling to engage our unique intersection, the sons of Issachar were "men who understood the times, with *knowledge* of what Israel should do" (1 Chronicles 12:32 NASB, emphasis added). Don't miss this! They embodied the words of Daniel: "The people who know their God will display strength and take action" (Daniel 11:32 NASB).[2] I firmly believe that one of the reasons we don't see many Christians engaging our culture in a redemptive way is because they don't have confidence that what they believe is actually true!

Luke begins his gospel offering knowledge of the truth: "It seemed fitting for me as well, having investigated everything carefully from the beginning, to write it out for you in consecutive order, most excellent Theophilus; *so that you may know the exact truth* about the things you have been taught" (Luke 1:3–4 NASB, emphasis added). John the apostle states, "These things I have written to you who believe in the name of the Son of God, so that you may know that you have eternal life" (1 John 5:13 NASB). And Peter commands us to "grow in the grace and *knowledge* of our Lord and Savior Jesus Christ" (2 Peter 3:18 NASB, emphasis added).

There is a crisis of knowledge today. Western Christianity desperately needs to recover the importance of the knowledge of God, pursue it, teach the next generation, and announce to the watching world that it is available. Biblical faith is not at odds with knowledge; in fact, it rests on the foundation of knowledge. Biblical faith acts on and actively trusts in the knowledge of God. Our knowledge of God increases so that we can exercise more faith! Faith is fundamentally about a commitment of the will based on what fills our hearts and minds.

An objection may be forming in your minds: But doesn't knowledge make people arrogant? It certainly can. But the opposite of arrogance is not ignorance, but humility. Since we are the recipients of the knowledge of God, there is absolutely no room for arrogance. "The trouble with the world," Mark Twain once wrote, "is not that people know too little, but that they know so many things that ain't so." Well said. Incidentally, the need for humility is another reason why spiritual formation is crucial to engaging our culture and why in the next two chapters we'll discuss how we can become more like the Jesus our world desperately needs. Jesus, who was perfect in knowledge, never hurt or abused anyone with it. Everyday Ambassadors recognize this and look to him as our model for engagement.

Knowledge is also critical because it helps eliminate defensiveness. Nancy Pearcey's comments are instructive:

> Generations of churched youngsters have been encouraged to shore up their religious commitment by sheer willpower, closing their eyes and ears to contrary ideas. This explains why so many churches are full of people who are closed-minded, dogmatic, harsh, and judgmental. Only people who understand that Christianity is true to the real world are capable of the relaxed confidence that allows them to be open, patient, and loving toward those who differ from them.[3]

The confidence to engage those who may disagree with us flows from the basis of knowledge.

SOME IMPORTANT QUESTIONS ABOUT KNOWLEDGE
What Is Knowledge?

Generally speaking, knowledge can be defined as "true belief based on adequate reasons." For the sake of clarity, I will be using "adequate reasons" synonymously with what philosophers typically call "justification."[4] Dallas Willard's summary is helpful: "We have knowledge of something when we are representing it (thinking about it, speaking of it, treating it) as it actually is, on an appropriate basis of thought and experience."[5]

For something to count as knowledge, (1) you must believe it; (2) the belief you hold must be true (that is, it accurately describes the way things actually are); and (3) this true belief must be justified or supported by adequate evidence based on thought and experience. Evidence comes in a *variety* of forms. The *amount* of evidence necessary to satisfy the "adequate reasons" condition for knowledge will be situation specific. Philosopher Garry DeWeese illustrates how this works with various types of knowledge claims:

> What counts as the right kinds of reasons depends on the nature of the proposition. I believe the sun is shining because I can see it and feel its warmth. I believe I had cereal for breakfast because I clearly remember it. I believe my wife loves me because she tells me so, shows me in many ways, and has stuck with me for a number of years. And I believe Tiglath-Pileser was a mighty king of Assyria who invaded Israel in 743 BC because I read about him in the Bible (2 Kings 15 – 16) and in reliable histories of Assyria. In all these cases the reason why I believe what I do are truth indicators. They are the right kinds of reasons to justify those beliefs.[6]

The key thing to remember is that every subject matter — whether math, gardening, or the spiritual life — has its own *particular* methods of knowing. So "we start with clear instances of knowledge, formulate criteria based on those clear instances, and extend our knowledge by using those criteria in borderline cases."[7]

Does Knowledge Require Bombproof Certainty?

Must we have bombproof certainty before we can say that we know something? Is it all or nothing—100 percent certainty (that is, it is impossible that I am wrong) or hopeless skepticism? I don't think so, because this dilemma is a false one. A skeptical approach to knowledge maintains that knowledge itself is impossible or that no beliefs can be justified *even if* they happen to be true. Not only is this view unlivable; it also seems self-contradictory, because even radical skeptics think they know enough to claim you are mistaken. Our beliefs come in degrees of confidence, and some beliefs are more central than others; logical certainty is available only in mathematics.[8] I may be very confident that God raised Jesus from the dead and have less confidence as to whether or not Christians ought to take the Lord's Supper every week, but my differing levels of confidence don't negate my beliefs. The all-or-nothing standard for knowledge gets us in trouble because it eliminates virtually everything that ultimately matters.

When it comes to God, one of the temptations is to withhold judgment until all the information is in and every possible issue has been investigated. To be honest, this is a pretty tall order. You will never know everything about everything. I sure don't. If you wait until then, well, you will be waiting a long time! And the question of God is too important. Just as an employer can't know if an employee will be reliable until hired, and a person can't know everything about a would-be spouse before they say "I do," so too you cannot experience God—really get to know him—until you have entered into a personal relationship.[9] Pastor John Ortberg offers some good advice: "There is no way to God that bypasses the call to let go [that is, to choose to trust him]. You may have many intellectual doubts, and it is really important to be honest about those, to talk about them and study. However, thinking and studying alone never remove the need to choose. The question of faith is never just an intellectual decision."[10]

Is Science Our Only Source of Knowledge?

With the rise and success of modern science (and these advances have been beneficial in many ways), some people have unfortunately come to believe that science, and science alone, offers true knowledge of reality. Famous atheist Bertrand Russell put it this way: "Whatever knowledge is attainable, must be attained by scientific methods; and what science cannot discover, mankind cannot know."[11] Initially, this sounds sophisticated and intelligent. You will hear variations of this slogan all over the place, and it is implied in most documentaries you see on TV. The only problem is that if it is true, we couldn't know it to be true. Why? Because the statement itself is not testable by the scientific method and is therefore by its own standard unable to be known! It's self-refuting. It's a statement that commits suicide.

We will get into this more in a later chapter, but science is not capable of providing *comprehensive* knowledge of reality. It does great with bacteria, supernovas, genes, and gravity, but it falters when trying to discuss virtue and vice, souls, free will, moral responsibility, success, joy, love, forgiveness, wisdom, salvation, redemption, hope, purpose, meaning, and beauty (just to name a few!). The scientism espoused by Russell, which is hand in hand with naturalism, must be resisted by Christians if we are to engage our world with the good news of the kingdom of God. We don't need to be bullied into thinking that if we can't examine something with a microscope or telescope, then we can't know it. For this is a self-evidently false statement.

Can We Know That God Exists?

Biblical faith is not belief in spite of the evidence but belief in light of the evidence. Science can neither prove nor disprove the existence of God, but it can point us in the right direction. Simply put, the beginning of the universe points to a Beginner; the fine-tuning of the universe points to a Fine-Tuner; the vast amount of information contained in living organisms (especially in DNA) points to an Information Giver. In addition to these scientific sources of knowledge, the existence of objective moral laws point to a Moral Lawgiver, and the existence of consciousness, free will, and the immaterial soul indicates that matter — studied through physics, chemistry, and biology — is not all there is. We could spend a whole book on each of these, but Christians can be confident in their knowledge that God exists.[12]

An Example of Moral and Spiritual Knowledge – Dealing with Anger

Have you ever been angry? Or, more accurately, when was the last time you were really angry? Can we gain knowledge of how to deal with our anger? Yes. Paul provides just that in his letter to the Ephesians: "Be angry, and yet do not sin; do not let the sun go down on your anger, and do not give the devil an opportunity ... Let all bitterness and wrath and anger and clamor and slander be put away from you, along with all malice. Be kind to one another, tender-hearted, forgiving each other, just as God in Christ also has forgiven you" (4:26–27, 31–32 NASB).

There is profound insight here that can set us free. We learn that anger and forgiveness are linked. When we fixate on anger, we give the devil an opportunity to secure a foothold of harmful influence in our life. Paul teaches that forgiveness breaks this foothold. But just when we are tempted to think that our story is different, that the wrongs done to us are too flagrant to be forgiven, he appeals to the fact that we have been forgiven by Christ when we didn't deserve it. The logic is clear: Our forgiveness of others is to be done in the same way ("just as") Christ has forgiven us. We don't forgive because they deserve it; we forgive because we have been forgiven.

Andy Stanley offers a concrete process for applying the knowledge rooted in this passage to breaking the power of anger in our lives. It is a practical way in which we guard our hearts (Proverbs 4:23). Here are the four phases (not steps, because they describe a process that is person and situation specific):

1. **Identify those you are angry at.** There is a big difference in trying to forget a debt and canceling a debt. We need to go back and make a list of those who have mistreated us, hurt us, and taken advantage of us. Odds are that our anger today is flowing out of much older wounds.

2. **Determine what they owe you.** Forgiveness needs to be specific, not vague. The people who hurt us took something from us—our innocence, an opportunity, money, our family, emotional security, trust. Make the list and be specific. This will take some time, but it is a crucial process we can't afford to skip.

3. **Cancel the debt.** After you name exactly what has been taken, it is time to cancel the debt. This means "deciding the offending party does not owe you anymore. Just as Christ canceled your sin debt at Calvary, so you and I must cancel the debts others have incurred against us."[13] If the offense is from a long time ago, it sometimes helps to physicalize this act of forgiveness—perhaps writing it all down on a piece of paper and then, with close friends or family present, burning the list as a symbol of canceling what the person owes.

   For the everyday offenses we encounter, Stanley suggests the following prayer habit:

   "Heavenly Father, _____ has taken _____ from me. I have held on to this debt long enough. I choose to cancel this debt. _____ does not owe me anymore. Just as you forgave me, I forgive _____."

   This will keep your heart free and clear. It is important to distinguish between forgiveness and reconciliation. In most cases, it is not necessary (or even beneficial) for the person to know that you have forgiven them because this process is about the anger growing *in your own heart.*

4. **Dismiss the case.** Thoughts of the offense and the offender will come back from time to time, but we must resolve not to reopen the case. It is done. "When memories of past hurts flood your mind, go ahead and face them. It's even OK to feel the emotions those memories elicit. But instead of reopening the case against your offender, take this opportunity to restate your decision: He/she doesn't owe me. Then thank your heavenly Father for giving you the grace to forgive."[14] Over time, the

emotions associated with this wound will diminish if we faithfully practice this habit. In the end, we must resist the urge to get payback. This is futile because in a sense we can't be paid back for what has been taken from us. What's more, "To cling to our hurt while waiting to be repaid is to allow the seeds of bitterness to take root and grow. When that happens, we allow the person who hurt us once to hurt us over and over again."[15] This temptation is subtle because we think we are making them pay for what they've done, when in reality the exact opposite is true. True freedom is possible only when we dismiss the case.

I don't know about you, but I could have used this bit of knowledge earlier in life. This is not just some take-it-or-leave-it self-help technique. God, through his inspired Word, offers us knowledge about how to break free from the power of anger and, in doing so, to become more like Jesus Christ. Anger is just one example. We could do the same thing with breaking the power of greed, envy, guilt, the nature of love (cf. 1 Corinthians 13), and a host of other things in life. But enough has been said to show that moral and spiritual knowledge is available to us. And equally important is recognizing that this knowledge is *just as real and legitimate* as the knowledge that when you combine sodium (Na) and chlorine (Cl), you get salt. Different methods, different subjects, same result — *knowledge*. And when we act in accordance with knowledge, we grow in our ability to successfully navigate reality.

An Example of Moral and Spiritual Knowledge – True Happiness

A monumental shift has taken place since the middle of the twentieth century. Happiness has been redefined to essentially mean that humans exist to have as many pleasurable experiences as possible. The leading authority on happiness today, Martin Seligman, observed a tenfold increase in depression in the baby boomer generation compared to earlier generations.[16] Why? Because they began living for themselves instead of for something bigger than themselves, as previous generations had done. Paul Campos sums it up well:

> Americans today are on average twice as rich, and far healthier, more youthful, and safer than our predecessors were a half century ago ... In other words, what is conventionally thought of as the American dream — that you will be better off than your parents, and that your children will in turn be better off than yourself — seems to keep coming true. There's just one little problem with this rosy scenario ... all this "progress" doesn't seem to have made Americans any happier.[17]

Living for yourself, according to the world's definition of happiness, will actually make you miserable and depressed. Teenagers today are more depressed than the boomer generation and complain mostly of being bored (think of the unprecedented technology and opportunities available to them that they can pursue at any moment!). Many of us have bought into this redefinition of happiness.

What a far cry from the classical definition of happiness as living a life of character and virtue, or from the biblical definition of living well before the face of God and living according to the pattern and teachings of Jesus. In fact, Jesus offers us knowledge of true happiness: "Seek first his kingdom and his righteousness, and all these things will be given to you as well" (Matthew 6:33).

EVERYONE'S A THEOLOGIAN

Theology has fallen on hard times these days. Many within the church think it's only relevant for the eggheads residing in the rarified air of ivory towers. But as theologian Erik Thoennes reminds us, "Knowledge without devotion is cold, dead orthodoxy. Devotion without knowledge is irrational instability. But true knowledge of God includes understanding everything from his perspective. Theology is learning to think God's thoughts after him."[18] Theology matters because "the most important thing about a man," writes A. W. Tozer, "is what comes into his mind when he thinks about God."[19]

If you have thoughts about God, then you are a theologian. The only question is whether you will be a good one. In the New Testament, Paul clearly teaches that Christians are to destroy speculations and everything raised up against the knowledge of God and take every thought captive to the obedience of Christ because the world system is at work in our culture (2 Corinthians 10:3 – 5). J. P. Moreland rightly reminds us, "The devil is waging war against the possibility of the knowledge of God. This is no time for the church to adopt an anti-intellectual approach to knowledge and faith."[20]

Contrary to the postmodern tendency to dismiss the possibility of knowledge, the Christian life requires both *propositional* (knowledge that) and *personal* (knowledge of) knowledge. God offers us both. One without the other results in deficient understanding. Yet our knowledge of whom we are worshiping and what we are personally experiencing is always guided and informed by the revealed propositional and narrative content of the Bible—which is, in fact, true.[21] Sound doctrine is not an add-on to the Christian life; it is the foundation. After all, the church, the body of Christ, is called to be the pillar and support of the truth (see 1 Timothy 3:15).

The goal of theology, then, is not simply to accumulate data about God. Rather, it should deeply affect us. David Clark paints a compelling picture: "When ... theology reaches full bloom, it blossoms into ... the wisdom of God. This leads us to passionate love for God, genuine worship of the Trinity, true community with fellow Christians, and loving service in personal evangelism and social compassion—all to the glory of God. That is what it means to know and love the true and living God. Absolutely nothing matters more."[22]

The acquisition of knowledge should help us along the path of becoming virtuous people, flourishing as followers of Jesus Christ. Knowledge, over time and with effort, becomes understanding. Understanding then describes the growing integration of our fragmented knowledge into an increasingly coherent picture of God and our world. And as we grow in understanding, we have the opportunity to grow in wisdom as well, which is the skillful application of knowledge and understanding to life. Solomon speaks of the blessing that accompanies this pursuit: "Blessed are those who find wisdom, those who gain understanding" (Proverbs 3:13; cf. 2:6). Knowledge is the crucial first step in this process.[23]

RECOVERING CHRISTIANITY AS A KNOWLEDGE TRADITION

As humans, we were designed to act on knowledge in everyday life. If you and I don't think the Bible and other sources of knowledge about God, morality, and the spiritual life are possible, and we are not growing in this knowledge, then following Jesus in everyday life will be next to impossible because we always default to what we know. Moreover, there appears to be no good reason to exclude the knowledge claims of Christianity simply because they are "religious." If they do not hold up to scrutiny, that is one thing. But Christianity, which is rooted in history, makes many claims, some of which are empirically testable while others are testable by nonempirical means. The crucial point is that Christianity rises to the level of being either true or false, and it can be known to be true or false (cf. Luke 1:1–4).

If Christianity is relegated to the realm of fairy tales, which may provide personal significance or meaning but not knowledge, then people will continue not taking the claims of Jesus or the Christian worldview seriously. If, however, people are invited to consider the claims of Christianity as a knowledge tradition, then chances are good that they may come to know the living God and live life according to the knowledge provided in his Word.

RESOURCES FOR ENGAGING YOUR INTERSECTION

Books

- *Knowing Christ Today: Why We Can Trust Spiritual Knowledge* by Dallas Willard
- *Philosophy Made Slightly Less Difficult: A Beginner's Guide to Life's Big Questions* by Garry DeWeese and J. P. Moreland
- *Unshakable Truth: How You Can Experience the 12 Essentials of a Relevant Faith* by Josh and Sean McDowell
- *Know the Truth: A Handbook of Christian Belief* by Bruce Milne
- *Kingdom Triangle: Recover the Christian Mind, Renovate the Soul, Restore the Spirit's Power* by J. P. Moreland

Websites and DVDs

- www.thinkchristianly.org – Think Christianly
- www.reclaimingthemind.org – Reclaiming the Mind Ministries
- www.biblicaltraining.org – Biblical Training
- www.bible.org – Bible.org
- *Unshakable Truth*, DVD
- *The Truth Project*, DVD

ENGAGING ISLAM

AN INTERVIEW WITH ALAN SHLEMON

Jonathan Morrow: Given your Assyrian family background and your experience speaking nationally on the topic of Islam, you bring a unique perspective to one of the most discussed topics today. There are many competing and even contradictory voices out there about what the true nature of Islam is, so how do we go about sorting out the truth?

Alan Shlemon: What matters to Muslims is authority. Yes, there are competing voices that purport to speak for Islam, but the ones that matter are those that rely on Islam's three most authoritative sources: the Qur'an, the Hadith, and the Sunnah. The Qur'an, which Muslims claim is the only reliable source of divine revelation, is the highest authority. The Hadith is a collection of written traditions that record what Muhammad said, did, or approved of. Though not considered the very words of Allah, the Hadith is still authoritative because that's where the Qur'an's broad principles are fleshed out with specific applications. The Sunnah is the life example set by Muhammad. Islam teaches that Muhammad is the perfect embodiment of Islam and the supreme example for right living.

These authoritative sources provide a standard for settling debates about what Islam actually teaches. Those claims that are consistent with the teaching in these texts pass the test. Those without basis in these sources cannot be trusted. For example, when the Queen of Jordan—herself a Muslim—comes on Oprah Winfrey's show and says Islam treats women as *equal* partners to men, this claim can be tested. As it turns out, though individual Muslims might treat women as equal to men, this is not the teaching of Islam's authoritative sources.

Jonathan: What advice would you give Christians to more effectively engage our Muslim friends and neighbors?

Alan: When it comes to engaging Muslims with the truth of Jesus, there's good news and bad news. The bad news is there's no magic bullet—no single approach that will work with every Muslim. The good news is that since there's no magic bullet, a range of approaches have merit, depending on the situation.

The problem isn't that Christians don't know the "magic" approach to sharing with Muslims; the real problem is that they rarely engage Muslims at all. This is a shame because Muslims are some of the easiest people to talk to about God, religion, and the Bible. It's like talking with an American about sports. It's virtually effortless. Many Christians are timid with Muslims, though, because they don't realize this.

Jonathan: You've developed a tactic that gives Christians confidence when talking to Muslims about Jesus and the Bible. Tell us about it.

Alan: As I mentioned earlier, virtually every conversation with a Muslim comes down to one issue: authority. No matter what approach you take to share the gospel, at some point you'll have to point to the New Testament to make your case. Muslims, however, believe the Bible is corrupt and unreliable. This is where the tactic comes in handy.

My approach hinges on a little-known fact. Though *Muslims* believe the Bible is corrupted, the *Qur'an* actually teaches that it is true and reliable. And since Muslims believe the Qur'an is an unassailable authority, you can enlist it as an ally and leverage its authority to your advantage. Here's the logic of the position:

- The Qur'an says the words of God cannot be changed or corrupted.
- The Qur'an says the Bible is the Word of God.
- Therefore, on the Qur'an's authority, the Bible could not have been changed or corrupted, as many Muslims claim.

There are many passages in the Qur'an that affirm the first premise but take surah 6:34 as an example: "There is none that can alter the words (and decrees) of Allah."

Likewise, many passages affirm that the Bible is a divine revelation from Allah (the second premise). Surah 29:46 tells Muslims not to argue with Christians and Jews. Instead, they are to say, "We believe in the revelation which has come down to us and in that which came down to you."

Notice that Muslims are commanded to believe in both the Qur'an ("which has come down to us") and the Bible ("that which came down to you"). Both "came down" from Allah as divine revelation, according to the Qur'an. If Muslims claim the Bible is corrupt, then they are rejecting the teaching of their own authoritative source, the Qur'an.

Muslims also face a different dilemma. If Allah *couldn't* protect the Bible from corruption, then he is inept because mere mortals were able to corrupt his words. If Allah *wouldn't* protect the Bible, then he is immoral for commanding his followers to believe in a corrupted and unreliable revelation.

Once Muslims acknowledge what the Qur'an claims about the Bible, then they may be more open to the teachings of the New Testament and the gospel message you plan to share.

Alan Shlemon is an author and public speaker for Stand to Reason. He has written *The Ambassador's Guide to Islam*, which describes his tactic more thoroughly. Besides his expertise in Islam, Alan is skilled at speaking on some of the most controversial issues of our day, including abortion, homosexuality, and stem cell research. He has trained thousands of adults and students across the country at churches, conferences, and universities. He has been a guest on both radio and television. You can learn more about Alan at www.str.org.

chapter seven

BECOMING LIKE THE JESUS THE WORLD NEEDS [I]

Jesus does not offer a new layer to your life. He invites you to a completely different life altogether.

J. P. Moreland, *The God Question*

THE LONGER I'M A CHRISTIAN, the more convinced I become that many people in the church today ebb and flow between frustration, exhaustion, and disillusionment when it comes to the spiritual life. The unspoken message is to pray more, read the Bible more, have more faith, attend church more often, profess whatever everyone professes, and, above all else, try harder. But trying really hard to live like Jesus without adopting his overall way of life — practices and priorities — will only lead to disappointment and discouragement. But I am getting ahead of myself.

Let's start with a fundamental question: Is it really possible to become more like Jesus? The biblical answer is yes. Scripture clearly teaches that our heavenly Father desires us to be increasingly "conformed to the image of His Son" (Romans 8:29 NASB). Furthermore, since we are constantly being spiritually formed in a way contrary to life with God, if we are to engage well and if our culture is to consider our message, then the church must make pursuing spiritual transformation a high priority (Romans 12:2). But how exactly does one go about this?

For most of my Christian life, I have known that I was supposed to read the Bible and pray. It wasn't always clear why or how — but I knew I needed to. And by

God's grace, over time I was growing. But I began to be frustrated by something. As I read pages of the New Testament, there seemed to be a significant gap between the life promised there and the kind of life I was experiencing (cf. 2 Peter 1:3–4). Can you relate? I have been a Christian for fifteen years now, but it has only been in the last couple of years that some important concepts concerning the spiritual life have begun to fall into place.

Several years ago, as I was reading a book by John Ortberg, I came across a quote that made me stop dead in my tracks. I had to reread it. And then I took out my pen and highlighter, marked the passage, and read it again:

> If I want to fully experience the love of Jesus, I must receive one of his most important gifts he sends me — his teaching. I must invite Jesus to be the personal Teacher of my life. I must trust that he is right — about everything. And that therefore where I disagree with him I must either be wrong or not yet understand what it was he was saying. I must allow Jesus to teach me how to live.[1]

This launched a personal journey to explore what the Bible teaches on this and what this looks like in everyday life. The fruit of this investigation, which I am imperfectly trying to live out, is what I will share in this chapter and the next.[2]

HOW WE LOST JESUS THE TEACHER

As evangelicals, we are good at recognizing Jesus as our Savior and Lord. And rightly so. But over the years, out of a well-intentioned commitment to preserve the deity and atonement of Christ in the controversy between fundamentalism and liberalism, Christians largely abandoned the idea of Jesus as teacher. The theme emerging from within liberalism was that Jesus was a good moral teacher, but not the Son of God. Unintentionally and over time, the role of Jesus' teaching began to be diminished because people wanted to make sure they affirmed his deity.[3]

In addition, somewhere along the way, the gospel of the kingdom of God that Jesus proclaimed was reduced to "minimal entrance requirements to get into heaven when we die."[4] I will flesh this out a little more in chapter 15, but the message should be that the rule of God — his kingdom — has arrived in Jesus. God's presence and power are now available to everyone in and through the person of Jesus. Up there is coming down here. Restoration is now possible at a personal, social, and cosmic level. That was his message, and that was what got him crucified. And his substitutionary death and his resurrection are what make this new kind of life possible. But forgiveness just sets the table for the meal; the meal is relationship with God and life in his kingdom.[5] The eternal kind of life now *and* forevermore (John 17:3).

Of course this includes heaven someday when God makes all things new; I don't want to diminish that for a second. But we have made Christianity all about someday and not today. Unless we move beyond this impoverished view of Christianity, there is little motivation or power to follow Jesus in the here and now. So let's think about this for a minute. If the gospel is *just* about being forgiven (as important as this is), and Jesus' death and resurrection accomplishes this for us, then doesn't discipleship seem as though it is optional or a bonus for the superspiritual among us? Perhaps we're missing something.

JESUS AS TEACHER

The Gospels clearly reveal that Jesus was a master teacher. They repeatedly affirm his identity as a rabbi who taught with authority. In fact, Jesus is called "rabbi" fourteen times and "teacher" forty times (for example, Luke 7:40). And he didn't just teach like everyone else. Matthew tells us, "When Jesus had finished saying these things, the crowds were amazed at his teaching, because he taught as one who had authority, and not as their teachers of the law" (7:28–29). This was not a slam on other teachers, because it was proper form to appeal to other authorities and other precedents in the law. But Jesus claims to hold the authority when he says things like, "You have heard that it was said ... but I tell you ..."

Does Jesus know what he is talking about? Really? I mean, we are in the twenty-first century. Dallas Willard observes that " 'Jesus is Lord' can mean little in practice for anyone who has to hesitate before saying, 'Jesus is smart.' He is not just nice, he is brilliant. He is the smartest man who ever lived."[6] In other words, Jesus has a PhD in everything—he is master of reality. He always has the best information about everything. He is the embodiment of the knowledge of God. Paul would later write that in Jesus Christ "are hidden all the treasures of wisdom and knowledge" (Colossians 2:3). Jesus possesses knowledge of reality, and his life, teaching, and example revealed in the Scriptures are a primary source for gaining spiritual and moral knowledge about the world in which we live. If anyone successfully navigated reality—lived according to knowledge—then Jesus of Nazareth certainly did.

BECOMING AN APPRENTICE OF THE MASTER

Everyone learns from someone. It is sometimes easy to deceive ourselves by thinking that since we graduated high school and college, we don't have teachers anymore. Not so. Every day, we all knowingly or unknowingly place ourselves under the influence and authority of various teachers—pop culture, TV, friends, family, coworkers. Usually there is no formal relationship to any one of these entities, ideas, or people; there are no tuition payments. But we are students nonetheless, and class is always in session.

But you and I have been offered the opportunity of a lifetime to sit at the feet of Jesus and follow in his footsteps. We are invited to be apprentices of Jesus—the God of the universe in human form! I think we have watered down the invitation to discipleship that Jesus offers. In the ancient world, most people were turned down from being a follower of a rabbi — only a precious few were invited to be a disciple. Yet Jesus makes this invitation to *everyone* who will accept it: "Come to me, all of you who are weary and carry heavy burdens, and I will give you rest. *Take my yoke upon you. Let me teach you*, because I am humble and gentle at heart, and you will find rest for your souls. For my yoke is easy to bear, and the burden I give you is light" (Matthew 11:28–30 NLT, emphasis added). A yoke is a way of life. Jesus is offering his way of life to us. He passionately desires to teach us how to live this new life in the reality of the kingdom of God.[7]

The rest of the New Testament affirms that Jesus is to be our example. Jesus himself said, "I have set you an example that you should do as I have done for you" (John 13:15). He also reminded us that "the student is not above the teacher, but everyone who is fully trained will be like their teacher" (Luke 6:40). Paul said that we should have "the same mindset as Christ Jesus" (Philippians 2:5) and invites us to imitate him as he imitates Christ (1 Corinthians 11:1; cf. Philippians 4:9). Peter reminds us, "To this you were called, because Christ suffered for you, leaving you an example, that you should follow in his steps" (1 Peter 2:21). And the author of Hebrews encourages us with these words: "Let us run with endurance the race that is set before us, fixing our eyes on Jesus, the author and perfecter of faith" (Hebrews 12:1–2 NASB).

So what is an apprentice? An apprentice, or Christ-follower, is someone in the process of learning how Jesus would live our lives if he were in our place. As apprentices, we are learning to live and respond as Jesus would if he were to face my unique circumstances, talents, gifts, job, relationships, opportunities, and challenges. This will undoubtedly be a rocky experience at first, but as we pursue this new kind of life, real change is possible. A lifelong apprentice to Jesus offers us some wisdom for our journey:

> When setting out as his apprentices, we will sharply encounter all of the harmful things that are in us: false thoughts and feelings, self-will, bodily inclinations to evil, ungodly social relationships and patterns, and soul wounds and misconnections. Our Savior and Teacher will help us remove these as we strive forward through the many-sided ministries of himself, his kingdom, and his people. All will be bathed in the Holy Spirit. The process of spiritual formation in Christlikeness is a process through which all the dimensions of our lives are transformed as they increasingly take on the character of our Teacher.[8]

That's good news for us and good news for the world!

SO, WHAT WOULD JESUS DO?

Now, honestly, there could be worse questions to ask, but this one really isn't very helpful. Let's say I am around someone who annoys me, and I'm getting impatient and frustrated (even angry). Now, apply the WWJD principle. Jesus would be patient and understanding. But I am not patient and understanding, nor do I even *want* to be just now! Have you ever tried to be patient in the moment? Obviously, something more than information and willpower are needed!

I submit that a better question is HDJDWHD: How did Jesus do what he did? (patent pending, but not holding my breath). What kind of practices, values, thoughts, priorities, relationships, and habits did Jesus arrange his life around so that he was able to live the life he lived? The simple fact is that "we cannot behave 'on the spot' as Jesus did and taught if in the rest of our time we live as everybody else does."[9] And all of us said — "Amen!"

TRAINING WISELY INSTEAD OF TRYING HARDER

When we examine the life of Jesus, a surprising pattern emerges: he trained to be able to accomplish the mission of the Father. Willpower alone will not produce this kind of life. In fact, I would go so far as to say that had Jesus not trained the way he did, then his final follow-through of obedience from Gethsemane to Golgotha would not have been possible. When he came home from the temple at age twelve, we don't hear of him again until he was thirty as he launched his public ministry, which lasted only three years. Therefore, if we want to grow as apprentices of Jesus, one of the foundational changes that must occur in our thinking is this: it isn't about "trying harder, but training wisely."[10]

To see this, we must first remember that Jesus was *human* in every way. He got hungry, thirsty, tired, and angry. Scripture teaches that he was tempted in every way, just as we are — except he did not sin (Hebrews 4:15). It also teaches that he learned obedience through his suffering (5:8 – 9). He grew in his capacity for obedience. Second, Jesus had a human mind. He grew in wisdom and stature (Luke 2:52), and he had limitations on his knowledge (Mark 13:32). Third, Jesus was completely dependent on the resources of God the Father (John 5:19) and on the Holy Spirit (Luke 4:1). Fourth, Jesus lived perfectly by faith (Hebrews 12:2). And finally, Jesus was saturated by the word of God and lived by it (Luke 4:1 – 14).

In addition, Jesus practiced certain spiritual disciplines or activities at various times in his life that enabled him to live the life he lived: solitude (Mark 1:35; 6:46), fasting (Matthew 4:1 – 11), frugality (Luke 9:58), prayer (Luke 6:12), secrecy (Matthew 6:1 – 7; Mark 4:1), submission (John 5:18 – 37), humility (Philippians 2:5 – 8), obedience (Luke 22:41 – 42), sacrifice (Hebrews 10:9 – 10), study (Luke 2:41 – 52), fellowship (Luke 22:14), confession (Mark 8:31; 14:36), worship (Luke 4:16; John 4:21 – 24), and Scripture meditation (Matthew 4:4 – 10).[11]

DEMYSTIFYING SPIRITUAL DISCIPLINES

You may have noticed I mentioned a word that is scary for some Christians — *disciplines*. Oh, no, not those! They are perceived as the lima beans of the Christian life. So consider this fair warning: we are now going to be talking about spiritual disciplines. And unfortunately, most of the time, mentioning spiritual disciplines does not lead to the transformation, hope, or freedom that God intends. Instead, it tends to produce a lot of guilt. For example, someone may say, "I know I should read Scripture and pray, and I already don't do those things—so why do I want to learn about fifteen other practices that I am not doing?" I feel that.

But I want to invite you to see spiritual disciplines with new eyes—as if for the first time. And be open to the idea that Jesus, Paul, Peter, Timothy, and countless other Christians who have practiced them through the ages have experienced God's power and presence in their everyday lives through the spiritual disciplines.

What the Spiritual Disciplines Are Not

It will be helpful to dispel a few myths about the spiritual disciplines. First, they are not "a barometer of spirituality."[12] We don't practice them so that we can say, "Wow, look how spiritual I am! I can do thirteen disciplines in one day." The measure of spiritual maturity is our ability to love God and people. Arrogance is not a fruit of the Spirit.

Second, they are not a way "to earn favor with God,"[13] to make him love us more (for example, performance spirituality), or to get spiritual brownie points. One of my biggest aha moments during my exploration was that the disciplines are for *us*, not God. No one is checking a box and keeping score. God certainly isn't. He is concerned with us becoming more like Jesus and growing in holiness (1 Peter 1:13–17).

What the Spiritual Disciplines Are

Right off the bat, we need to acknowledge that Paul commands us to discipline ourselves "for the purpose of godliness; for bodily discipline is only of little profit, but godliness is profitable for all things, since it holds promise for the present life and also for the life to come" (1 Timothy 4:7–8 NASB; cf. 2 Peter 1:5–10). They are essential for our growth and not optional when it comes to the Christian life.

A discipline is "any activity I can do by direct effort that will help me do what I cannot now do by direct effort."[14] For example, we practice scales on a piano to learn to play music—not to get really good at playing scales. I don't practice grammar to get really good at grammar. I study vocabulary and grammar *so that* I can learn to speak a new language and experience the whole new world that language opens up. The eternal kind of life is like learning a new language.

The best definition of the spiritual disciplines I've come across is this one from Dallas Willard: "The indirect means that allow us to cooperate in reshaping the personality—the feelings, ideas, mental processes and images, and the deep readinesses of soul and body—so that our whole being is poised to go with the movements of the regenerate heart that is in us by the impact of the gospel Word under the direction and energizing of the Holy Spirit."[15]

But how do we know which spiritual discipline to practice? Here's a suggestion. We must learn what particular barriers keep us from living this kind of life. And then we must discover what particular practices, experiences, or relationships can help us overcome these barriers. For example, if I struggle with hurry, then the discipline of solitude and silence will be really helpful for me. If I struggle with being content, then the discipline of gratitude will be really helpful. Disciplines of abstinence (for example, solitude, silence, and fasting) help weaken and break the power of internal or external forces that are pressing in on us to conform us against life with God. Disciplines of engagement (for example, study, celebration, and service) help us to immerse ourselves more fully in the life God offers.[16]

GOD, THE ANSWER IS YES ...

In light of all we've covered, I want to revisit the quote from the opening section of this chapter:

> If I want to fully experience the love of Jesus, I must receive one of his most important gifts he sends me—his teaching. I must invite Jesus to be the personal Teacher of my life. I must trust that he is right—about everything. And that therefore where I disagree with him I must either be wrong or not yet understand what it was he was saying. I must allow Jesus to teach me how to live.[17]

I need to trust that Jesus is right about everything. I must submit to him as the one who knows what is real and good and true moment by moment. I must decide to hear and do what Jesus teaches (Matthew 7:24–25; cf. James 1:22). Or as Andy Stanley defines submission, "God, the answer is yes ... now what's the question?"[18] As apprentices of Jesus, this should become our mission statement for life.

THE GREAT OMISSION

Oh, and one more thing. All the stuff we talk about in this and the next chapters is what we are supposed to teach others about (cf. Matthew 11:28; 28:20). This is what it means to make disciples—introducing people to Jesus so they can learn from him, live with him, and be like him. We have left out part of the Great Commission—"teaching them to observe all that I commanded you." We are called first and foremost to be apprentices of Jesus ourselves, and then we are called to make disciples. And the "making disciples" part involves teaching them how to do what Jesus said and assumes we have learned and are increasingly learning to do this ourselves.

Transformation, not perfection, is what we must be committed to as we engage people and move into cultural moments. If we don't, then when we do engage, people will resist our message because they will see a glaring disconnect between our life and our message. The reality is, we can sit in church and hear good sermons for years and years and not grow in our maturity.

Jesus came to earth announcing that a new kind of life was now available—*eternal life in the kingdom of God*. And this new kind of life encompasses *all* areas of life. The idea of Jesus as Lord and Savior is foundational, but seeing him as our Teacher is central to our growth as his disciples. Jesus invites us to be his students and apprentices, to learn from him how to live and then to teach others how to do the same. Discipleship and spiritual formation are not optional. For us to have the power to engage well, we must be with Jesus so that we can become like him in the context of community. In the next chapter I'll take a closer look at how the process of spiritual formation works, from the inside out.

RESOURCES FOR ENGAGING YOUR INTERSECTION

Books

- *The Me I Want to Be: Becoming God's Best Version of You* by John Ortberg
- *Renovation of the Heart: Putting on the Character of Christ* by Dallas Willard
- *Everybody's Normal Till You Get to Know Them* by John Ortberg
- *Spirit of the Disciplines: Understanding How God Changes Lives* by Dallas Willard
- *Divine Conspiracy: Rediscovering Our Hidden Life in God* by Dallas Willard
- *Spiritual Disciplines Handbook: Practices That Transform Us* by Adele Calhoun
- *The Complete Book of Discipleship: On Being and Making Followers of Christ* by Bill Hull

Websites and DVDs

- www.metamorpha.com – An online community for spiritual formation
- www.monvee.com – Monvee (online spiritual growth tool)
- www.dwillard.org – Dallas Willard's website
- www.biblicalspirituality.org – Donald Whitney's website
- *In the Dust of the Rabbi* by Ray Vanderlaan, DVD
- *The Me I Want to Be*, DVD

SPIRITUAL FORMATION AND THE EVERYDAY CHRISTIAN

AN INTERVIEW WITH KYLE STROBEL

Jonathan Morrow: Metamorpha.com is an online community for spiritual formation that you cofounded. Can you explain what Christian spiritual formation is and why you began this ministry?

Kyle Strobel: Christian spiritual formation is simply God's work to sanctify believers into the image of Christ. The *spiritual*, in spiritual formation, is the Holy *Spirit's* work to form Christ in us. Life in the Spirit doesn't undermine our action, but allows us to live freely in grace, where our freedom is freedom to love both God and neighbor. Jesus' life, in the Spirit, is now our own life as members of his body who are being built up into him, our Head.

We started Metamorpha.com because we believe people have tried to think rightly, look rightly, and act rightly, but have failed to come to God truly, authentically, and personally. Spiritual formation, at its heart, is coming to Christ at the cross by faith alone and by his grace alone. Our task, therefore, is learning dependence on God and trust in his way over our own. Our goal is to provide ways for people to open their hearts more fully to the God who has come to us in Christ Jesus and who invades our hearts by his Spirit.

Jonathan: Christians can become disillusioned and frustrated with their lack of spiritual growth. The New Testament seems to assume it is really possible. How do Christians grow spiritually in everyday life?

Kyle: The frustration most Christians experience is what we might call "spiritual feedback" from their effort to grow themselves rather than resting in the work of God for them and in them. This feedback stems from a false understanding of the gospel, a kind of prosperity gospel, where they assume that if they do all the right things, God will grant them excitement, success, happiness, etc. This is often most acute for pastors, who assume that if they preach "rightly," have the "right" doctrine, and do all of the "right" programs, then their ministries will flourish.

When they don't, they assume they are not good enough or savvy enough, or else are being punished for former sins. They turn, in other words, not to grace or dependence, but to self-loathing and self-help.

Turning instead to Christ and his work on the cross entails trusting in his way over the ways of the world, which means that the Christian life won't merely be building up, but also tearing down the structures and idolatries of the heart. This breaking down can be thought of as tilling the soil of one's heart, and God does this work by his Spirit through his Word and community. We can think of this in terms of Jesus' voice speaking through his Word, penetrating our hearts by his Spirit, and helping us discern his voice within his community.

Jonathan: What do you see as the most significant challenge Christians face from a culture that seeks to undermine our attempts to grow spiritually?

Kyle: In my mind, the two places in Scripture I immediately turn to are Philippians and James. In both of these books, we are confronted with worldly values, beliefs, and social structures that undermine the gospel. Specifically, in Philippians we are given examples and patterns of those who have lived before us, especially Christ, who used his status and position to walk the way of the cross.

Our culture trains us to get what we want when we want it and seeks to form us into consumers who have it "their way right away." Spiritual formation entails a willingness to pray "not my will, but yours be done." It demands, in John Calvin's words, a knowledge both of God and of self, where we come to grasp his holiness *as well as* our sin. Our temptation will be either to ignore our sin and try to cover it up with something else or to use God for our own ends rather than for his. Many want God for what he can do for them, while fewer are interested in Christ as Lord and King. The countercultural reality of the gospel is that we are called as citizens of another realm even as the very material reality of this world seeks to draw our attention.

> **Kyle Strobel** is a speaker, writer, and practitioner of spiritual formation and community transformation who seeks to think theologically and evangelically about spiritual formation, doctrine, and the church. He is the cofounder of Metamorpha Ministries (Metamorpha.com), the author of the book *Metamorpha: Jesus as a Way of Life* (Baker, 2007), and coeditor of *A Guide to Christian Spiritual Classics* (Downers Grove, IL: InterVarsity, forthcoming). Kyle has his PhD in systematic theology from the University of Aberdeen, writing a dissertation on "Jonathan Edwards's Trinitarian Theology of Redemption."

chapter eight

BECOMING LIKE THE JESUS THE WORLD NEEDS [II]

A thoughtless or uninformed theology grips and guides our life with just as great a force as does a thoughtful and informed one.

Dallas Willard, *The Spirit of the Disciplines*

IF OUR CULTURE is to seriously consider the good news we are commanded to make known, then we must intend to become more like the Jesus our culture desperately needs. To be an apprentice of Jesus Christ simply means that we are learning from him how to live our lives if he were in our place. Our heavenly Father's desire for us is clear: "As obedient children, do not conform to the evil desires you had when you lived in ignorance. But just as he who called you is holy, so be holy in all you do" (1 Peter 1:14–15). Obedience leads to holiness and holiness leads to life. As we do what God says, we'll become more like him; and as we become more like him, we will experience the life he offers.

In this chapter we will examine the dynamics of how we become more like Jesus and grow in holiness from the inside out. This will help us to not be so easily deceived by the lies of the world system. However, this is not an easy task because there are many moving parts that interact quickly—thoughts, feelings, emotions, desires, will, and then actions. Sometimes it helps to slow it down so we can take a better look.

This is why I'm a fan of the show *Time Warp* on the Discovery Channel. The premise of the show is simple: take an HD high-speed video camera with super slow motion, and film ordinary occurrences in life that seem quite unremarkable. Yet slowed down to 675,000 frames per second, you can see a bullet slowly penetrating a series of aluminum cans, a water balloon wrapping around a person's face before it pops, and a martial arts expert's hand grotesquely bending as he breaks concrete—pretty amazing stuff!

The effect would be equally amazing if we could somehow slow down our internal world, second by second, moment by moment, and decision by decision, as we either choose life with God or life apart from God. For the most part, we can. The New Testament offers various distinctions that help us understand exactly what is going on when we act on *this* desire and not *that* one. And if we see how things work and what areas influence other areas, then we can more intelligently cooperate with God's Spirit in the dynamic process of spiritual transformation.

After studying this, lights started to come on for me.[1] I began to more clearly see what was going on within me and, more importantly, what needed attention if I was to grow in a particular area. But the place to start is the heart because this is where our Teacher started when he taught about the spiritual life.

WE LIVE FROM OUR HEARTS

In order to avoid legalistic and guilt-inducing "performance Christianity," it's vital to grasp the fact that holiness begins on the inside (that is, "the heart") and works its way outward (that is, "our behavior"). Here is a common scenario: Joe tries really hard to behave—by sheer willpower alone—and when he fails (and he will), he thinks that God has failed him, Christianity isn't true, or the Christian life may work for someone else who is really spiritual but not him. For a while he feels guilty about not trying harder, but eventually he just stops trying. Sure, Joe will continue to attend church—after all, that is what good Christians do, and it happens to be one of the behaviors he can actually control—but he has given up hope that the life described in the New Testament is possible for him. All of this results in a diminished life and undercuts meaningful engagement with our culture. We must aim at the heart because in the end, behavior modification is both ineffective and exhausting.

Solomon, the wisest man who ever lived, carefully studied and wrote about many topics. So when we come across a passage where he writes "above all else," our ears ought to perk up! "Above all else, guard your heart, for everything you do flows from it" (Proverbs 4:23). Our hearts equal our lives. Picking up on this theme, Jesus teaches that "the things that proceed out of the mouth come from the heart ... For out of the heart come evil thoughts, murders, adulteries, fornications, thefts, false witness, slanders" (Matthew 15:18–19 NASB).

On another occasion, Jesus taught, "No good tree bears bad fruit, nor does a bad tree bear good fruit. Each tree is recognized by its own fruit. People do not pick figs from thornbushes, or grapes from briers. A good man brings good things out of the good stored up in his heart, and an evil man brings evil things out of the evil stored up in his heart. For the mouth speaks what the heart is full of" (Luke 6:43–45). Our behavior is the outworking of what's really going on in our heart. To sum up, the Bible teaches that the heart is the core of our being, the CEO of our inner life, from which all of our actions flow. We live from our hearts, but as we will discover, transformation begins with the mind (Romans 12:2).

THE INTERWORKINGS OF THE HEART: FLESH, DESIRE, WILL, AND MIND

Flesh

In the New Testament, the biblical term *flesh* most often describes the natural tendencies, abilities, and desires we have as embodied humans, which have been formed according to the evil in the world and are set against God. It comes as a surprise to many Christians, however, that the flesh is not *inherently* evil. We know this because Adam and Eve both had a flesh that God created good, and so did Jesus Christ in the incarnation. Jesus experienced the natural bodily desires we do (for example, feeling hungry and tired), yet did so *without sin*.

The flesh is rooted in desire and intertwined with our body in the form of habits (cf. Romans 6:11–14).[2] Since the fall, our flesh has been corrupted by sin, obsesses over and fixates on what it desires, is weak, and is at war with our own spirit and the Holy Spirit.[3] Our bodies have been trained to respond in certain ways without our even thinking about it. All of us have formed habits to manage life in a fallen world. We must retrain our bodies to act in accordance with the kingdom of God by the power of the Holy Spirit. Because we have been born again, it is now possible to replace automatic bodily responses toward selfishness with patience and kindness. We do this by wise training, not by trying harder.[4]

Desire

Desires are simply the things we want. God created us with desires that ultimately will only be satisfied in him. C. S. Lewis captures this point well: "If I find in myself a desire which no experience in this world can satisfy, the most probable explanation is that I was made for another world. Probably earthly pleasures were never meant to satisfy it, but only arouse it, to suggest the real thing."[5]

Desire is a good thing. The psalmist says that God "will fulfill the desire of those who fear Him" (Psalm 145:19 NASB). David also says to "delight yourself in the LORD; and He will give you the desires of your heart" (Psalm 37:4 NASB). We run into trouble when evil desires govern our lives and enslave our will (Romans 8:6). This happens subtly. We can desire things that are good—sexual intimacy, food, and pleasure—but when we make them ultimate (which is idolatry), we are enslaved.[6]

Will

The will is the human capacity or power to choose, originate, do, and act. When the Bible speaks of self-control (a fruit of the Spirit; Galatians 5:23) and self-determination, it has our will in mind. The book of Proverbs tells us that "like a city whose walls are broken through is a person who lacks self-control" (Proverbs 25:28). Much of our society, with its pursuit of pleasure on the basis of strong feelings and desires, is a testimony to this proverb.

It is imperative to distinguish desires and feelings from our regenerate will. Here's why. In Christ, we no longer have to do what we currently desire. It will be helpful to note two aspects of the human will—the impulsive will and the reflective will.[7] The *impulsive will* is best seen in the child who wants what she wants—right now. See the doughnut, must have the doughnut. Nothing else exists in the entire universe except that doughnut! There is an inability to see past the desired object to anything else. The *reflective will* is at work when we can come to the place where we can "do what we don't want to do" (for example, homework) and "not do what we want to do" (for example, eat ice cream for dinner every night). We want to be able to choose what is best.

The good news is that we can now do this! Peter instructs the believer:

> His divine power has given us everything we need for a godly life through our knowledge of him who called us by his own glory and goodness. Through these he has given us his very great and precious promises, so that through them you may participate in the divine nature, having escaped the corruption in the world caused by evil desires.
>
> 2 Peter 1:3–4

Because this is true, we can make sense of the command to "abstain from fleshly lusts which wage war against the soul" (1 Peter 2:11 NASB). We can choose not to do what we now desire—indeed, we must if we are to grow up in Christ. The goal is to choose not what we *want* but what is *good*. A critical point to grasp is that the will is *completely dependent* on the thoughts and feelings present in our minds at the time of any particular choice.

Mind

The biblical term *mind* describes our thoughts and emotions—we can't have one without the other. Our thoughts consist of ideas (for example, happiness) and images (for example, a peace sign). Our "first freedom" as human beings is to choose what we dwell on, what occupies our minds.[8] So while we can't just choose to feel a certain way, we can direct our minds to pretty much whatever we want, like a beach or the mountains.

Here is a fundamental truth of the spiritual life: If we never think of the things of God throughout the day, then our will cannot act on them. Every thought we have either leads us toward life with God or away from life with God. Our beliefs and our thought life provide the live possibilities for us to choose in the day in, day out experiences of life. If our thoughts are mostly directed away from God, then our choices most likely will be as well—and repeated choices become ingrained habits. Renewing our mind is fundamental to being an apprentice of Jesus. "Do not conform to the pattern of this world, but be transformed by the renewing of your mind" (Romans 12:2). We live from our hearts, but transformation *begins* with the mind. This is how we get off the merry-go-round of "see, want, get." Dallas Willard reminds us, "The process of spiritual formation in Christ is one of progressively replacing destructive images and ideas with images and ideas that fill the mind of Jesus himself."[9]

Even though we can get into ruts in our thinking and form bad habits, the good news is that *we really can change*. We can form good habits of thinking by dwelling on what is true, honorable, and good (Philippians 4:8). However, we cannot change our beliefs and feelings *directly* by willpower alone. Change is accomplished *indirectly* by exposing our minds to new images, ideas, and thoughts. By using our first freedom, we can "choose to take in the Word of God, and when we do that, beliefs and feelings will be steadily pulled in a godly direction."[10]

This truth finds confirmation in modern neuroscience. People with obsessive compulsive disorder have been able to literally rewire their brains and neural pathways by directing their minds to other thoughts over time (yes, the mind is *distinct* from the brain; brain states are correlated with mental states, but they are not identical).[11] You can literally form new neural pathways through renewing your mind as you repeatedly tell yourself the truth from God's Word.[12] As the prophet Isaiah wrote, "You will keep in perfect peace all who trust in you, all whose thoughts are fixed on you!" (26:3 NLT; cf. Psalm 16:8–11).[13]

Robert McGee offers a helpful pattern for replacing lies with the truth:

1. Agree with God that we have been deceived, believed a lie, and need to repent for doing so.
2. Allow God to show us how destructive this lie has been in our lives.
3. Choose to reject the lie we have been believing for so long, and commit ourselves to believe what God says to be true.
4. Be willing to stand on the truth that God disclosed to us about ourselves instead of using our normal responses.[14]

A great application is to regularly focus our mind on our identity in Christ, which will help free us from seeing our sense of worth as tied to performance and success.

We can regularly meditate on truth as we face problems and wrestle with insecurities: "I am a child of God" (John 1:12). "I have been completely forgiven" (Colossians 1:14). "I am God's handiwork" (Ephesians 2:10). "Nothing can separate me from the love of Christ" (Romans 8:39). How marvelously liberating these thoughts are to dwell on!

WHAT ROLES DO GRACE AND THE HOLY SPIRIT PLAY IN SPIRITUAL TRANSFORMATION?

Grace is God acting in your life to enable you to accomplish what you cannot accomplish on your own (it's not just unmerited favor).[15] And God's grace is available whenever we ask for it. As we act, fueled by grace, we are transformed. Grace eliminates the need to earn God's forgiveness and love, but it does not preclude our effort in the Christian life. Moreover, we are not waiting on the Holy Spirit so that we can obey. Rather, if we are in Christ (Colossians 3:1–3), then the Holy Spirit is *already* at work and waiting for us to jump on board. Our job is to keep in step (Galatians 5:25). The Holy Spirit is absolutely essential all along the way—from our new birth to glorification. But we must still act; the spiritual life is not passive (Philippians 2:11–12). And as we act, our whole person (thoughts, feelings, will, bodily habits, etc.) begins to be conformed to the pattern of Christ. Our worldviews begin to change in fundamental ways.

RELATIONSHIPS ARE THE CONTEXT FOR CHANGE

Everyone is hardwired to connect. God created us for community, first with himself and then with others. David Benner goes so far as to say that "if you are making significant progress on the transformational journey of Christian spirituality, you have one or more friendships that support that journey. If you don't, you are not. It is that simple."[16] The author of Hebrews exhorts us, "And let us consider how we may spur one another on toward love and good deeds, not giving up meeting together, as some are in the habit of doing, but encouraging one another" (10:24–25). This is just one of the numerous "one another" passages in the New Testament (see, for example, Romans 13:8; Galatians 6:2; Ephesians 4:32; Colossians 3:16; James 5:16). The Bible knows nothing of lone-ranger spirituality. All of us need a place to belong, to connect, to be known and loved unconditionally, to be challenged, encouraged, and forgiven as we live out our calling.

CIRCUMSTANCES ARE THE CATALYSTS FOR CHANGE

I wish there was a way to grow spiritually without challenges and tests. But alas, there is not. Everyday circumstances are the unpredictable laboratory of change. James reminds us, "Consider it pure joy, my brothers and sisters, whenever you face trials of many kinds, because you know that the testing of your faith produces perseverance. Let perseverance finish its work so that you may be mature and complete, not lacking anything" (1:2–4; cf. Romans 5:1–5). Our tendency is to view circumstances as the enemy, when in fact they are opportunities to experience life with God, to cooperate with him in what he wants to do in these very moments. To be honest, I've got a long way to go. But I am increasingly recognizing how God is using everyday circumstances to form me into the image of his Son.

OVERCOMING HURRY SICKNESS

Dr. Richard Swenson is a futurist who writes about the social and personal factors that afflict America. Dr. Swenson has diagnosed the problem of our day as "overload." If you were to take an MRI of our lives, here is what you would see: "We have too many choices and decisions, too many activities and commitments, too much change creating too much stress. We have too much speed and hurry. We have too much technology, complexity, traffic, information, possessions, debt, expectations, advertisements, and media. We even have too much work."[17] And all God's people said — "Amen!" When we no longer have any margin in our lives, no space between our load and our limits, then we are in a constant state of overload. And that is not a healthy place to be.

There is perhaps no greater barrier to spiritual transformation and cultural engagement today than the lack of time. If we are to be who God calls us to be, we must ruthlessly eliminate hurry from our lives.[18] God's word instructs us "to number our days that we may get a heart of wisdom" (Psalm 90:12 ESV). Paul admonishes us to "look carefully then how you walk, not as unwise but as wise, making the best use of the time, because the days are evil" (Ephesians 5:15 – 16 ESV). We can have the best of intentions, but if there is no time to think, study, reflect, pray, cultivate relationships, or engage with others — then it simply won't happen. It can't. John Ortberg writes, "For many of us the great danger is not that we will renounce our faith. It is that we will become so distracted and rushed and preoccupied that we will settle for a mediocre version of it. We will just skim our lives instead of actually living them."[19] Probably the most spiritual thing we can do is to start taking our time back by building some margin into our lives.

LEARNING THE LANGUAGE OF GOD'S KINGDOM

By this point, you may be saying, "OK, I'm in. I need to change and want to change — but *how* do I change?" What follows is a habit that we can all learn and apply to *any* area of life. Once you begin to apply it thoroughly to one area, it becomes much easier to apply to other areas. There are three parts to this approach — Vision, Intention, and Means.[20]

To make this more concrete, think of a teenager who just turned sixteen. She has formed a vision for a certain way of life — how wonderful it would be to have a car to drive all her friends around in and to be free from the watchful eye of Mom and Dad (Vision). She then *decides* that she must have this car — doing whatever it takes to get it (Intention). Finally, she arranges her life around making this car a reality — she does chores for extra money, mows grass, and does odd jobs (Means). This pattern (VIM) is the same for learning a new language, dealing with anger, addressing lust, or anything else you can think of.

Vision: What is my picture of reality?

Our vision is our picture of reality. What is "real" in this situation? (Incidentally, there is always a "counterfeit picture of reality" when we experience temptation.) Ultimately, our vision needs to be something like this: living in the reality of God as our heavenly Father, enjoying his creative goodness and love, his power and presence — the eternal kind of life he invites us into right now (John 17:3). Our vision is shaped as we renew our minds (Romans 12:2) and direct our thoughts toward God.

Intention: Have I actually decided to pursue this vision?

Sometimes we are confronted with a picture of reality but never decide to actualize it. You don't just halfway learn Chinese — you either commit to it or not. Spiritual transformation works the same way. Either you want to grow or you don't. Either you want to do what is necessary to deal with your anger or you don't. We actually have to *intend* to live as Jesus lived.

Means: How do I need to arrange my life to make this vision a reality?

This is where we experiment and get creative. We begin to introduce practices and habits that help us implement this God-saturated vision in our lives (1 Timothy 4:7). Means are the final step. So many times we start doing stuff and trying harder without attaching it to a vision of life. If I want to experience God, then I need to meditate on his words more often and build into my schedule times of solitude and silence.[21]

PUTTING IT ALL TOGETHER

As this chapter comes to an end, here are a few summary principles: First, *who you want to be must be determined before what you need to do.* We must have a vision of the kind of life that we actually want; without this, much of our effort will be in vain. Second, *everyone is becoming something.* We are either becoming more like Jesus or more conformed to the pattern of this world — nothing stays the same. Third, *everyone learns from someone.* As we saw in the last chapter, becoming an apprentice of Jesus is the best decision we can make.

Finally, we must ask this question: How do I need to live (that is, arrange my life) in order to become who I want to be? This is where spiritual disciplines and margin come in, but it is essential to see that they must be tied to a compelling vision. Without this vision, Christians fall into the traps of legalism and performance Christianity. Means are effective only in the context of a compelling vision once we have decided to become this kind of person.

I encourage you to be on the lookout for comparison. You are God's handiwork (Ephesians 2:10) with a unique set of experiences, temperament, needs, calling, and season of life. We all need to grow, and the ingredients are the same, but he has us all at different places. This mind-set will allow us to have greater compassion for those who are either young in their faith or do not yet know Christ.

RESOURCES FOR ENGAGING
YOUR INTERSECTION

Books

- *Renovation of the Heart: Putting On the Character of Christ* by Dallas Willard
- *The Divine Conspiracy: Rediscovering Our Hidden Life in God* by Dallas Willard
- *It Came from Within* by Andy Stanley
- *Overcoming Emotions That Destroy* by Chip Ingram and Dr. Becca Johnson
- *The Search for Significance: Seeing Your True Worth through God's Eyes* by Robert McGee
- *Love Your God with All Your Mind: The Role of Reason in the Life of the Soul* by J. P. Moreland
- *A Minute of Margin: Restoring Balance to Busy Lives* by Richard Swenson
- *The Me I Want to Be: Becoming God's Best Version of You* by John Ortberg

Websites and DVDs

- www.metamorpha.com—An online community for spiritual formation
- www.monvee.com—Monvee (online spiritual growth tool)
- www.dwillard.org—Dallas Willard's website
- www.biblicalspirituality.org—Donald Whitney's website
- *The Me I Want to Be*, DVD
- *The Divine Conspiracy*, DVD

MAKING THE CASE FOR LIFE

AN INTERVIEW WITH SCOTT KLUSENDORF

Jonathan Morrow: As the founder of Life Training Institute, you have written articles, published a book, and participated in debates all over the country making the case for the pro-life position. In your view, is the abortion debate complex?

Scott Klusendorf: No, it's not, really. It comes down to just one question: *What is the unborn?* Unfortunately, many people ignore this question and simply assume the unborn are not human. For example, Nadine Strossen, former president of the ACLU, asserted in a recent debate that we must respect freedom of conscience and allow women a right to choose. Well, maybe. But choose what? Suppose the topic were killing toddlers in the name of trusting women? Would Nadine argue for freedom of conscience for those parents who wish to unjustly kill their kids? Again, only by assuming the unborn are not human can she argue this way. Pro-life advocates, meanwhile, contend that elective abortion unjustly takes the life of a defenseless human being. This simplifies the abortion controversy by focusing public attention on just one question: *Is the unborn a member of the human family?* If so, killing him or her to benefit others is a serious moral wrong. Conversely, if the unborn are not human, elective abortion requires no more justification than having a tooth pulled.

Jonathan: Can you talk about the importance of using arguments from philosophy and science when making the case for life in the public square?

Scott: In short, it's absolutely crucial. While Christians accept religious truth claims as real and knowable, secularists do not. The trick is to communicate biblical truth by using arguments unchurched people cannot reject out of hand. I always make a pro-life case using science and philosophy.

Jonathan: Can you briefly summarize what that pro-life case looks like?

Scott: Sure. Scientifically, we know that from the earliest stages of development, the unborn are distinct, living, and whole human beings. True, they have yet to grow and mature, but they are whole human beings nonetheless. Leading embryology textbooks affirm this. (For a summary of the scientific case, go to www.caseforlife.com.)

Philosophically, there is no morally significant difference between the embryo you once were and the adult you are today. Differences of size and development are not relevant in the way that abortion advocates need them to be. For example, everyone agrees that embryos are small—perhaps smaller than the dot at the end of this sentence. But since when do rights depend on how large we are? Men are generally larger than women, but this hardly means they deserve more rights. Body size does not equal value. In reply, some assert that self-awareness makes us valuable human beings. But if that's true, newborns and those in reversible comas fail to qualify. In short, although humans differ immensely with respect to talents, accomplishments, and degrees of development, they are nonetheless equal because they share a common human nature.

Jonathan: How can Christian leaders and pastors become more involved in defending the unborn?

Scott: Here's what a pro-life pastor looks like. First, he preaches a biblical view of human value—namely, that humans are valuable because of whose image we bear rather than because of some function we perform. Second, he equips his people to engage the culture with a robust but graciously communicated case for life, using the brief scientific and philosophic case summarized above. Third, he restores broken lives through consistent cross-centered preaching. Wise pastors avoid the twin extremes of heavy-handed (and graceless) preaching on the one hand, and ignoring sin on the other. Instead, they opt for a biblical third alternative. They preach that abortion is sinful and then point to the remedy—the cross of Christ. Finally, pro-life pastors confront their fears about driving people away should they preach on a controversial but essential topic. My own speaking experience confirms that when the abortion issue is presented persuasively and compassionately, the vast majority of people will applaud the pastor rather than crucify him.

Jonathan: What is the greatest opportunity or challenge facing the pro-life movement today?

Scott: There's a short-term challenge and an even tougher long-term one. Short-term, we must engage politically at a whole new level. Let's stop beating around the bush. One major political party promotes abortion wholesale and wants your tax dollars to do it. That party must be defeated at the ballot box. The other major party more or less supports pro-life legislation but needs to do a better job standing up for innocent human life. That party should be supported but challenged to do better—much better. As my friend Greg Koukl puts it, given a choice between a first-class arsonist and a second-class fireman, you go with the second-class fireman—all the while challenging him to do better! Long-term, we must systematically train more Christian youth. I speak in Protestant and Catholic high schools all over the United States. Over and over again, students tell me they've never heard a pro-life talk like mine. At each place, students see pictures depicting abortion and hear a compelling case for the pro-life view. Gatekeepers such as teachers and administrators worry the kids can't handle abortion-related content, but the gatekeepers are wrong. I'm often told by students, "Gee, I finally know how to defend what I believe. Thank you!"

> **Scott Klusendorf** is the founder and president of Life Training Institute and the author of *The Case for Life* (Crossway, 2009). He travels throughout the United States and Canada training pro-life advocates to defend their views in the public square. Scott is a graduate of UCLA and holds an MA in Christian apologetics from Biola University. His website is www.prolifetraining.com.

chapter nine

CAN WE DO THAT IN CHURCH?

Instead of engaging ... [the] secular world, most Christians have taken the easy way out. They have retreated into a Christian subculture where they engage Christian concerns. Then they step back into secular society, where their Christianity is kept out of sight until the next church service. Without realizing it Christians have become postmodernists of a sort: they live by the gospel of the two truths. There is religious truth reserved for Sundays and days of worship, and there is secular truth, which applies the rest of the time.

Dinesh D'Souza, *What's So Great about Christianity*

THE LOCAL CHURCH IS GOD'S VEHICLE to reach the world with the good news of Jesus Christ. It is also the primary place where Christians are to be equipped for the ministry. Among other things, biblical churches proclaim Christ, preach the word (2 Timothy 4:2), and equip Christ-followers (Ephesians 4:12). Having said this, there is much flexibility in how we operate on a Sunday morning. In this chapter, I especially speak to church leaders who have influence over the flow, emphasis, and content of church services.

Now, I am not arguing that we get rid of the sermon, prayer, worship, and Communion; these are central elements to the corporate gathering (Acts 2:42). But I am suggesting that there is room to creatively engage the cultural moments of our day, which in turn help people wrestle honestly with important questions and give them confidence to interact about the things of God in the spheres of influence God has placed them in. However, our mind-set will have to change. As busy as people are today, most Christians will attend worship on Sunday morning, and that's about it. If they are not getting it there, then the odds are that they aren't getting it. We typically do doctrinal and apologetic studies that explore why Christians believe what they believe at a time other than Sunday mornings (if at all). Unfortunately, the people who may need this exposure and training the most aren't there to receive it.

CREATING SAFE SPACE FOR DOUBTS AND QUESTIONS

It is becoming harder to distinguish the mental maps of those within the church from those outside the church. In light of this fact, church leaders need to create environments, sermons, and small groups where people can be honest about the doubts they have and what they really believe, not just what they say they believe.[1] If believing something means we are ready to act as if it is true, then there are a lot of beliefs that we are only professing and not embracing. All of us can relate to this tension at some level. The fact is that everybody has questions. But what most people don't know is what to do with these questions. Where can they be asked? And what happens when questions about God, the Bible, or Christianity turn into doubts? Real Christians aren't supposed to doubt, are they?

The church needs clear teaching on dealing with doubt. First, the opposite of faith is unbelief, not doubt. Unbelief is when someone sets themselves against a position or belief (the new atheists like Christopher Hitchens and Richard Dawkins, for example). Doubt resides in the middle and is a natural part of being human because part of what it means to be human is to have limitations. Every one of us has limitations in energy, time, and knowledge. All of us experience doubts at one time or another simply because we cannot know everything about everything.

But we also need to distinguish between three kinds of doubt. First, there are *genuine intellectual doubts* where we need to find reasonable answers to our questions (the key here is to be as specific as possible regarding the nature of your doubt). Second, we can have *emotional doubts*, which have nothing to do with gaining more information. These can be caused by experiencing disappointment, failure, pain, or loss; having unresolved conflict or wounds from the past that need to be addressed; letting unruly emotions carry us away for no good reason; being spiritually dry and relationally distant; and being afraid to truly commit to someone (whether that "someone" be God or another person). Finally, there is doubt that stems from *lack of growth*. If we are not pursuing God by reading his Word, not studying what we believe and why, not living in community with others, and not looking for opportunities to share our faith and to serve—or if we are allowing sin to drive us away from God's presence—then doubt creeps in because our faith is withering rather than flourishing. Obedience is a necessary ingredient to "feel" our faith (please note I did not say that God loves us more if we obey).

But we have a problem in this area, and J. P. Moreland and Klaus Issler offer some compelling analysis about why:

> People do not feel safe in expressing doubt or lack of belief about some doctrinal point — even the question of whether they actually believe in God. The result is that people hide what they actually believe from others, and even from themselves, all the while using faith-talk to avoid being socially ostracized in their local fellowship ... We have unconsciously created a situation in which people do not know how to distinguish what they believe from what they say they believe ... They substitute community jargon for authentic trust.[2]

There is a big difference between what most people say they believe and what they really believe.

The problem with doubt is that if unresolved, over time it erodes our confidence in God. There are many Christians sitting in churches right now who are ready to throw in the towel. Others may not have prayed — really prayed — in months or years. Some find themselves with nagging questions that no one has given them reasonable answers to but are afraid to bring it up because of how it would look.

So what is the solution? We must intentionally "create safe, honest, nondefensive fellowships in which people are given permission to be on a faith journey, with all the warts, messiness and setbacks that are part of such a journey."[3] Is your church a safe place to doubt and explore belief?

CONNECT THE DOTS

As often as you can, connect the truth about which you are preaching or teaching to something going on in the world — usually a headline. For example, if you are interacting with *The New York Times*, *Time* magazine, or *Newsweek*, you are modeling effective engagement for everyday Christians. Moreover, you are building confidence, because most Christians have the idea that Christianity cannot really compete in the marketplace of ideas. Dallas Willard writes:

> The crushing weight of the secular outlook ... permeates or pressures every thought we have today. Sometimes it even forces those who self identify as Christian teachers to set aside Jesus' plain statements about the reality and total relevance of the kingdom of God and replace them ... The powerful though vague and unsubstantiated presumption is that something has been found out that renders a spiritual understanding of reality in the manner of Jesus simply foolish to those who are "in the know." But when it comes time to say exactly what it is that has been found out, nothing of substance is forthcoming.[4]

While its readership continues to decline, *The New York Times* still carries a lot of weight in our culture. A Christian pastor engaging with it provides confidence to Christians as they live out their worldview. The unspoken message is that the Christian faith is intellectually credible. And for far too long Christians have lived on the outskirts of responsible intellectual existence. But things are beginning to change (see Paul Copan's interview in chapter 5).

CREATE A SUNDAY MORNING INTERSECTION

I suggest that you can creatively equip your church by incorporating intersections into the regular rhythms of your worship gatherings. Intersections are eight- to ten-minute segments (outside of the sermon) that address cultural moments. My experience has been that the monthly repetition of speaking to the entire congregation on Sunday mornings about the truth of the Christian worldview in the context of cultural moments is having a positive impact. The culture within our church is slowly changing. People are coming to see that it really is OK to talk about big questions and doubts here. We don't have to fear the next big headline. Moreover, if done well, it increases the confidence of Christians so that they will engage. I am fortunate to have elders who are supportive of this vision. This kind of engagement may be a stretch for your church, but the "we have always done it this way" mentality is a bad reason to miss out on these cultural moments. Because every church is unique, this is not the only way to do it, but it may spur some ideas. Let me give you an example of an intersection dealing with a cultural moment.

"IDA" GOES TO CHURCH

Are you familiar with *Darwinius masillae*? You may know it by another name—Ida.

The same week Ida catapulted on the scene amid a media frenzy about "the Missing Link" having finally been found, I taught an intersection responding to it on the Sunday before *The Link* documentary showcasing Ida was to air on the History Channel. I used PowerPoint slides with images and quotes (each heading in what follows represents a new slide).

Pop Quiz

Who is this? I showed a picture of Ida. Many in the audience could recognize the fossil due to the media blitz that week. Ida, the most complete primate fossil ever found (95 percent), was discovered two decades ago in Messel Pit, Germany, and has been dated at about 47 million years old.

Scientific Media Blockbusters

This story was big. You know this is so when Google changes its search engine icon to incorporate a drawing of Ida. Here were some of the headlines: The New York Times: "Seeking a Missing Link, and a Mass Audience." National Geographic: "MISSING LINK" FOUND: New Fossil Links Humans, Lemurs?" And a Time magazine article that surprisingly read, "Ida: Humankind's Earliest Ancestor! (Not Really)." I encouraged our church to let the dust settle. (As it turned out, Ida was all hype and no link [and so was Ardi, who followed soon after].)[5]

Why All the Hype?

This is an interesting question. If neo-Darwinian evolution is so well established and the fossil record so clear already, then why all the hype? Aside from the opportunity to make a little money, the media blitz tries to overshadow the lack of evidence in the fossil record. Rather than pointing to hard evidence, this looks similar to the Discovery Channel's flop *The Lost Tomb of Jesus* and the nonexistent evidence undergirding Dan Brown's claims in *The Da Vinci Code*.

What Story Do the Rocks Tell?

Darwin recognized that the gravest objection to his theory was the fossil record. And 150 years later, it is still a grave objection (though you wouldn't know it by looking at most biology textbooks). As the eminent Harvard paleontologist Stephen J. Gould pointed out, the two dominant features in the fossil record are:

- **stasis.** Most species exhibit no directional change during their tenure on earth. They appear in the fossil record looking much the same as when they disappear; morphological change is usually limited and directionless.
- **sudden appearance.** In any local area, a species does not arise gradually by the steady transformation of its ancestors; it appears all at once and fully formed.[6]

Regarding the theory of natural selection that is built on incremental changes over a long period of time, the fossil record does not bear this out. The fossils all show up fully formed and at the same geological moment. This is known as the Cambrian Explosion. (Imagine if all of geological time were represented by a twenty-four-hour day, the vast majority of body plans appear suddenly during a two-minute span.)[7] Organisms that are thought to have evolved from one another show up in the fossil record side by side and fully formed.

Common Ancestry or Common Design?

One argument for Darwinian evolution and particularly common ancestry is that organisms exhibit similar features over time. But this could just as easily be explained by appealing to common design. For example, take the first Mac, the iPod, iPhone, Mac Book Pro, and iPad. They are all distinct but show similar design features. These similar features alone cannot decide the question of evolution because both common ancestry and common design explain the common features we see.

A Darwinian Bedtime Story?

Henry Gee, a science writer for *Nature* and a believer in Darwinian evolution, is honest about what the fossils can show: "No fossil is buried with its birth certificate ... That, and the scarcity of fossils, means that it is effectively impossible to link fossils into chains of cause and effect in any way." Headlines talk of missing links, "as if the chain of ancestry and descent were a real object for contemplation and not what it really is: a completely human invention created after the fact, shaped to accord with human prejudice ... To take a line of fossils and claim they represent a lineage is not a scientific hypothesis that can be tested, but an assertion that carries the same validity as a bedtime story—amusing, perhaps even instructive, but not scientific."[8]

Go Deeper

For more on this topic, see my website (www.thinkchristianly.org) and the book *Understanding Intelligent Design: Everything You Need to Know in Plain Language* by William Dembski and Sean McDowell.

And that was it. But please don't miss the importance of this. The same week that people were being bombarded with headlines proclaiming the missing link and the unassailability of Darwinian evolution, the church provided a thoughtful ten-minute response and helped equip Christians to think about this discovery and the broader cultural issue of Darwinian evolution. We were connecting Sunday morning with Monday through Friday and offering the confidence that we are a church that talks about such things. Two final thoughts: First, you never know who is going to walk into your church and what kind of influence they may have. And second, people have questions (especially the next generation) and want to learn; if not in church, then where will they find thoughtful Christian answers to their questions?

Now it may not be feasible to always put a ten-minute segment into your worship flow for the morning because of time constraints and multiple services, but a regular intersection morning might be an alternative. Perhaps dedicate one Sunday morning every three months to engaging a cultural moment of worldview and apologetic interest and spend a whole morning on it (see the topics in part 3 for ideas and resources). Also, make books and articles available to people so they can go home with something and do further study. This approach retains the centrality of expository preaching, yet it models high-level engagement with cultural moments.

FOLLOW THE LEADER

A final word to leaders and pastors reading this book. What you value and emphasize, your congregation will eventually come to value and emphasize. How you engage issues will shape how they will engage issues (this also applies to your tone and respect for those with whom you disagree). If you think it is important, over time they will as well. Part of this is just how the sociology of knowledge works. You are called to help your congregation think Christianly about the world they live in. As leaders, we must recover a vision for this high calling (Hebrews 13:17). For good or ill, it all starts with you. Set the pace. Do the hard work necessary, and watch your spiritual posture and gestures. But what an opportunity we have! Be creative ... engage.

RESOURCES FOR ENGAGING YOUR INTERSECTION

Books

- *God in the Dark: The Assurance of Faith beyond a Shadow of Doubt* by Os Guinness
- *Communicating for Change* by Andy Stanley
- *Lies That Go Unchallenged in Popular Culture* by Charles Colson and James Stuart Bell
- *Lies That Go Unchallenged in Media and Government* by Charles Colson
- *Pop Goes the Church: Should the Church Engage Pop Culture?* by Tim Stevens
- *The Politically Incorrect Guide to Darwinism and Intelligent Design* by Jonathan Wells

Websites and DVDs

- www.thinkchristianly.org – Think Christianly
- www.str.org – Stand to Reason
- www.leestrobel.com – Lee Strobel's website
- www.intelligentdesign.org – Intelligent Design
- *Expelled: No Intelligence Allowed* by Ben Stein, DVD
- *The Reason for God* by Tim Keller, DVD

GOD, DARWIN, AND CULTURE

AN INTERVIEW WITH SEAN MCDOWELL

Jonathan Morrow: It is commonplace to hear about the "overwhelming evidence" for evolution. Have you found this to be the case? Can you talk a little about the role that Darwinism plays in our culture?

Sean McDowell: There's a well-known joke for lawyers that says when the facts are on your side, argue the facts. However, when you don't have the facts, use emotion and state your case with absolute certainty. This is precisely what is going on with claims about the "overwhelming evidence" for evolution. We live in an information age, and materialist theories such as Darwinism are slowly going the way of the Dodo. Intelligent design (ID) is on the move. Many Darwinists know this, which is why they focus their primary attacks on ID being religiously motivated or based on ignorance and avoid engaging the actual arguments. But they can ignore the substance for only so long.

People often ask, "Couldn't God have used evolution?" Certainly. God can create however he wants to. Yet it's important to remember that Darwin intentionally devised a materialist explanation that excluded God from the process. *Nature* is the selecting mechanism, not God. If God somehow guided the process of evolution, we are no longer talking about Darwin's theory but about some form of intelligent design. And if God is not part of the process, then it's a short step to removing him altogether.

While I have significant reservations about evolution (see my *Understanding Intelligent Design* with William A. Dembski), my bigger concern is the role Darwinism now plays in society. Evolution has become an ideology. It is the creation myth that justifies the dominant worldview in Western culture — naturalism.

Since evolution is viewed as the "creative" force, then all aspects of nature must be "Darwinized." Thus, we have books such as *Literary Darwinism*, *Financial Darwinism*, and *Evolution and Ethics*. Everything, including morality, religious belief, psychology, sexuality, marriage, and more, must be seen from this perspective. These ideas are disseminated to young people through our universities. This is why atheist philosopher Daniel Dennett called Darwinism a "universal acid." He's right. If evolution were true, then everything demands a Darwinian explanation. But if evolution were false, then this would be a colossal mistake.

There is a temptation to avoid this controversial topic in the church. Why not just talk about Jesus? Remember, the Christian story makes sense only if we were created by God and then rebelled. Otherwise, what's the need for a Savior?

Belief in God as the Creator is not simply blind "religious" faith but something we can *know* to be true (Psalm 19:1 – 2). I've seen young people come alive when they discover the evidence for intelligent design. It gives us confidence in our faith as well as in the God of the Scriptures. This is not a truth we simply store away in our minds, but one that transforms how we think about ourselves and other people. We *really* are made in the image of God, who loves us and has a plan for our lives. We can see the divine fingerprint from the tiniest cell to the depths of the universe.

Jonathan: From your perspective as a Christian high school teacher who also speaks to thousands of students each year, how well prepared do you think students are to leave our churches and live out their faith in college and beyond?

Sean: This question is the driving force of my ministry. We've all heard the statistics of young people leaving their faith in college, and it rightly concerns us. There may not be a silver bullet to fix this problem, but there are some areas which we must address.

Part of the problem is that the worldviews of this churched generation are largely unbiblical. According to the National Study of Youth and Religion, 18 percent of conservative Protestant youth have either a deistic or pantheistic view of God, 48 percent believe many religions may be true, and 42 percent are not assured of the existence of evil spirits. We need to teach substance. But we must connect this truth to their lives and relationships.

Young people are also relationally hurting. Many are lonely, depressed, and searching for real meaning. It's difficult for young people who struggle with broken relationships and have emotional baggage to develop a biblical worldview. Many kids leave the church because they never built healthy relationships with their parents or other Christian adults. If we want to teach the biblical worldview effectively, we must first help kids get emotionally healthy.

This is why I deeply believe in mentoring. Jesus was a mentor. My hope is that mentoring will become as normal in the church in the future as small groups are today. Young people simply cannot survive temptations and intellectual challenges without caring, involved adults coming alongside to guide them.

> **Sean McDowell** is an award-winning educator, speaker, and author. A popular speaker at camps, churches, schools, and conferences nationwide, Sean has spoken for organizations such as Focus on the Family,

Campus Crusade for Christ, and Youth Specialties. He has cowritten or edited several books, including *Understanding Intelligent Design*, *Is God Just a Human Invention?*, *Evidence for the Resurrection*, and *More Than a Carpenter*, and has contributed to *YouthWorker Journal*, *Decision Magazine*, and the *Christian Research Journal*. Visit him at www. seanmcdowell.org.

part three

AREAS WE MUST ENGAGE

chapter ten

JESUSANITY VERSUS CHRISTIANITY

We need to understand that public discussion of the Christian faith has changed—permanently. So the next time you hear an earth-shattering announcement about Jesus from the media, don't get angry. Rather, take three deep breaths, sit down with your Starbucks coffee, and watch how the announcement is treated on blogs and other media. Above all, prepare yourself for the opportunities it presents.

Darrell Bock, "When the Media Became a Nuisance"

WHO WOULD HAVE THOUGHT THAT A MAN from such a small town would have had such a big impact on the world? It's hard to find people who don't at least respect Jesus. For the most part, people like Jesus. The problem arises when trying to figure out precisely which Jesus they have in mind.

"Western culture," says New Testament historian Ben Witherington, "is a Jesus-haunted culture, and yet one that is largely biblically illiterate ... Almost anything can pass for knowledge of Jesus and early Christianity in such a culture."[1] Unfortunately, many Christians are in the same boat (consider the confusion that followed the release of Dan Brown's *The Da Vinci Code*). And if Christianity rises or falls with the person and work of Jesus—and it does—then this confusion about Jesus is not good.

Darrell Bock, a prominent evangelical New Testament scholar and coauthor of *Dethroning Jesus*, sums up the cultural conversation about Jesus in terms of Jesusanity versus Christianity. If you can understand and explain this distinction, then you can help people consider the eternal kind of life that the *real* Jesus offers.

JESUSANITY VERSUS CHRISTIANITY

One evening while living in Dallas, I was on a date with my wife and was walking past a storefront, only to discover Jesus staring back at me—a bobblehead Jesus, that is. I had seen bobbleheads of NFL players and rock stars before, but I didn't realize that Jesus had reached bobblehead status! Fast-forward a few years to when I was kicking off our Christmas series at our church. Want to know who was helping me preach that morning? Yep, bobblehead Jesus standing on a stool (I am happy to report that I was neither fired nor struck by lightning). To help make the Jesusanity versus Christianity distinction more concrete, I read out loud to our church the ad from the back of the box he was packaged in:

> The name Jesus means God saves. The term Christ is a title for anointed of God. For Muslims and some Jews, Jesus was a prophet. Buddhists say he was enlightened. Hindus call him an Avatar (the incarnation of a deity in human form). And Christians hail him as the Son of God. Although he is understood in many different ways, everyone seems to agree that he was an extraordinary man.[2]

Now I would take "extraordinary," but is that what Jesus was after? Today in our thoroughly pluralistic culture, Jesusanity is what is most often practiced. Jesus is respected as one of the great religious leaders—even the best religious leader of all time—but he does not have *unique* status. For many people today, both inside and outside the church, Jesus is not unique; he is simply one among many (recall from the introduction that 57 percent of evangelicals think there are other ways to God than through Jesus). Respected? Yes. Street cred? Check. But if we take the New Testament documents seriously, Jesus wasn't aiming for respect. His messianic mission was far larger than that.

In stark contrast to Jesusanity, Bock summarizes that Christianity "involves the claim that Jesus was anointed by God to represent both God and humanity in the restoration of a broken relationship existing between the Creator and his creation."[3] Only Jesus the Messiah can address humanity's deepest need, the forgiveness of our sins so that we can be reconnected with God and enjoy the eternal kind of life we were made for (Mark 2:1–12; 8:27–30; John 17:3). In Christianity, Jesus is worshiped; in Jesusanity, he is simply respected. The difference could not be more important for our world.

TWO BIG QUESTIONS PEOPLE HAVE ABOUT JESUS

It used to be that there were only two certainties in life—death and taxes. Now you can add a third. Every Easter and Christmas there will be TV documentaries aired on the Discovery and History Channels, ABC, and CNN, as well as full-color articles in *Newsweek*, searching for the lost Jesus of history, examining banned books of the Bible, and seeking the "real" origins of Christianity (read: conspiracy and cover-up). Now this is an opportunity because people are talking about Jesus. But it's also a challenge because—well, remember our Jesus-haunted culture?

For far too long, Christians have viewed the Bible as a magical book that descended from the clouds in calfskin leather disconnected from real life and history. Moreover, many assume it just isn't polite to ask serious questions of the Bible, even if they don't understand it. After all, only people who lack faith experience doubts or have questions, right? Consequently when books get published that go to number 1 on Amazon, or Ivy League scholars show up on TV debunking the New Testament portrait of Jesus, people are left with a dilemma: muster up more faith (whatever that means) in the teeth of this new evidence or slowly come to regard Jesus as little more than a children's bedtime story. Christians and non-Christians alike have honest questions about who Jesus is, but most have no idea how to begin sifting through the different views of Jesus. The church has failed them in this regard.

For some, "the Bible says so" will carry the day.[4] But for most, this will not cut it in the face of impressive-sounding scholars who used to believe in fairy tales too (and if they have British accents, then everybody knows they can't possibly be wrong!). So people have no other options but to Google "Jesus"—which, to be honest, is a crapshoot. They may come across something credible, but it is far more likely they will stumble on skeptical websites not based on sound scholarship.[5]

In light of this new reality, here are two questions about Jesus we need to talk about in our churches.[6]

Do Lost Gospels Provide a More Historically Accurate Portrait of Jesus?

In 1945, fifty-two papyri were discovered at Nag Hammadi in Lower Egypt, and some of these texts had the word *gospel* in the title. Scholars have known about these and other second- through fourth-century documents for a long time, but only recently has the general public been introduced to them. This has caused quite a bit of controversy and speculation. Why? Our culture is generally skeptical of authority and enjoys a good conspiracy theory; sprinkle in some high-definition documentaries, and, presto, your recipe for confusion is complete!

The first time I heard about these "lost gospels," it honestly made me nervous—until I read them. The juiciest of the apocryphal writings is probably the *Infancy Gospel of Thomas*. Here are some things I discovered about Jesus' childhood: he called a child an "unrighteous, irreverent idiot" (3:1–3). Another child bumped into Jesus, which aggravated him so much that Jesus struck him dead (4:1–2). Evidently those who provoked *childhood Jesus* fell dead a lot (14:3).

The Gospel of Thomas wins the most scandalous passage award: "Simon Peter said to them, 'Let Mary leave us, for women are not worthy of life.' Jesus said, 'I myself shall lead her in order to make her male, so that she too may become a living spirit resembling you males. For every woman who will make herself male will enter the kingdom of heaven'" (Saying 114).[7] Does anything else really need to be said?

Quite honestly, there is a world of difference between the writings in the New Testament and these so-called "missing gospels." Historically and literarily, these lost gospels simply don't stand up to careful scrutiny.[8] Moreover, these gospels were not lost to the early church; early Christians knew about them and rejected them for good reasons (e.g., Irenaeus in AD 180). While historically interesting, these lost gospels offer us nothing significant about the historical Jesus. The writings in the New Testament are still the earliest and most reliable witnesses to the words and works of Jesus. Christians often needlessly fear the unknown. We can change that. Portions of these texts can be read out loud in church so that people can see the differences for themselves.

Before we move to the next question, I need to say something about Gnosticism (the Greek word *gnosis* means "knowledge"). Gnosticism can get kind of complicated, so here's the big idea: There is a fundamental opposition between the spiritual world (good) and the material world (evil), and "salvation" is based on the acquisition of special knowledge. This chart reveals how different Gnosticism is from the orthodox Christianity of the New Testament documents. Once people understand the basics, they will be able to spot it when it shows up in documentaries, articles, or college classrooms.

Orthodox Christianity of the New Testament	Gnosticism of the Lost Gospels
There is only one God and Creator.	There are multiple creators.
The physical world, body, soul, and spirit are good.	The physical world and body are evil. *Only* spirit and soul are good.
Jesus is fully human and fully divine.	Jesus only *appeared* human; he was only a spirit being.
Jesus came to restore relationships broken by sin.	Ignorance, not sin, is the ultimate problem.
Faith in Christ by grace alone brings salvation (available to all).	"Special knowledge" brings salvation (available to only a few).

But Did Jesus Actually Claim to Be God?

While it is true that we have no record of Jesus saying the words, "I am God," there is solid historical and textual evidence Jesus claimed to be God and that people understood him to be making that claim.

First, devotion to Jesus Christ *as God* emerged in a Jewish monotheistic context, and this must be accounted for. Larry Hurtado of the University of Edinburgh has exhaustively researched the origins of devotion to Jesus in earliest Christianity and makes this critical observation:

> Certainly, various deities were reverenced in the Roman period, and it was in principle no problem to enfranchise another divine figure in the religious 'cafeteria' of the time. But it was a major and unprecedented move for people influenced by the exclusivist monotheistic stance of Second-Temple Judaism to include another figure singularly alongside God as recipient of cultic devotion in their worship gatherings.[9]

In other words, this wasn't just like adding another god to the pantheon out of novelty. The cultural tide of Judaism would have been strongly against worshiping any other gods but Yahweh. Something quite remarkable would have had to occur to account for this radical change. Perhaps being raised from the dead would qualify?[10]

Moreover, Jesus took himself to be equal with the Father. We see this in the authority he claimed for himself. Only God has authority over the law and Sabbath, to forgive sins, and over the final judgment. And yet, Jesus claimed he had authority over each of these (Mark 2:1 – 12; 2:23 – 28; 8:35 – 38). The clearest example of his self-understanding occurs when he is on trial before the Jewish leaders and, quoting from Daniel 7:13 – 14, refers to himself as the Son of Man (Mark 14:60 – 62). In the Daniel passage, the Son of Man is in the presence of the Ancient of Days (God himself) and is given authority by him (cf. Psalm 110). The Jewish leaders — who knew their Scriptures well — got the message loud and clear (cf. Mark 14:63 – 64).

Finally, there is a large body of textual evidence that emerges from the Hebrew Scriptures and the New Testament documents that Jesus was God. In the excellent book *Putting Jesus in His Place: The Case for the Deity of Christ*, authors Robert Bowman and Ed Komoszewski develop a memorable acronym that helps people understand and share this evidence with others (**H.A.N.D.S.** — Jesus shares the **H**onors, **A**ttributes, **N**ames, **D**eeds, and **S**eat of God).

Citing these kinds of reasons to support Jesus' deity allows us to engage the critical scholars who talk about Jesus in the media and in the university classroom. The conversation is now more sophisticated than just citing Bible verses for Jesus' deity, and Christ-followers need to be prepared.

A NEW DAY IN THE CULTURAL CONVERSATION ABOUT JESUS

As Darrell Bock explained in the epigraph at the beginning of the chapter, the way academic news filters down to the general public has forever changed. We need to help Christians understand that before coming to hasty conclusions or getting nervous about a recent discovery or new book that gets all the hype of a blockbuster movie, we should let the dust settle. *Everything* is "a show" in our culture; we love to be entertained. (Have you watched how the news is reported lately?) So once the initial media splash has occurred, watch how scholars respond and interact with the *actual* evidence. This will take study, preparation, and patience. But Christian leaders cannot remain silent when the evidence for Jesus is so compelling and his message so life changing. When all is said and done, the truthfulness of Christianity rises or falls on the identity of Jesus.

RESOURCES FOR ENGAGING YOUR INTERSECTION

Books

- *Reinventing Jesus: How Contemporary Skeptics Miss the Real Jesus and Mislead Popular Culture* by J. Ed Komoszewski, M. James Sawyer, and Daniel B. Wallace
- *The Case for the Real Jesus: A Journalist Investigates Current Attacks on the Identity of Christ* by Lee Strobel
- *Dethroning Jesus: Exposing Popular Culture's Quest to Unseat the Biblical Christ* by Darrell L. Bock and Daniel B. Wallace
- *Putting Jesus in His Place: The Case for the Deity of Christ* by Robert Bowman and Ed Komoszewski
- *The Heresy of Orthodoxy: How Contemporary Culture's Fascination with Diversity Has Reshaped Our Understanding of Early Christianity* by Andreas J. Kostenberger and Michael Kruger
- *Four Portraits, One Jesus: An Introduction to Jesus and the Gospels* by Mark L. Strauss.

Websites and DVDs

- www.patheos.com/community/bibleandculture – Ben Witherington's blog
- http://blogs.bible.org/blog/12 – Darrell Bock's blog
- www.reasonablefaith.org – Reasonable Faith, William Lane Craig
- www.leestrobel.com – Lee Strobel, Investigating Faith
- *The Case for Christ*, DVD
- *Jesus: Man, Messiah, or More?*, eight-part DVD

STUDENTS AND
REAL-WORLD APOLOGETICS

AN INTERVIEW WITH BRETT KUNKLE

Jonathan Morrow: A lot of churches and youth ministries take mission trips. But odds are good that they haven't taken a mission trip quite like the ones you organize. Can you share about your unique approach and the response you get from students and youth leaders?

Brett Kunkle: We've designed an apologetics mission trip to Berkeley, California, and a theological mission trip to Salt Lake City, Utah. We first do classroom training and then we immerse students in real-life apologetics and theological experiences. In Berkeley we bring in atheists to argue against the Christian worldview, training students to respond along the way. In Utah we create opportunities to dialogue with Mormons on theological issues like the Trinity and the nature of salvation (for more, go to STRplace.org).

Worldview training cannot be confined to the classroom. After training, we must get young people engaged in the real world, actually living out the mission of Jesus. These trips do exactly that. And the response from students and youth leaders has been phenomenal. When a group completes one mission, the leaders almost immediately book the next. They're simply that transformative in students' lives.

Jonathan: As the student impact director for Stand to Reason, you interact with lots of high school and college students each year. What are the questions asked most frequently? What are the topics that student ministries simply *have* to cover with their students?

Brett: Actually, the typical student has a lack of questions. Of course, deep down they have serious questions. But that's the problem; most spiritual questions are deep down, situated in the background of their lives. Why? Because spiritual and moral issues aren't taken to be areas of knowledge, like the sciences, but mere preferences, like our choice of ice cream flavors. And how much serious thinking do we devote to preferences in ice cream? Not much. Students aren't thinking as seriously or as often about spiritual subjects as they are about their school subjects, so spiritual questions quietly fade to the background of life.

This spiritual apathy results from students' woeful confusion about knowledge, truth, and belief. And this confusion results from the relativistic thinking they're infected with. But these are foundational issues. Get truth wrong, and a lot of other ideas go awry. To prepare youth adequately, student ministries must build a solid foundation of truth for young people. Belief alone is not sufficient to get at the truth. Christianity isn't just true for me because I believe but not true for those who don't believe. Rather, students must see truth as grounded in reality and become convinced that Christianity is *true*—it's not merely a preference, but knowledge of reality. Worldview training will do just that and is therefore essential to youth discipleship.

Jonathan: We've all found ourselves in situations where we didn't know what to say. When it comes to having spiritual conversations with others, can you talk about the importance of tactics in helping people think clearly about the biggest questions in life?

Brett: Spiritual conversations require clear thinking. Clear thinking requires careful reasoning and sound logic. When *both* guide our discussions, we're in a good position to separate truth from error. And ultimately, arriving at the truth is the goal of every spiritual conversation. Tactics are simply tools of clear thinking, allowing us to discover the truth about life's biggest questions.

For instance, when Christians claim to know the truth about almost any matter, we're labeled as narrow-minded or intolerant. Declare that Jesus is the only way to God, and watch the sparks fly. But such name-calling obscures truth.

To clear away confusion, a simple tactic—what we at Stand to Reason call the "Columbo tactic"—is vital. Rather than begin with a defensive statement, we begin with a clarification question: "What do you mean by that?" To make progress, we need to know what is meant by narrow-minded or intolerant. Typically, the objector has some self-contradictory idea in mind, which muddies their thinking and creates an intellectual obstacle to the truth. The Columbo tactic can remove the barrier, thus opening the heart to truth.

> **Brett Kunkle** is the student impact director at Stand to Reason. Brett has more than seventeen years of experience working with youth and speaks to thousands of students and adults across the country. In addition, he has built a dynamic youth training website at www.STRplace. org. Brett is currently completing a master's degree in philosophy of religion and ethics at Talbot School of Theology. He lives with his wife and four children in Newport Beach, California.

chapter eleven

TRUTH, TOLERANCE, AND RELATIVISM

The differences between religions are worth debating. Theology has consequences: It shapes lives, families, nations, cultures, wars; it can change people, save them from themselves, and sometimes warp or even destroy them. If we tiptoe politely around this reality, then we betray every teacher, guru and philosopher — including Jesus of Nazareth and the Buddha both — who ever sought to resolve the most human of all problems: *How then should we live?*

Ross Douthat, "Let's Talk about Faith"

I'M NOT A BUMPER STICKER KIND OF GUY (although my wife and I have seriously debated putting a "we used to be cool" sticker on our car!). But I keep running into one particular bumper sticker. Maybe you've seen it? It reads: "COEXIST" (with the letters replaced by various religious symbols). At one level, this sentiment is praiseworthy. People should do their best to get along with those with whom they disagree. But given that globalization and immigration have dramatically changed the religious landscape of the United States and that our culture is regularly saturated with slogans like the one uttered by Oprah — "There are millions of ways to be a human being and many paths to what you call 'God'" — I don't think this is what most people have in mind by "coexist."

In our society, personal preference reigns supreme, including in the realm of religion. You like chocolate, and I like strawberry — there is no one true religion or one that is better than another. After all, someone's personal experience, taste in ice cream, or religious preference can't possibly be mistaken, right? This sentiment is part of postmodernism's impact.

Let me first clear up a misconception. Christianity is not the enemy of diversity. The Bible teaches that God created humanity in all its wonderful diversity, and the new heaven and the new earth will one day be filled with people from every tongue, tribe, and nation. (In fact, if the trajectories hold true, by 2050 there will be more Christians in the global South—Africa and Asia—than in the West.)[1] But religious relativism is a bad idea on several levels, not the least of which is its failure to respect the fundamental teachings of most religions.

TRUTH MATTERS

In his fascinating book *The Decline of the Secular University*, C. John Sommerville observes, "We used to talk about truth, but now we talk about tolerance."[2] And if this is the case while in the university, then how much more so when people get out? Truth is a basic fact of existence. Even though people seem confused about what truth is these days—or skeptical about the possibility of truth—deep down they have an awareness of truth. There is a way things are; truth is what you bump into when you are wrong. The classic commonsense notion of truth is when what I say or believe corresponds to the way things really are (that is, reality).

People want the truth about reality. Will this medicine heal my sickness? Will the brakes work on my car? Does my life really matter? If God is there, does he love me ... does he care? Can I really find forgiveness to erase my brokenness and shame? What happens when I die? But given our cultural situation, there is just less confidence that truth is available in religion and ethics. Recall the unbiblical notion of a "fact/value split," where science deals with publicly accessible "facts" while religion deals with socially constructed reality, or "values." Our culture's dubious attitude toward religion stems in part from allowing clever slogans to shut down meaningful conversations about truth. But if truth is the only sure foundation on which to build a life, then we need to press through these slogans and sound bites with clear thinking:

- There is no truth. (Is that a true statement?)
- We can't know truth. (Is that a truth you know?)
- All truth is relative. (Is that truth claim also relative?)
- You have your truth and I have my truth (Is this true for both of us?)
- I don't believe anything unless it can be proven scientifically. (What scientific experiment taught you that truth?)

These are as common in the classroom as they are in the media we consume, but all of these popular slogans are self-refuting. That is, if they are true, then they are false! It would be like saying, "I cannot speak a word of English," or "My brother is an only child." Not only is relativism self-refuting; no one reacts this way when their rights or values are violated. They want justice. They want truth to win out.[3] And this is as it should be.

As Christians, we ought to be passionate about knowing the truth because God is passionate about making it known. Jesus promised that knowing the truth sets people free for life (John 8:32). And the New Testament calls the body of Christ to function as "the pillar and foundation of the truth" (1 Timothy 3:15). C. S. Lewis put it this way:

> Christianity claims to give an account of the facts — to tell you what the real universe is like. Its account of the universe may be true, or it may not, and once the question is really before you, then your natural inquisitiveness must make you want to know the answer. If Christianity is untrue, then no honest man will want to believe it, however helpful it might be; if it is true, every honest man will want to believe it, even if it gives him no help at all.[4]

TWO POPULAR MYTHS WE NEED TO EXPOSE
All Religions Basically Teach the Same Thing

This one gets a lot of airtime and was the assumption smuggled into Oprah's comment above. But only a little reflection shows that it is false. Ravi Zacharias, who was born in India and intimately knows what it is like to grow up in a very different religious context than in America, explodes this myth by observing the following:

> The truth is that all religions are not the same. All religions do not point to God. All religions do not say that all religions are the same. In fact, some religions do not even believe in God. At the heart of every religion is an uncompromising commitment to a particular way of defining who God is or is not. Buddhism, for example, was based on Buddha's rejection of two of Hinduism's fundamental doctrines. Islam rejects both Buddhism and Hinduism. So it does no good to put a halo on the notion of tolerance and act as if everything is equally true. In fact, even all-inclusive religions such as Bahaism end up being exclusivistic by excluding the exclusivists![5]

Let's illustrate how this plays out with an example: Jesus is the only way to God (cf. John 14:6). Now Judaism, Islam, and Christianity all *disagree* on this. As Christians, we should tolerate our Jewish and Muslim friends by doing our best to represent their views fairly and treat them with respect. But there is a fact to consider. Either Jesus was not the Messiah (Judaism), was the Messiah (Christianity), or was a great prophet (Islam) — but not all three. They can all be false, but they can't all be true!

The Story of the Blind Men and the Elephant

Odds are you have encountered this one. It's a cultural favorite to show that reality is determined by perspective. The parable tells of a group of blind men who one day meet an elephant. One touches the trunk, another the tail, another the tusk, another the ear, and so on. Later, as they describe to each other what they felt, they find they all disagree — hard, soft, squishy, rough, and so forth Therefore, no one knows what the elephant is really like. We may have partial truths, but not the whole truth. Religion and people's experiences of God are like the blind men and the elephant. If the story is told well, it can be very convincing. But Lesslie Newbigin deftly points out the fatal problem with this story that undermines its conclusion:

> In the famous story of the blind men and the elephant ... the real point of the story is constantly overlooked. The story is told from the point of view of the king and his courtiers, who are not blind but can see that the blind men are unable to grasp the full reality of the elephant and are only able to get hold of part of it. The story is constantly told in order to neutralize the affirmations of the great religions, to suggest that they learn humility and recognize that none of them can have more than one aspect of the truth. But, of course, the real point of the story is exactly the opposite. If the king were also blind, there would be no story.[6]

So rather than saying that all religions teach the same thing, this myth actually claims that no religion has the truth. But one could know this only if they could see all of reality — the whole elephant. So what appears at first glance to be a humble statement ends up concluding that all of the devout adherents of the world's major religions — billions of people — have it wrong! If this doesn't count as arrogance, I'm not sure what does.

But isn't it arrogant or even immoral to claim to know the truth? Leaving aside the fact that those who make this claim think *they* know the truth and you are mistaken, Alvin Plantinga, one of the leading philosophers of religion of our day, responds to this charge by asking:

> Suppose I think the matter over, consider the objections as carefully as I can, realize that I am finite and furthermore a sinner, certainly no better than those with whom I disagree, and indeed inferior both morally and intellectually to many who do not believe what I do; but suppose it still seems clear to me that the proposition in question is true [for example, that Jesus Christ is the only way to God]: can I really be behaving immorally in continuing to believe it?[7]

The point is well-taken. People can certainly be arrogant as they hold the truth or condescendingly tell others what they think is the truth and the reasons for it, but it does not follow that they are arrogant for making a truth claim. Again, this is why Peter reminds Christians to speak "with gentleness and respect" (1 Peter 3:15).

TAKING A LESSON FROM
TIGER WOODS AND BRIT HUME

In 2009, Tiger Woods was in the news for his adultery and other rumors of promiscuity and immorality. At one point in the public discussion, political commentator Brit Hume of Fox News suggested that Woods, a Buddhist, should consider embracing Christianity. Of Buddhism he said, "I don't think that faith offers the kind of forgiveness and redemption that is offered by the Christian faith." Well, that went over like a lead balloon! And Hume was immediately labeled a bigot (among other things). But as Ross Douthat put it in a perceptive *New York Times* op-ed piece, "What Hume said wasn't bigoted: Indeed, his claim about the difference between Buddhism and Christianity was perfectly defensible. Christians believe in a personal God who forgives sins. Buddhists, as a rule, do not. And it's at least plausible that Tiger Woods might welcome the possibility that there is Someone out there capable of forgiving him, even if Elin Nordegren and his corporate sponsors never do."[8]

Did you recognize the hidden assumption that all religions are basically the same or that no single one of them is to be preferred? Christians need to be able to engage these kinds of cultural moments with the substance of what they believe. It will take courage and some training—but we can help people move beyond the popular slogans and myths to the truth.

PROCLAIMING A RADICALLY INCLUSIVE
AND EXCLUSIVE MESSAGE

While civility is a virtue, the goal is not for everyone to agree. Indeed, Christians who take their cues from the Bible will find a lot in a fallen world to disagree with. In the end, we must recognize that Christianity is both radically inclusive and exclusive at the same time. It is *inclusive* because anyone can become a follower of Christ. No one is excluded by social status, gender, race, or IQ, and the offer is completely free. But Christianity is also *exclusive* because any truth, by definition, is exclusive. Moreover, Jesus says, "If you do not believe that I am the one I claim to be, you will indeed die in your sins" (John 8:24, my paraphrase; cf. 1 Timothy 2:3–5). Apologist Brett Kunkle clarifies: "Jesus offers both the diagnosis *and* a cure. Sin is the disease we are all infected with and Jesus is the one true cure. So, why is Jesus the only way? Because Jesus is the only medicine that can cure the spiritual disease—sin—that is killing us."[9]

But it is here where Christians are being conformed to the culture. Recall in the introduction that 57 percent of evangelical adults agreed with the statement: "Many religions can lead to eternal life." We've got some work to do.

Christians must learn to winsomely and boldly present these two realities in an increasingly diverse religious landscape. Truth and tolerance can coexist. But we must recover the classic idea of tolerance, which encourages us to learn to understand and respect one another, even though we have deep disagreements. When we don't, it gets ugly—fast! But false tolerance just to get along helps no one. Truth is too precious to be ignored.

RESOURCES FOR ENGAGING YOUR INTERSECTION

Books

- *True for You, But Not for Me: Countering the Slogans That Leave Christians Speechless* by Paul Copan
- *Truth Matters* by Brett Kunkle
- *Choosing Your Faith: In a World of Spiritual Options* by Mark Mittelberg
- *Tactics: A Game Plan for Discussing Your Christian Convictions* by Greg Koukl
- *Jesus among Other Gods: The Absolute Claims of the Christian Message* by Ravi Zacharias
- *The Reason for God: Belief in an Age of Skepticism* by Tim Keller
- *The Baker Pocket Guide to World Religions: What Every Christian Needs to Know* by Gerald R. McDermott
- *Reclaiming the Center: Confronting Evangelical Accommodation in Postmodern Times* edited by Millard J. Erickson, Paul Kjoss Helseth, and Justin Taylor

Websites and DVDs

- www.str.org – Stand to Reason
- www.reasonablefaith.org – Reasonable Faith
- www.rzim.org – Ravi Zacharias
- www.thinkchristianly.org – Think Christianly
- *The Case for Faith*, DVD

JESUS AMONG
WORLD RELIGIONS

AN INTERVIEW WITH CRAIG HAZEN

Jonathan Morrow: Christians live in a pluralistic culture where it can be difficult to talk in an inviting way about the uniqueness of Jesus among all of the various religious options. As a professor of comparative religions, you have developed an approach that will help Christians better engage in discussions about Jesus. Can you share a little about this?

Craig Hazen: If I run into someone who has a fondness for religion or is even on some sort of religious quest and is exploring the various world religions, I have a way of focusing the discussion in a disarming way. It is a technique that also puts on display the features of Christianity that make it unique among all other religious options.

When I run into a religious seeker, I make a bold claim that "any thoughtful person on a religious quest would obviously start the quest with Christianity." It will immediately sound to the seeker like I am trying to favor Christianity out of personal bias. But I follow up quickly by saying, "Let me give four reasons why it makes a lot of sense to start your exploration with Christianity."

First, Christianity is *testable*. Objective evidence for it or against it can be offered, and the evidence means something. For instance, the New Testament declares that if Jesus was not raised from the dead, our faith is worthless. So, if there is no good reason to believe that Jesus really did rise from the dead, then Christianity can be dismissed, and we can move on to something else. Of course, if anyone does take an unbiased look at the evidence for the resurrection of Jesus, they will be surprised just how strong the case is.

Second, in Christianity *salvation is free*. The contrast here is that salvation or enlightenment requires an awful lot of effort in other religions, but in Christianity it is a free gift from a loving God.

Third, in Christianity you get a *tight worldview fit*. That is, Christianity paints a picture of the world that matches the way the world really is. Take for instance, the issues of evil, pain, and suffering. Most Eastern religions such as Buddhism and Hinduism conclude that evil, pain, and suffering are not real; rather, they are illusions. But we all know that pain and suffering are real—we experience them every day. Christianity has never shied away from facing up to the reality of evil, pain, and suffering. Hence, Christianity seems more in line with the way the world really is, at least on that issue.

Fourth, Christianity has *Jesus at the center*. This may sound like it is stacking the deck in favor of Christianity. But it isn't because the point is that everyone seems to want to make Jesus a part of their religion. Clearly Jesus is *the* universal religious figure. Everyone wants to claim him as their own. Therefore, it makes perfect sense that if a person is on a religious quest, she would want to start her quest with the religion that has always had Jesus firmly planted at the center, namely, Christianity.

So these are four reasons why it would be smart to start a religious exploration with an in-depth examination of Christianity.

Jonathan: Sometimes Christians find themselves with a desire to go deeper in their ability to defend their faith, only to discover their options for quality training are limited because of where they live. Can you share how people can receive top-notch training in Christian apologetics and worldview without having to relocate?

Craig: We have developed the premier graduate degree in Christian apologetics at Biola University, and it can be done at a distance. All that is required are two short visits to our campus in southern California, and the rest of the course work can be done through stimulating graduate seminars and specialized classes online. It has become wildly popular, and we've seen our graduates go on to make an impact through teaching, writing, speaking, missions work, broadcasting, doctoral studies, and much more. We also have a Distance Learning Certificate Program that is open to everyone. To find out more, just go to www.biola.edu/apologetics or call 1-888-332-4652.

> **Craig J. Hazen** is a professor of comparative religion and Christian apologetics at Biola University and director of the Christian Apologetics Program. He is the editor of the journal *Philosophia Christi* and author of several books, including the acclaimed novel *Five Sacred Crossings*. Hazen holds a PhD in religious studies from the University of California and has won a range of awards for his teaching and research. He has lectured in the White House and on Capitol Hill and is a former cohost of a national radio talk program. To see a full list of his writings and lectures, visit www.craighazen.com.

chapter twelve

TAKING THE BIBLE SERIOUSLY

To stay away from Christianity because part of the Bible's teaching is offensive to you assumes that if there is a God he wouldn't have any views that upset you. Does that belief make sense?... If you don't trust the Bible enough to let it challenge and correct your thinking, how could you ever have a personal relationship with God? In any truly personal relationship, the other person has to be able to contradict you.

Tim Keller, *The Reason for God*

THROUGHOUT THE CENTURIES, Christians have responded to numerous challenges seeking to undermine the authority and relevance of the Bible. Some things never change. While the twentieth-century debate centered on the nature and implications of biblical inspiration and inerrancy[1], the action has now shifted to two other significant challenges. First, critics like evangelical-turned-agnostic Bart Ehrman claim that the text of the New Testament has been corrupted and changed. The second challenge, which receives more press, argues that the Bible is culturally outdated and that its offensive archaic interpretations should give way to a hermeneutic of love, tolerance, and inclusion.

I'll address these in turn and then conclude by taking a closer look at the hot-button issue of what the Bible has to say about homosexuality. One thing is crystal clear: our culture is talking about the Bible with a sophistication that exceeds that of most people in the church. This is so primarily because we don't talk about such things in church. However, the fact that our society is talking about the Bible presents another opportunity for Christians to engage and seize a cultural moment. Part of cultivating a thoughtful faith means learning how to take the Bible seriously and then being able to teach others to as well (see 2 Timothy 2:15).

HAS THE NEW TESTAMENT TEXT BEEN CORRUPTED AND CHANGED?

To begin with, Christians need to know that none of the original manuscripts of either the Old or New Testaments are still in existence. All that remain are imperfect copies. Although this is exactly the same situation of every other ancient work of literature—no one has the originals—it is this little bit of news that writers like Ehrman have popularized. When I taught a seminar on this topic at our church, Christians who had grown up in the church had never heard this, and they found it a little disconcerting. (Incidentally, it is much better for Christians, and especially youth, to hear challenging ideas for the first time in the church, where they can process them, rather than on CNN, the History Channel, or in the classroom.) While this revelation may come as a surprise, we don't have to become skeptics regarding ancient texts. Scholars use the copies we have to reconstruct the original Old and New Testaments. Generally speaking, the more copies available to examine and the closer they are to when the originals were written, the better. This practice of reconstruction is known as textual criticism.[2]

We can't offer a full treatment here, but we must answer two critical questions. First, do scholars have enough copies of the New Testament to work with in order to reconstruct the text? And second, have the New Testament texts been corrupted beyond recovery?

Regarding the number of copies, New Testament textual critic Dan Wallace authoritatively answers this question:

> The wealth of material that is available for determining the wording of the original New Testament is staggering: more than fifty-seven hundred Greek New Testament manuscripts, as many as twenty thousand versions, and more than one million quotations by patristic writers. In comparison with the average ancient Greek author, the New Testament copies are well over a thousand times more plentiful. If the average-sized manuscript were two and one-half inches thick, all the copies of the works of an average Greek author would stack up four feet high, while the copies of the New Testament would stack up to over a mile high! This is indeed an embarrassment of riches.[3]

Regarding corruption beyond recovery, Bart Ehrman claims, "There are more variations among our manuscripts than there are words in the New Testament."[4] He uses the number of 400,000 textual variants (the entire Greek New Testament contains only 138,162 words). While his account of textual variants is technically accurate, the statistic is highly misleading to those unfamiliar with textual criticism. Daniel Wallace breaks down the kinds of variants into four categories:[5]

1. *spelling differences.* The great majority of variants (70 to 80 percent, or 320,000) are spelling errors and easily correctable upon manuscript comparison.

2. *minor differences that involve synonyms or do not affect translation.* These differences include whether or not definite articles are used with proper names (for example, "The Joseph or The Mary" in Luke 2:16) or words are transposed (word order is very important in English, but in an inflected language such as Greek, word order isn't nearly as important).

3. *meaningful but not viable differences.* Sometimes a single manuscript will differ from the rest of the manuscripts that contain the same alternate reading (for example, 1 Thessalonians 2:9 either reads "gospel of God" or "gospel of Christ").

4. *meaningful and viable differences.* These meaningful and viable differences are not things like "Jesus was a liar" or "Jesus was the Devil." One of the most famous differences is Romans 5:1, which either reads "let us have peace with God" or "we have peace with God." The manuscripts are quite evenly divided in this case.

We need to be honest about how we got the Bible, but we also need to give people confidence in it. Wallace summarizes: "Less than 1 percent of all textual variants are both meaningful and viable, and by 'meaningful' we don't mean to imply earth-shattering significance but rather, almost always, minor alterations to the meaning of the text."[6] This comes out to less than 4,000 of the original 400,000 variants *having any real significance at all for the meaning of a verse.* And regarding the verses where questions remain, "significant textual variants that alter core doctrines of the New Testament have not been produced."[7] Bottom line: Despite what you may hear in news stories recycled every Christmas and Easter, we can trust that what was written then is what we have now.

IS THE BIBLE CULTURALLY OUTDATED?

For better or worse, the Bible is a cultural text. And people are struggling today with how to read it. Magazines like *Newsweek* are informing the general public (and in this particular case advocating) that the Bible is culturally obsolete and outdated. Here is an excerpt from the December 2008 cover story *The Religious Case for Gay Marriage* by Lisa Miller:

Most of us no longer heed Leviticus on haircuts or blood sacrifices; our modern understanding of the world has surpassed its prescriptions. Why would we regard its condemnation of homosexuality with more seriousness than we regard its advice, which is far lengthier, on the best price to pay for a slave? . . . A mature view of scriptural authority requires us, as we have in the past, to move beyond literalism. The Bible was written for a world so unlike our own, it's impossible to apply its rules, at face value, to ours.[8]

For some Christians, this is where appeals to blind faith or personal feeling come in — but these responses don't cut it in the public square. When we only emote and don't offer reasons for our views, this serves only to reinforce the stereotype that Christians are ignorant, dogmatic, and closed-minded.

Since homosexuality is such a prominent topic right now, given the gay marriage debate, I'll address it below. But for now, should Christians take the Bible literally? *Maybe.* It really all depends on what someone means by the term *literally.* Notice Lisa Miller's assumption in the article that immature people take the Bible literally.

Here's the big idea: People can take the Bible seriously without having to read it in an overly rigid or hyperliteral way. They can still be faithful to the text. So if someone tries to dismiss you with, "Oh, you're just one of those fundamentalists who takes the Bible literally," the way to respond is to say, "Well, I actually try to take the Bible seriously on its own terms." Someone may disagree with the teaching of the Bible (and they are certainly free to do so), but intellectual honesty compels us to play by the normal rules of language and to read biblical passages in light of their cultural and literary context.

To illustrate, consider one of Jesus' favorite ways of communicating to his first-century Jewish audience — hyperbole, or exaggeration. Hyperbole is effective because it jolts people into paying attention and grasping the big idea. If you read Jesus' statement, "If anyone comes to me and does not hate father and mother, wife and children, brothers and sisters . . . such a person cannot be my disciple" (Luke 14:26) in a woodenly literal manner, you are going to miss his point. Jesus didn't want us to hate anyone. His followers were to love their parents and even take the more radical step of loving their enemies. His point here was that a person's most important relationship in life was to be with God; it was a matter of priorities. This is how to take the Bible seriously.

Dealing with passages that seem culturally strange or offensive

When it comes to offensive, troubling, or confusing texts, Pastor Tim Keller offers helpful advice to both practicing Christians and those exploring Christianity for the first time: "I counsel them . . . to slow down and try out several different perspectives on the issues that trouble them. That way they can continue to read, learn, and profit from the Bible even as they continue to wrestle with some of its concepts."[9] The guiding principle is that sometimes the Bible does not teach what it appears to teach at first glance. It would be a shame to punt the Bible after only an initial read. Give it some thought, read credible Christian scholars on the passage, and then, after some time, evaluate it.

A clear illustration of this principle is found in the issue of slavery and the Bible. When you come across passages that say, "Slaves, obey your earthly masters with respect and fear" who doesn't cringe a little? But more context and study reveal a much different picture. Contrary to your first impression, the Bible does not teach that God views slavery as a good thing. Moreover, you will discover that slavery in ancient Israel was vastly different from what occurred during colonial America.[10] And finally, as we grow in our understanding of the biblical text, cultural background, and the reality of life in a world messed up by sin yet into which God was and still is speaking, we see that, far from enthusiastically endorsing slavery, God's people *tolerated* it with unheard-of compassion and humaneness until it could finally be abolished.[11]

Another helpful principle to remember is that the Bible does not necessarily endorse what it accurately records. The Bible records many things that it does not endorse—though it describes those situations accurately. For example, the Bible records people lying, but it does not endorse lying. Or take the practice of polygamy in the book of Genesis. The patriarchs had multiple wives, but the narrative always highlights the painful consequences of this practice. God's creation norm is one man with one woman for a lifetime (Genesis 2:24). Yet another example is that Israel often went to war without God's blessing and suffered for it. You get the idea. Some things are endorsed in Scripture, while others are merely accurately described. Careful study is required to be able to tell the difference.

Specific Guidelines for Understanding the Old Testament Law Today

As the *Newsweek* article revealed, the Old Testament is what is usually cited to demonstrate that the Bible is culturally regressive. Unfortunately, most people, Christians included, are clearly not prepared to understand and apply the Old Testament. So here are some helpful guidelines in interpreting the Old Testament Law.

The Interpretive Journey
1. Grasp the text in their town. What did the text mean to the biblical audience?
2. Measure the width of the river to cross. What are the differences between the biblical audience and us?
3. Cross the principle-izing bridge. What is the theological principle of this text?
4. Cross into the New Testament. Does the New Testament teaching modify or qualify this principle, and if so, how?
5. Grasp the text in our town. How should individual Christians apply the theological principle in their lives?

First, we need to teach and follow the interpretive journey (see chart).[12] A lot of confusion immediately evaporates as we apply sound principles of interpretation to the passage in question. Unfortunately, most Christians have never been trained in these principles.

Next, we need to understand that seemingly arbitrary laws served an important function in ancient Israel. At first glance, laws like "Do not cook a young goat in its mother's milk" (Deuteronomy 14:21) and "Do not plant your field with two kinds of seed. Do not wear clothing woven of two kinds of material" (Leviticus 19:19) seem ridiculous. But as biblical scholars Gordon Fee and Douglas Stuart explain:

> These and other prohibitions were designed to forbid the Israelites to engage in fertility cult practices of the Canaanites. The Canaanites believed in what is called sympathetic magic, the idea that symbolic actions can influence the gods and nature. They thought that boiling a kid in its mother's milk would magically ensure the continuing fertility of the flock. Mixing animal breeds, seeds, or materials was thought to "marry" them so as magically to produce "offspring," that is, agricultural bounty in the future ... Knowing the intention of such laws—to keep Israel from being led into the Canaanite religion that stood so utterly over and against God and his character—helps you see that they are not arbitrary, but crucial and graciously beneficial.[13]

THE BIBLE AND HOMOSEXUALITY

It is here that our conversation about how to interpret the Old Testament merges with an issue widely discussed in our culture—homosexuality. When Christians appeal to passages like Leviticus 18:22 to argue that homosexual behavior is a sin, they are often met with the charge of "picking and choosing" random verses that support their view and leaving out others. Is this true? I don't think so, but I'll come back to this after I lay some groundwork. Christians are now under the New Covenant. The Law of Moses (that is, the Mosaic covenant), while important for teaching us about God's redemptive history through Israel, is not binding on Christians *unless* the principle, law, or command is reaffirmed or restated in the New Testament (Romans 6:14–15; 10:4; Galatians 3; Hebrews 8–9). God made a conditional covenant with the people of Israel in the Old Testament that was specific to them and their national status with God as their king (that is, theocracy). The Law was good in the sense that it accomplished God's design for it, and we can and should learn from it (2 Timothy 3:16–17). However, the Mosaic Law was temporary, not ideal, and not "reflective of God's ultimate intentions for his people" (for example, the New Covenant).[14] This does not mean that God has changed or that what pleases him has changed; rather, as Fee and Stuart observe, "God expects of his people—us—somewhat different evidences of obedience and loyalty from those he expected from the Old Testament Israelites. The *loyalty* itself is still expected. It is *how* one shows this loyalty that has been changed in certain ways."[15]

So, should Christians not appeal to Leviticus 18:22 because it is part of the Law? In this case, appealing to it is still legitimate because Genesis 19, a pre-Law text, and New Testament texts such as Romans 1:26–27; 1 Corinthians 6:9–10; and 1 Timothy 1:9–10 restate the same moral principle expressed in the Levitical law.

Christians need to know what the Bible teaches regarding the passages that address homosexuality and the pro-gay movement's revisionist interpretations of them. Miller, after enlisting some of these arguments, concludes: "Religious objections to gay marriage are rooted not in the Bible at all, then, but in custom and tradition."[16] In a matter of a few paragraphs, she dismisses traditional arguments that homosexual behavior is a sin by pointing to more progressive scholars' revisionist interpretations. I will address the most common ones below in the chart.[17] Christians certainly need to know the biblical view and be able to argue for it, but knowing the biblical view is not enough. As Alan Shlemon rightly states, we must know the truth *and* speak it with compassion.[18] I would also add one more requirement for meaningful engagement on this issue. We must be sure that we are addressing the right questions at the right times because there are three different aspects to this cultural discussion that we need to keep straight.

First, we need a solid understanding of what the Bible actually teaches regarding homosexuality. The Bible's uniform teaching is that homosexual *behavior* is condemned (see comparison chart below). Second, we need to rethink how Christians and churches respond to those who struggle with same-sex attraction (which I address in chapter 13). And finally, we need to clarify how we go about making the case for traditional marriage in the public square for the public good (which I address in chapter 16). Each sphere requires a different approach.

Revisionist Interpretations	Traditional Biblical Responses
Genesis 19:4–9: The sin of Sodom was inhospitality, attempted gang rape, or general wickedness—not homosexual behavior.	Lot's response, offering his two virgin daughters instead of the men, and his plea to "don't do this wicked thing" indicate that the Hebrew *yada'* ("to know") in this passage is sexual in nature. Several other biblical passages refer to the sexual nature of Sodom's sin (2 Peter 2:6–7; Jude 7; cf. Ezekiel 16:49; in the Apocrypha, 3 Maccabees 2:5; Jubilees 16:6). Arrogance, idolatry, and pride were certainly involved as well. God's righteous judgment fell on the *overall* wickedness of Sodom.

Leviticus 18:22; 20:13: *Idolatrous* homosexual behavior (for example, temple prostitution), not homosexual behavior per se is what is condemned as an abomination. Moreover, Christians pick and choose which parts of the Levitical law to apply.	Regarding the "pick and choose" argument, see the discussion of the Mosaic Law and the New Covenant above. Under Levitical law, homosexuality was one of many abominable practices punishable by death. This passage is addressed to the Israelites (Leviticus 18:2), not just the priests. More than idolatry and cultic regulations for ritual purity are being addressed in this passage because the surrounding context, in addition to condemning child sacrifice, also condemns other sexual sins—adultery, incest, and bestiality. Surely Moses is not saying these are OK as long as they are not associated with idolatry or temple worship, is he? Moreover, God calls other practices not associated with idolatry or pagan worship "detestable" in Proverbs 6:16–19 (haughtiness, lying, false witness, etc.).
Jesus says nothing negative about homosexuality. In fact, Jesus favorably mentions homosexuals as "eunuchs" (Matthew 19:12) and also healed a centurion's male lover (Matthew 8:5–13).	First, Jesus was not silent; he defined the "one flesh" marriage union heterosexually as between a male and a female (Mark 10:6–9). But if his silence works in favor of homosexual behavior, then why not other behaviors that Jesus never mentioned, like incest, cannibalism, or wife beating? Does his silence legitimize them too? Also, the Gospels are limited in what they record from Jesus' ministry (John 21:25). This line of thinking assumes that the words contained in the Gospels are *more authoritative* than the rest of the New Testament. Such thinking is false. Regarding eunuchs, the meaning of the word rules out any homosexual connotation. Jesus, as he does on so many occasions, shows compassion for the outcasts of society (like the eunuch). Regarding the male lover, the text clearly says that the centurion loved his servant. But nothing indicates sexual love is in view *contextually*. Even if it were, Jesus' healing of him does not mean that he approves of his behavior. Jesus healed many sinful people.
Romans 1:26–27: Paul was not talking about homosexuals here, but (1) heterosexuals who abandon their "nature" (that is, sexual orientation) by practicing homosexuality; (2) homosexuality within the context of idolatrous worship; or (3) sex with boys (pederasty) or multiple-partner, risky sexual relationships (that is, noncommitted, loving homosexual relationships).	This is the clearest and most comprehensive treatment of homosexual behavior in the Bible. It's also the only passage that specifically addresses female homosexuality. The biblical context is important when addressing various revisionist interpretations. In Romans 1–3, Paul demonstrates the *universality* of human sinfulness and that *every person* is under God's righteous judgment. This is the main point—homosexual behavior is just one of many illustrations: (1) First, this argument, if it invokes sexual orientation, is highly anachronistic. Scientific discussions about being "born gay" began only in the late twentieth century, and the available data is highly inconclusive. Second, "natural desires"

are not what Paul is discussing here. "Against nature" (*para physis*) in this context refers to the created order. Furthermore, Paul appeals to the natural "function" (*chresis*) of males and females. The vocabulary he uses for male (*arsen*) and female (*thelys*) highlights their specific genders. Paul is arguing on the basis of how males and females are biologically and anatomically designed to operate sexually. Men were designed to function sexually not with men but with women. Males and females were designed by God to "function" together in a sexually complementary way. Paul's word choice could not have been clearer. Homosexual behavior is a clear violation of God's creational order and complementary design of male and female, along with the command to be fruitful and multiply (Genesis 1:26–27; 2:18–24). (2) If idolatry was the only moral limitation of homosexual behavior, then what of the *other* twenty-three sins addressed between verses 20–31? The logic would seem to require them being morally OK as long as they're not practiced in an idolatrous manner—which is absurd. Regarding the "doing what comes naturally" argument, these other sins come naturally to us as well; we're all inclined toward pride, lying, envy, greed, etc. An inclination or even strong desire does not make a behavior morally right or authorize us to act on it. (3) If Paul was only concerned with condemning adult male sex with young boys (pederasty), then he would have used the Greek word commonly used for this practice. Finally, Paul's argument leaves no room for "loving, committed, and responsible homosexual relationships" because he uniformly condemns the *behavior itself*, not merely what are described as risky or irresponsible expressions of certain homosexual behaviors.

1 Corinthians 6:9–10 (cf. 1 Timothy 1:9–10): Paul was not condemning homosexual behavior as a whole, only male prostitution and immoral behavior in general. The particular terms Paul used (*arsenokoites*) and (*malakos*) refer to specific behaviors condemned and are not a blanket condemnation of all homosexual behavior.	Paul's clear and comprehensive teaching in Romans 1 should be recalled as the backdrop for this passage (see also 1 Timothy 1:9–10). Here Paul is contrasting the unrighteous versus those who have been made righteous because of the work of Christ. Homosexual behavior is *but one* of the ways that unrighteousness is manifested. Paul uses two words in verse 9 that clarify his argument: "effeminate" (*malakos*) and "homosexuals" (*arsenokoites*). In Roman society it was permissible for male Roman citizens (usually the elite) to be involved sexually with male non-Roman citizens (for example, slaves). It was not uncommon for male slaves to be purchased to be used as passive sexual partners.

> The word translated "effeminate" (*malakos*) refers to this passive sexual relationship. Regarding the second word, translated "men who have sex with men" (*arseno-koites*), critics argue that this means "male prostitutes." This isn't the case because Paul actually coined this word to clearly make his point. He uses the Greek translation of the Hebrew Scriptures (OT; Septuagint [LXX]) from the prohibition of homosexual behavior in Leviticus 18:22. He takes the two words (*arsen*) "male" and (*koite*) "bed" from Leviticus 18:22 and combines them to form this new word (*arsenokoites*) to describe sex between men in 1 Corinthians 6:9. Paul's countercultural statement condemns both forms (passive and active) of homosexual behavior common in Corinth. This argument also applies to Paul's use of *arsenokoites* in 1 Timothy 1:10.

AN OPPORTUNITY FOR RADICAL LOVE

Before this chapter concludes, two things remain to be said. First, homosexual sin, while a serious offense to God, is not worse than other sins. Heterosexual adultery is equally repugnant to God. So is lying. Second, redemption from the power and habits of sinful behavior is possible because of the work of Jesus Christ. This is true of all sin—whether heterosexual or homosexual. This is Paul's point: "And that is what some of you were. But you were washed, you were sanctified, you were justified in the name of the Lord Jesus Christ and by the Spirit of our God" (1 Corinthians 6:11).

The Bible will seem culturally out of step with our society. But as Christians we must prepare ourselves to stand our ground on the truth of Scripture while at the same time compassionately moving toward those who struggle with same-sex attraction with the radical love Christ offers to us all.

RESOURCES FOR ENGAGING YOUR INTERSECTION

Books

- *Dethroning Jesus: Exposing Popular Culture's Quest to Unseat the Biblical Christ* by Darrell L. Bock and Daniel B. Wallace
- *How to Read the Bible for All Its Worth* by Gordon D. Fee and Douglas K. Stuart
- *Grasping God's Word: A Hands-On Approach to Reading, Interpreting, and Applying the Bible* by J. Scott Duvall and J. Daniel Hays
- *Is God a Moral Monster? The New Atheists and the Strange World of Old Testament Ethics* by Paul Copan
- *The Complete Christian Guide to Understanding Homosexuality* by Joe Dallas and Nancy Heche
- "Homosexuality: Know the Truth and Speak It with Compassion" by Alan Shlemon in *Apologetics for a New Generation* edited by Sean McDowell
- *The Questions Christians Hope No One Will Ask: (With Answers)* by Mark Mittelberg

Websites and DVDs

- www.csntm.org – Center for the Study of New Testament Manuscripts
- www.str.org – Stand to Reason
- www.exodusinternational.org – Exodus International
- www.joedallas.com – Joe Dallas's website
- www.bible.org – Bible.org

EXPLORING REASONS
FOR FAITH

AN INTERVIEW WITH WILLIAM LANE CRAIG

Jonathan Morrow: Many Christians sometimes fear that someone somewhere has found an argument or discovered evidence that Christianity is false. As a Christian philosopher of religion, you have spent your life wading through deep intellectual waters that the ordinary believer will never navigate. Have you seen your faith confirmed and strengthened by your studies?

William Lane Craig: Even though exploring philosophical issues raised in connection with a Christian worldview has been challenging, and studying the New Testament documents with respect to the historicity of Jesus' resurrection has led to some changes in my beliefs, I must say that the result of my philosophical and theological studies has been overwhelmingly confirmatory. When I graduated from college, I thought there were no good arguments for God's existence; now I think there are several. The arguments for atheism appear weak by comparison. Moreover, although since becoming a Christian I always believed in the fact of Jesus' resurrection, I was pleasantly surprised how remarkably strong a historical case can be made for the fundamental reliability of the Easter narratives. Attempts to bar the resurrection hypothesis as the best explanation of the evidence strike me as quite weak, as do most of the naturalistic, alternative explanations. So my Christian faith has been greatly buoyed by my studies.

Jonathan: You are the founder of ReasonableFaith.org. Why did you begin this ministry and what has the response been?

Craig: Frankly, I became frustrated with the competence of those constantly trotted out by the media as spokesmen for the Christian faith. I yearned to hear an intelligent, articulate presentation and defense of the Christian worldview. I believed it was high time that we Christians do something to present a more credible image of who we are and what we stand for. For that reason we established our web-based ministry Reasonable Faith. The burden on my heart is to provide in the public arena an intelligent, articulate, and uncompromising, yet gracious Christian perspective on the most important issues concerning the truth of the Christian faith. We've been greatly encouraged by the expressions of thanks from believers and nonbelievers alike for the material posted on the site. It's gratifying to see the fruit of changed lives as a result of this ministry.

Jonathan: What do you see as the greatest challenge Christians are facing from our culture today?

Craig: It seems to me that religious pluralism or relativism is the burning theological issue of our day. The religious pluralist holds that no one particular religion is true, but that all, or most, religions represent equally valid approaches to the divine. Christian particularism has now become politically incorrect, and its proponents are vilified as intolerant, bigoted, and narrow-minded. I suspect that the popularity of religious pluralism in this theological sense is in great measure the cultural fallout of scientific naturalism, which holds that science gives us the objective truth about reality, whereas religious beliefs are merely expressions of personal taste and sentiment. If religious statements are not putative statements of fact but merely expressions of personal preference, then to regard one particular religion as true and therefore uniquely valid would be as perverse as thinking that, for example, vanilla is objectively better-tasting than chocolate. We need to present Christian truth claims as statements of putative fact, having an objective truth value and supported by argument and evidence.

> **William Lane Craig** is research professor of philosophy at Talbot School of Theology in La Mirada, California. He has authored or edited over thirty books, including the award-winning *Philosophical Foundations for a Christian Worldview* (with J. P. Moreland); *Theism, Atheism, and Big Bang Cosmology* (with Quentin Smith); *Assessing the New Testament Evidence for the Historicity of the Resurrection of Jesus*; *On Guard*; and his signature book *Reasonable Faith*. Visit his website at www.reasonablefaith.org.

chapter thirteen

RECOVERING GOD'S DESIGN FOR SEX

> If we think of sex as only a physical activity to be engaged in at our pleasure, and only for our pleasure ... If we think our makeup is limited to satisfying appetites, we'll conclude that we can engage in sexual activity, enjoy it at a physical level, and totally disassociate these acts from the rest of what we are as human beings — but we'll be sadly mistaken.
>
> Joe S. McIlhaney Jr. and Freda McKissic Bush, *Hooked*

FIFTY YEARS HAVE COME AND GONE since the sexual revolution. How's that worked out for us? The short answer is, "Not good." The slightly longer answer is, "*Really* not good." Andy Stanley writes:

> Nothing has stolen more dreams, dashed more hopes, broken up more families, and messed up people more psychologically than our propensity to disregard God's commands regarding sexual purity. Most of the major social ills in America are caused by, or fueled by, the misuse of our sexuality. If issues related to sexual impurity — adultery, the shrapnel associated with adultery, addiction to pornography, AIDS and other sexually transmitted diseases, abortion, the psychological effects associated with abortion, sexual abuse, incest, rape, and all sexual addictions — were to suddenly disappear from society, imagine the resources we would have available to apply to the handful of issues that would remain.[1]

When it comes to sex, our culture now takes the consumer approach. Dr. Jennifer Roback Morse, author of *Smart Sex: Finding Life-long Love in a Hook-Up World*, observes that "sex is a purely private matter, in the narrowest sense of private. Sex is a recreational activity, a consumer good. My consumption of this good, my enjoyment of this activity, is a completely private matter that should be viewed as any other good and activity."[2]

Oh, and by the way, what do people do with consumer goods that no longer satisfy? They trade them in for a newer model or a better deal. In short, sex exists to satisfy me, and as long as you do that, then I will keep you around. But there is no permanence to it, no unique or lasting bond. Such is our hook-up culture. Sex is reduced to a purely physical act for my immediate pleasure without the baggage of future commitments.

GOD'S DESIGN FOR SEX

There is nothing casual about sex, and deep down we all know it. Sex is powerful because God designed it that way. Yes, contrary to popular opinion, God invented sex! Unfortunately, the way sex is typically talked about in church doesn't help change this misperception. Usually, it will be some variation of "Just don't do it before marriage because God says so." We can do better.

In stark contrast to the consumer mind-set of sex that prevails in our culture, God's design for sex reflects who we are as human beings at the deepest level. We are hardwired to connect and to love. And a departure from God's design ends up hurting everyone. It's not a message we hear often, but it's true nonetheless. Christianity is not about what we have to say no to; it's about what we get to say yes to. Big difference. Once people investigate the Bible for themselves and get past the misconceptions, they will find that God is not a prude or a killjoy, and Christians aren't against pleasure or fun.

Professor of Christian ethics Dennis Hollinger contends there are four biblical purposes for sex.[3] The first purpose is *oneness*. God created a husband and wife to bond with one another for life (Genesis 2:24; 1 Corinthians 7:3 – 5). I get you, and you get me — at the deepest, most intimate level. Our relationship is unique and exclusive. What we experience together, no one else experiences with either of us. Every time a husband and wife have sex, their oneness is reaffirmed. Oneness begins on the wedding night and continues throughout their marriage. The benefits of this for each other and for the family are obvious — husband and wife are attached to one another for the other's good and eventually the good of their children.

The second purpose of sex is *procreation*. God intended sex to move outward. Thus we are reminded of the creation mandate to "be fruitful and increase in number" (Genesis 1:28). Children are a unique expression of the oneness of husband and wife and are a gift from the Lord (Psalm 127:3; 128:2 – 4). Every sexual act carries the potential of creating human life. In reality, there is nothing casual about sex.

The third purpose of sex is *love*. Love by its very nature longs to express itself physically in marriage (Ephesians 5:25–33). Hollinger summarizes, "True sexual love is in the context of a loving, committed relationship, a set-apart covenantal relationship that is willing to bear potential fruit of the action … Sex is not 'making love.' It is giving love, expressing mutual and personal love."[4]

The fourth purpose of sex is *pleasure*. God is not against pleasure, but he does call us to seek pleasure in ways that are ultimately good for others and ourselves. God created sexual pleasures for us to enjoy in the marital context:

> Drink water from your own cistern,
> > running water from your own well.
> Should your springs overflow in the streets,
> > your streams of water in the public squares?
> Let them be yours alone,
> > never to be shared with strangers.
> May your fountain be blessed,
> > and may you rejoice in the wife of your youth.
> A loving doe, a graceful deer—
> > may her breasts satisfy you always,
> > may you ever be intoxicated with her love.
>
> Proverbs 5:15–19

Notice the bride inviting her husband to enjoy their wedding night:

> Awake, north wind,
> > and come, south wind!
> Blow on my garden,
> > that its fragrance may spread everywhere.
> Let my beloved come into his garden
> > and taste its choice fruits.
>
> Song of Songs 4:16

The Bible says plenty more, but you get the point. We need to teach this in our churches, especially to the next generation. God is not trying to keep them from pleasure; he wants them to have the maximum pleasure that comes only in the secure and intimate context of marriage.

But sex is not ultimate; only God is. Our common human problem is making idols out of what is good in and of itself by making it ultimate in our lives. As wonderful as sex is, it too can become an idol of the heart.

God designed sex to be between one man and one woman for a lifetime so that they can experience love, intimacy, oneness, safety, trust, pleasure, and delight, and for this to serve as the context in which children can grow up in a safe, loving environment where they will have the best opportunity to flourish as human beings. Set next to this backdrop, consumer sex is seen for what it really is—a hollow imitation that promises far more than it can fulfill. The author of sex offers a far more compelling vision.

THIS IS YOUR BRAIN ON SEX

Many people already know that sex outside of the context of lifelong marriage and with more than one partner is risky. There is no shortage of statistics on sexually transmitted diseases, nonmarital pregnancies, elevated emotional and psychological disorders related to sexual behavior during the adolescent years and with multiple partners, and devastating life consequences for unwed teenage mothers. But we need to say it again. Did you know that 70 million Americans live with some form of sexually transmitted infections? To put this in perspective, there are 300 million people in the United States. This number of cases is not static; every year 19 million *new* cases are contracted.[5] And the collateral damage of consumer sex is staggering.

But a message we need to spread far and wide, a message that comes as a surprise to many people, is that contemporary neuroscience supports the biblical view of sex. Consumer sex only has two rules: (1) Both people must consent, and (2) practice safe sex. But there are no condoms to protect your brain and heart; there's no pill for that. There's no magic formula to stave off the depression you experience after you have been sexually active and then break up. No one tells young people that having sex early on in life—often and with multiple partners—actually works against them being able to bond with a future spouse when they are finally ready to "settle down."

Modern neuroscience is revealing that the most important human sex organ is the brain. As we've seen, one of the purposes of sex is to unite two people for life. Science has recently confirmed that this bonding takes place on a neurochemical level. A key neurochemical important to healthy sex and bonding is oxytocin. The release of oxytocin generates trust with another person. In fact, one study showed that sniffing oxytocin during a game involving finances caused people to be more trusting with their money.[6]

While oxytocin occurs in both genders, it is most prominent in women.[7] A woman's body is flooded with oxytocin during labor and breast-feeding. The presence of oxytocin produces a chemical impact on the mother's brain that a woman experiences as the "motherly bond" with her child. A woman's body is also flooded with oxytocin during intimate physical touch and sexual activity, causing her to desire touch again and again with the man to whom she has bonded, generating an even stronger connection.[8] Oxytocin helps build the trust that is essential for a lasting, healthy relationship.

Few women realize that during each sexual encounter, oxytocin floods their brain and creates a partial bond with each person they have sex with. This bond is not *just* a feeling or an emotion to get over; it is a physiological and neurological connection that has formed in the brain and is extremely painful to break. More-over, oxytocin is "value-neutral because it is an involuntary process that cannot distinguish between a one-night stand and a lifelong soul mate."[9] In *Hooked*, Dr. Joe McIlhaney (founder of the Medical Institute of Sexual Health) and Dr. Freda McKissic Bush explain the devastating effects of promiscuous sex:

> An individual who is sexually involved, then breaks up and then is sexually involved again, and who repeats this cycle again and again is in danger of negative emotional consequences. People who behave in this manner are act-ing against, almost fighting against, the way they are made to function. When connectedness and bonding form and then are quickly broken and replaced with another sexual relationship, it often causes damage to the brain's natural connecting or bonding mechanism.[10]

McIlhaney and Bush use the vivid illustration of tape losing its stickiness after it is repeatedly applied and removed to compare what is going on in our brains. More could be said and should be; in fact, every pastor, youth pastor, and parent ought to read *Hooked*. This issue cannot be ignored, and Christian leaders and parents need to become informed. And when you talk about God's design for sex, utilize the neurological facts when you make your case. People may not initially care what the Bible says. But if you connect the dots so they see that the biblical portrait of sex correlates with the latest neuroscience research, then you have helped them overcome a hurdle and see yet another area in which a Christian worldview makes the best sense of our human experience.

TWO STRUGGLES WE DON'T TALK ABOUT IN CHURCH: PORNOGRAPHY AND SAME-SEX ATTRACTION

God's vision for sex is hard enough for most of us to talk about in church. Even more difficult are two sexual issues that make people uncomfortable — pornography and same-sex attraction. My goal is not to single them out for special shame or indicate that anyone who struggles with these must be really sinful. I want to address issues that people are typically left to figure out for themselves. We need to help people apply the gospel to these sexual struggles, to let everyone know that God is not content to leave any of us where we currently are. Let me say as clearly as I can: We are all broken; we just express our brokenness in different ways.

Pornography

Our culture is saturated with pornography; it is everywhere. According to Cov-enant Eyes, a company that specializes in accountability software, by age eighteen, 90 percent of boys and 60 percent of girls have been exposed to Internet pornography.[11] Estimates are that the financial size of the worldwide sex industry is $57 billion ($12 billion comes from the United States).[12] This dehumanizes and objectifies people—mostly women—and numbs people to overall healthy sexual expression. It is slowly killing both adult and young men—though many don't realize it. Feminist Naomi Wolf, in her article "The Porn Myth," bluntly states the effect of the universal accessibility of porn. "For the first time in human history, the images' power and allure have supplanted that of real naked women. Today, real naked women are just bad porn."[13]

All the ingredients exist for a perfect storm in this area, and here is the formula:

Personal autonomy as the goal of human existence
+ the belief that the satisfaction of my immediate desires will make me happy and feel better
+ the anonymity and accessibility provided by the Internet
= a recipe for disaster.

The temptation of pornography is the satisfaction of a legitimate desire in an inappropriate way. Pornography and sex addiction are definitely heart issues. But there is a way out. God can change our hearts, but we must cooperate with him in this process. I'll get to this in a minute. We first need to look at pornography's devastating effects on the brain.

In his illuminating and hopeful book *Wired for Intimacy*, William Struthers explains:

> As men fall deeper into the habit of fixating on these images, the exposure creates neural pathways. Like a path is created in the woods with each successive hiker, so do the neural paths set the course for the next time an erotic image is viewed ... The neural circuitry anchors this process solidly in the brain ... Repeated exposure to pornography creates a one-way neurological superhighway where a man's mental life is over-sexualized and narrowed. It is hemmed in on either side by high containment walls making escape nearly impossible.[14]

But this is not the whole story. Thankfully the process of neurological formation and the way to break free from this self-destructive habit are parallel. Struthers writes:

> But if this corrupted pathway can be avoided, a new pathway can be formed. We can establish a healthy sexual pattern where the flow is redirected toward holiness rather than corrupted intimacy. By intentionally redirecting the neurochemical flow, the path toward right thinking becomes the preferred path and is established as the mental habit. The path to recovery relies on the very rules that govern how the wounds were initially created.[15]

That is good news indeed! This is yet another reason why renewing our minds and thinking Christianly are vital for us all (Romans 12:2).

But how do we change our thinking? How are new pathways created? The same way all spiritual transformation takes place. Dallas Willard describes it this way: "Spiritual transformation into Christlikeness results from getting the right *Vision* of reality and goodness, the right *Intention* and decision (to actually become like Christ), and adequate *Means* to carry out the intention."[16] I don't mean it will be easy, but if God is who he says he is, and if the gospel is true — change really is possible. But we must begin by transforming our vision of humans being used to satisfy our desires. For example, men need to strengthen their belief that women are not toys but are image bearers who are precious to God, and they are somebody's daughters. We must decide that we actually don't want this practice anymore and are willing to arrange our lives differently in order to break this habit. No one drifts into life change. Community is essential in this process. But it begins with the individual.

Same-Sex Attraction

We've already established that homosexual behavior is condemned in the Bible (as is any other form of sexual immorality such as adultery or pornography). Christians who struggle with same-sex attraction will not be magically healed by quoting Bible verses that condemn homosexual behavior. If they are still attending church, they probably know their behavior is not in line with God's design for sex. This does not mean that we don't speak the truth in love — only that we shouldn't single them out. And they don't need to be lectured on the politics of same-sex marriage.[17]

Every Christian needs to do two things with regard to those in their churches who struggle with same-sex attraction. Alan Chambers, president of Exodus International, writes:

> As we consider ministering to those whose lifestyle we don't understand, we must always remember to offer them the same grace, understanding, and love that Christ offered us. There isn't a special antidote for ministering to those with same-sex attractions any more than there is for ministering to those with an unhealthy love for money, food, heterosexual sin … or whatever. The same God who sent His Son for you sent His Son for the homosexual. It really is that simple.[18]

Sometimes we can make things more complicated than they need to be.

The second thing we must do is to erase the idea from our vocabulary that "being gay is a choice." People don't choose to feel gay any more than people choose to feel straight. It is more complicated than that, as Chambers explains:

I haven't ever met anyone who woke up one morning and simply decided, out of life's great big buffet, to be gay. I don't think such a choice has ever been made. When we make this false assumption, we invalidate the complexities of this issue and undermine the individual's struggle with it by assuming that same-sex attractions can be chosen like someone chooses to wear brown shoes rather than black ones. Such assertions are offensive and insulting.[19]

Current research indicates that same-sex attraction is neither genetically determined nor arbitrarily chosen.[20] Rather than a single cause, there seems to be a constellation of possible factors—from inborn traits that may find expression in certain environments to attachments triggered by relationships with parents (or lack thereof). We need to recognize that "it is possible to accept the possibility that inborn elements contribute to homosexuality without legitimizing homosexuality itself."[21] Al Mohler's advice on this issue is helpful:

> Christians must be very careful not to claim that science can never prove a biological basis for sexual orientation. We can and must insist that no scientific finding can change the basic sinfulness of all homosexual behavior ... This does not alter God's moral verdict on homosexual sin (or heterosexual sin, for that matter), but it does hold some promise that a deeper knowledge of homosexuality and its cause will allow for more effective ministries to those who struggle with this particular pattern of temptation.[22]

The reality is that we live in a fallen world in which sin affects all of us at physical, genetic, psychological, relational, and emotional levels. There are plenty of sinful desires we should not act on or consider "natural" that can be overcome as we grow more like Christ. This is the hope and power of the gospel—we can struggle well.

As Christians and recipients of God's love, we have an opportunity to incarnate God's radical love in this area. But it will require a change in mind-set. If you are a teacher or preacher, you need to recognize that you are always sending a message. If you joke about homosexuality or single it out as the worst of all sins from the pulpit or in casual conversation, it reinforces and legitimizes that way of thinking in people's minds because the teacher or the pastor said it. It also drives those who struggle deeper underground. We need to send a clear message: For those who struggle in silence, please reach out for help. You are not alone. God does not hate you. In fact, he couldn't love you more. You are welcome here at our church.

SETTING MORAL BOUNDARIES IS NOT OPTIONAL

Regarding sexual immorality, God does not pull any punches. He loves us and wants what is best for us, and he sees what we cannot see:

> Flee from sexual immorality. All other sins a person commits are outside the body, but whoever sins sexually, sins against their own body. Do you not know that your bodies are temples of the Holy Spirit, who is in you, whom you have received from God? You are not your own; you were bought at a price. Therefore honor God with your bodies.
>
> 1 Corinthians 6:18–20

So how do we do this? The reality is that someone else will set your moral boundaries if you don't.[23] Every immoral decision can be traced back to a series of unwise decisions. For example, there is nothing wrong with computers or the Internet. Being alone, late at night, with the computer and the Internet is not in and of itself immoral. But is it wise for you? Answer honestly these kinds of questions. Decide well in advance of any temptation to say no to what you know is unwise. Set a clear moral boundary, well back from the danger zone, so that your conscience can send you a warning message before any real damage is done.

In the right circumstances and context, fire is a good thing (like a fireplace). But wisdom reminds you not to light a fire on your living room floor that can burn down your house and consume your life. This is how *all* sexual immorality works. If you light that fire, you will get burned.

THE BOTTOM LINE

Let's talk about sex in church. Everyone else already is. So let's talk clearly about how to catch God's vision for healthy lifelong sexuality, how to cooperate with God in changing unhealthy sexual habits, and how to set moral boundaries that keep us from blowing up our own lives and the lives of those we love. This is an area where our identity as Kingdom Citizens should look very different from the message of the world. As we engage cultural moments, we offer genuine knowledge of how sexuality should work.

RESOURCES FOR ENGAGING YOUR INTERSECTION

Books

- *Smart Sex: Finding Life-Long Love in a Hook-Up World* by Jennifer Roback Morse
- *The Meaning of Sex: Christian Ethics and the Moral Life* by Dennis P. Hollinger
- *Hooked: New Science on How Casual Sex Is Affecting Our Children* by Joe S McIlhaney and Freda McKissic Bush
- *How and When to Tell Your Kids about Sex: A Lifelong Approach to Shaping Your Child's Sexual Character* (part of the God's Design for Sex series, ages three to fourteen) by Stanton Jones
- *Sex Is Not the Problem (Lust Is): Sexual Purity in a Lust-Saturated World* by Joshua Harris
- *The Best Question Ever* by Andy Stanley
- *Wired for Intimacy: How Pornography Hijacks the Male Brain* by William Struthers
- *The Complete Christian Guide to Understanding Homosexuality: A Biblical and Compassionate Response to Same-Sex Attraction* by Joe Dallas and Nancy Heche

Websites and DVDs

- www.ruthinstitute.org – The Ruth Institute
- www.medinstitute.org – The Medical Institute for Sexual Health
- www.familylife.com – Family Life
- www.exodusinternational.org – Exodus International
- www.covenanteyes.com - Covenant Eyes Internet Monitoring
- *The Song of Solomon* by Tom Nelson, DVD

STRENGTHENING
MARRIAGES AND FAMILIES

AN INTERVIEW WITH DENNIS RAINEY

Jonathan Morrow: As the founder of Family Life, you are passionate about effectively developing godly marriages and families who change the world one home at a time. What do you see as the greatest challenge facing marriages and families today?

Dennis Rainey: I see three challenges. First, there has been a loss of the fear of God within families today. This reverential awe of God is the foundation of wisdom, morality, and life. A W. Tozer said, "The most important thing about you is what you think about God." The loss of the fear of God has given birth to hundreds of lesser evils in marriages and families. One of these evils is the loss of accountability to God and to our spouse. A second challenge is the reality of living in a culture that is redefining marriage, family, and life. The result is couples and families embracing cultural norms, *not* biblical standards. And third, all of the above has spawned a "culture of divorce." Divorce is now seen, for the most part, as an acceptable alternative to marriage. What used to be the "seven-year itch" has now been cut in half, with the divorce rate peaking after only a little more than three years of being married. We need to replace the "*D* word" with the "*C* word"—commitment for a lifetime. Marriage is not a contract, but a covenant.

Jonathan: In 2007, the National Center for Health Statistics revealed that nearly 40 percent of babies born in the United States were delivered by unwed mothers (1.7 million children). How can Christian leaders and local churches compassionately move into and speak into the growing issue of fatherlessness in America?

Dennis: Three ways: First, we must teach what the Bible has to say about children—that they are a gift from God, that we are stewards of them for a time, and that we must train, disciple, and equip them with wisdom, which is godly skill in everyday living. Second, we must address the issue of passivity in men by training and equipping them in biblical manhood. Men need to be mentored by older men who can demonstrate what sacrificial, loving leadership looks like. These men need to be shown what faith, courage, and taking responsibility looks like in this culture with their wives and families. And when they fail, these men need to be called to step up by these mentors. Third, the Christian community needs to be the leader in the culture of embracing and proclaiming a message of being "pro-life *and* pro-parents."

Jonathan: If you had three minutes with every pastor and church leader in America, what would you want them to know about ministering to families in today's world?

Dennis: I would want them to understand that the crisis of broken families is so huge and urgent that they can no longer afford to do ministry as usual. What we are currently doing is *not* working. We need a fresh revolutionary approach that can virally impact every home in our nation. I have been in ministry now for forty years, and more than ever, I believe the solution to the marriage and family crisis is not found in asking pastors to work harder, preach more, or do it themselves. In fact, I think the solution is found in these leaders giving away a portion of their ministry by equipping and unleashing an army of laypeople who can do marriage and family ministry. I believe there are literally hundreds of thousands of laypeople who are rusting out for lack of three things: (1) a clear challenge that they can be used by God to see people's lives transformed, (2) simple yet compelling training on how they can be effective, and (3) some "heaven class" tools and resources that work. If they want more information on how to challenge, train, and equip laypeople, go to www.familylife.com and click on LifeReady.

> **Dennis Rainey** is the president and CEO of FamilyLife (www.familylife.com). Dennis has authored or coauthored more than two dozen books, including the bestselling *Moments Together for Couples* and *Staying Close*. Dennis serves as the senior editor of the HomeBuilders Couples Series, which has sold over 2.5 million copies and has been translated into forty-seven languages. A powerful and effective communicator, Dennis can be heard daily as cohost of the nationally syndicated radio program *FamilyLife Today*.

chapter fourteen

ENGAGING OUR MEDIA-SATURATED UNIVERSE

We know that film, art, television, literature, the Internet, and the other forms of entertainment and expression have the power to shape and influence culture. This is why businesses advertise: it works! They know full well that a well-crafted image or a string of carefully fashioned words has the power to change minds and hearts.

Francis Beckwith, *Politics for Christians*

"MEDIA EXPOSURE," CONTENDS GEORGE BARNA, "has become America's most widespread and serious addiction."[1] Perhaps you wouldn't go quite that far. But there is a lot of truth in that statement. We all twitch for our iPhones and Blackberries when we step away from the device — "Did I miss something? Let me check!" Think about this: "Two decades ago, the average child under eighteen spent about fifteen to twenty hours per week digesting media content. Today, it has nearly tripled to almost sixty hours per week of unduplicated time." To put this into perspective, Barna states, "They now devote more time to media than to anything other than sleep."[2] *Time* magazine calls them Generation M: M for multitasking.[3]

What kind of effect is this having on us as individuals? Are our brains being altered? Tech writer Nicholas Carr wonders aloud, "Is Google making us stupid?"[4] Shane Hipps, author of *Flickering Pixels*, argues, "We become what we behold ...

Our thinking patterns actually mirror the things we use to think with."[5] He goes on to explain:

> When we watch television, we are oblivious to the medium itself. The flickering mosaic of pixilated light washes over us, bypassing our conscious awareness. Instead, we sit hypnotized by the program — the content — which has gripped our attention, unaware of the ways in which the television, regardless of its content, is repatterning the neural pathways in our brain and reducing our capacity for abstract thought.[6]

I have felt this. After watching a lot of TV, I usually don't feel like springing into thoughtful engagement.

And then there is the impact of the content itself. George Barna writes, "Out of more than 3,500 medical and behavioral research studies exploring the association between media violence and violent behavior, only 18 have *not* shown a correlation."[7] People are busy, and TV and the Internet have become surrogate parents to Generation M (and in some cases, the primary caregiver). Barna makes this sobering observation:

> By the time a person reaches the age of twenty-one, it is estimated that they will have been exposed to more than 250,000 acts of violence through television, movies, and video games. They will have viewed more than 2,000 hours, on average, of pornographic images that reduce the dignity and value of human life. They will have listened to several thousand hours of music in which the lyrical content promoted anger, hostility, disrespect for authority, selfishness, and radical independence.[8]

As humans, we are deeply emotional beings. Our emotions are fluid and easily molded, able to take one shape and then another a second later (this is because they are correlated with thoughts). Emotions are prone to being squeezed by all the stuff we come into contact with on a daily basis. What most people don't realize is that movies, TV, and YouTube have the ability to mold and condition our emotions. Producers and directors shoot, think, plan, direct, and edit based on their desire for our emotions to take a certain shape. Depending on the intent of the director and the content of the media, this can be a good or bad thing. To highlight but one example, the founding chairman of MTV bluntly said, "What we've introduced is nonnarrative form; we rely on mood and emotion. We make you feel a certain way as opposed to you walking away with any particular knowledge."[9] News flash: when you watch movies, TV, and surf the Internet, you are not merely being entertained; you are being shaped! Incidentally, given our vision (*Vision*) of life with God, this is one of the main reasons that we should all commit (*Intention*) to building periodic disciplines of solitude and silence (*Means*) into our lives. As

John Ortberg writes, "Solitude is the one place where we can gain freedom from the forces of society that will otherwise relentlessly mold us."[10]

Like waves washing perpetually over a rock on the beach, extended media exposure can dull the edges of our minds. While our minds require sharpening (the mind is very much like a muscle that strengthens with use), movies and TV often subtly condition our emotional responses so that over time, we find our beliefs being changed. For example, when was the last time in a movie or sitcom you saw a positive portrayal of a Christian pastor or leader or of a thoughtful, competent, and responsible father. When were you presented with a healthy portrait of marriage and sexuality? On the other hand, have you ever seen a homosexual character portrayed negatively in a film or TV show? When was the last time you saw a successful businessman portrayed with integrity, or even as the hero? I could go on and on. If visual ideas can do this to current beliefs we hold (that is, our worldview), what about those things we have never really thought of before? The answer is quite simple. Our default beliefs become set without our even realizing it. We are, as Dallas Willard suggests, "constantly hammered by the innumerable fists of an 'information society' and an inescapably media-saturated social consciousness set squarely against the reality of the kingdom of God."[11] The world system on display. Idea systems embedded in images are one of our Enemy's favorite tools. It is not an overstatement to conclude that the entertainment culture keeps most Christians desensitized and distracted.

Now after reading this, you may think that all film, TV, and entertainment is evil and that, by way of application, I am going to recommend that you take a baseball bat to your flat screen, blow up your TiVo, flush your iPhone, and run for the mountains. But you would be wrong. My hope in sharing this is that we will be sobered to the reality of our intersection with culture. Armed with an honest picture of reality, we are now ready to move toward critical and discerning engagement. But this takes reflection, self-control, study, and self-awareness.

THE SOCIAL MEDIA REVOLUTION

Facebook now has well over 500 million active users. If Facebook were a country, it would be the third largest in the world (China, India, Facebook, United States). The average user has 130 friends and spends 55 minutes each day on the site.[12] There are over 100 million users on Twitter, with 50 million tweets sent each day. And Flickr, DIGG, and Technorati have their own populations. You get the idea. In just a few short years, the way people connect, communicate, and interact has been forever altered.[13]

So how can we think Christianly about social media? Here are two suggestions. First, Facebook can be a great way to "connect" (I put that in quotes because there is a wide range of depth and interaction) to people you wouldn't normally talk to because of the long distance of geography. People move all the time, so it can be a helpful way to keep up with family and friends.

Facebook can be a time drain. Before you know it, you have been sucked in and have wasted an hour on trivial feed updates. Ask yourself how much time you spend on Facebook. It's a stewardship issue. Is most of your interaction trivial, or is there some meaningful interaction? Don't get me wrong. I'm not suggesting that people publish dissertations on their status updates, but we could do without the "I'm going to the bathroom now." Also, you do know that Facebook owns, logs, and analyzes all the information you post, right? There is no such thing as Facebook privacy. And wisdom must be exercised with those you choose to friend on Facebook. There is a growing trend of virtual and actual affairs through Facebook.

Media Help for Parents

Finally, a word to parents regarding social media, Internet use, entertainment, movies, and music. If you love your children, you must be prepared to do what is "good" for them rather than what they like or want. Your children need you. They are not mature enough to make these choices on their own. They are up against savvy marketers who know how to push their emotional, peer pressure, and hormone-driven buttons (this is the case well into the teenage years, when they are still under your roof). So here are some bits of media wisdom:

1. Do not just authorize a credit card on your children's iTunes account to which they have access without consulting you. Instead, go through this progression of song choice: choose for them, choose with them (review lyrics together), and then, once they demonstrate discernment, give them freedom to choose for themselves.

2. No TVs or computers in children's/teens' bedrooms—you are only asking for trouble here. Keep the computer in a public place in the home, limit screen time, and put an Internet filter on your network.[14] Maybe develop a ratio of screen time to active play or to reading a book so that they are exercising their bodies and minds. (Oh, and by the way, since they will adopt the habits they see you practicing, how is *your* ratio?)

3. You need to have a sheet with all of your children's passwords to their computer log-ins for Facebook, Twitter, and other social media; iTunes—*everything*. There is nothing—within the confines of the law—that a child/teenager needs absolute and final privacy on. This doesn't mean you are always in their business, but you can be if you need to be. Social media access is a privilege, not a right. You should find the balance between privacy and freedom on the one hand, and responsibility and accountability on the other. As the parent, you are the one who needs to set and enforce healthy and wise boundaries.[15]

4. You need to be "friends" (with full profile-viewing privileges) with your kids on their social networks. There is a natural accountability to this, but the more important reason is to connect with your kids. Again, don't become a nuisance or deliberately embarrass them, but your presence in their social world is important. Also, if they communicate online, then you can communicate with them online through the humorous, sad, disappointing, and trivial things shared on Facebook—it is a shared experience with your child. Another by-product is that you will be aware of the people influencing your child. As Proverbs 13:20 states, "Walk with the wise and become wise, for a companion of fools suffers harm." As we noted earlier, their friends will determine the direction and quality of their lives.

5. It would be wise to have your children "check in" their cell phones with you for the night before bedtime—say at nine o'clock—and then they can get them back from you in the morning as they leave for school. This will reduce the possibility of "sexting" (sexual pictures kids take of themselves to text to others), which typically occurs late at night. Moreover, kids don't need to be texting all night long unsupervised. They need time to unplug, rest, and give their already overstimulated brains a break from technology. It should go without saying that the later the hour gets, the less wisdom teenagers typically exercise. Finally, you need to have access to their text messages history to skim periodically as a way of accountability. If they delete the history so that you can't read it, then they should lose the privilege for a while. Again, the key thought in this is that they don't need to be texting stuff that wouldn't be appropriate to be read by you.

SEE YOU AT THE MOVIES

Talking about movies and entertainment in Christian circles can be a bit dicey. As I thought about this a few years ago, I came across an excellent book by award-winning screenwriter Brian Godawa titled *Hollywood Worldviews*. He makes some wise and experienced observations, which provide helpful guidelines for our consumption of media. We don't want to fall into either of two extremes. We don't want to completely withdraw or cut ourselves off from culture (he calls this "cultural anorexia"). Nor do we want to completely immerse ourselves in culture (he calls this "cultural gluttony"). Which one do you tend to lean more toward? (See the questions in the box.)[16] We want to engage our minds and be selective, critical, and thoughtful as we watch movies.[17] The goal is not to be amused. We are Everyday Ambassadors looking to build bridges between kingdom and culture.

Are you a Cultural Glutton?
1. Do you watch every movie that interests you without considering beforehand whether its subject matter is appropriate?
2. Do you think movies and television are only entertainment and don't communicate any real messages?
3. How many hours a week do you spend on entertainment? Compare this with how many hours a week you read the Bible or other spiritual growth material.
4. How many times have you enjoyed a movie that you later came to realize was offensive to your beliefs or worldview?

Are you a Cultural Anorexic?
1. Do you generalize all movies as "worldly" or consider any depiction of sin as wrong without concern for the context?
2. Are you unable to appreciate anything good in a movie because of some bad you see in it?
3. Do you consider art and entertainment to be a waste of time and therefore spend all of your leisure time on "spiritual" activities?
4. How many times have you been incapable of interacting with those around you because you were out of touch with their cultural experience?

A FRAMEWORK FOR THOUGHTFULLY ENGAGING FILM

Here is a three-step framework we can apply to all the movies we watch.[18] First, there is the *form of the film*: Was this film written, produced, and directed with excellence and skill? What are the artistic elements to note? Next, we move on to the *content of the film*: What is the message of the film? Who is the hero and what does he or she believe? (The director usually wants you to embrace this idea.) Who is the villain? (Directors usually locate the ideas they want you to reject here.) What was the worldview content of the film itself? (Remember our five basic categories of questions from chapter 4.) Finally, there is the *function of the film*: What purpose does this film serve within the broader culture? How is it being used? Are the purposes noble and good? As we'll see below, a film with good purposes ought to redemptively portray aspects of our fallen world, demonstrating, for instance, that adultery is ultimately a bad thing.

Let's briefly apply this framework to *Avatar*, the bestselling box office movie ever, grossing over $2.7 billion worldwide.[19]

- **Form**: This $500 million film is a technological wonder, employing 3-D, stunning cinematography, and vivid creativity. However, the script is full of cliché-filled dialogue and two-dimensional characters (it has been compared to *Dances with Wolves* in outer space). So in this regard, it's a mixed bag. But you can't say it didn't resonate with the audience.

- **Content**: Avatar is full of worldview elements. It is multicultural, with allusions to Christian, Hindu, Native American, animistic, and pantheistic themes. It resonates with the spirit of our day in two key respects: (1) the new green religion (Earth worship and environmentalism), and (2) its aversion to capitalism and anything Western.
- **Function**: Director James Cameron clearly wanted to use this film to make a statement. As Godawa observed, Cameron is a brilliant mythmaker, which resonated globally with audiences. Listen to his comments at the film's London premiere: "We have this tendency to just take what we want. And that's how we treat the natural world as well. There's this sense of we're here, we're big, we've got the guns, we've got the technology, therefore we're entitled to every d*** thing on this planet. That's not how it works, and we're going to find out the hard way if we don't wise up and start seeking a life that's in balance with the natural life on Earth."[20] Filmmakers always have an agenda. Of course we *should* care for the environment. But, for Christians, this is so because it is God's good creation and we are stewards, not because the environment is God.

PRINCIPLES FOR MAKING WISE ENTERTAINMENT CHOICES

Which movies should Christians see? No R-rated films? Should we see only movies made by professing Christians with explicitly Christian themes? What kind of music or video games should we consume? This area can get contentious, but let me give a few general observations, biblical principles, and questions that can help guide us. Obviously, we can't develop every nuance and justify each claim, so I encourage you to pick up Brian Godawa's book *Hollywood Worldviews* as you form your own convictions.

First, *given my own past experiences and current struggles, is it wise for me to watch this film, play this game, or listen to this music?* This isn't a question of what is wise for everyone, but what is wise for me. We all have unique temptations and struggles — and our Enemy is aware of them and is scheming to defeat us (Ephesians 6:11; cf. 2 Corinthians 2:11) — and we are really good at self-deception (Jeremiah 17:9; James 1:14 – 15). Images stick with us for better or worse — especially for the males of the species. So don't just let everything in there. Know your propensities. If you are not already doing so, take the time to preview films, music, and games at sites like Screen It! or Plugged In online before you consume them.

Please don't legislate your personal convictions and weaknesses as the standard for everyone else; there are things that bother me that don't bother other people (see

Romans 14). If you have ever found yourself saying, "That stuff doesn't bother me," then there's a good chance you've been desensitized, and that is a dangerous place to be. There is a difference between being discerning enough to know which movies you will allow yourself to see and becoming so numb to evil that it no longer bothers you.

Second, *will this film, song, or game enrich my life in some way and lead me toward life with God, or will it diminish my life and lead me away from life with God?* This is the "everything is lawful but not beneficial" principle. I like how the New Living Translation captures Paul's advice: "You say, 'I am allowed to do anything'—but not everything is good for you. You say, 'I am allowed to do anything'—but not everything is beneficial" (1 Corinthians 10:23 NLT). Yes, I have freedom. But freedom exists for me to do what is virtuous, not for me to do whatever I want. Does this glorify God and enrich me as an apprentice of Jesus? (1 Corinthians 10:31). Or does it cause a brother or sister in Christ to stumble? If so, I should abstain (cf. Romans 14:13). And does my consumption of this movie, TV show, or video game put me under its control? Does it dominate me, my thoughts, and my time? If so, stop. For as Paul commands believers, "'I have the right to do anything'—but I will not be mastered by anything" (1 Corinthians 6:12).[21]

YES, BUT WHAT ABOUT SEX, VIOLENCE, AND PROFANITY?

Should we consume media that has these elements? Sex, violence, and profanity are part of our imperfect world, and they were part of the fallen biblical world as well. In fact, a case could be made that the Bible would probably get an R-rating in some areas and even an NC-17 in others (for example, see the end of the book of Judges).[22] So how does the Bible redemptively record these kinds of elements? Brian Godawa offers three observations:

1. The Bible does not use evil for exploitation. The intention of the inspired storyteller is to expose evil for what it is, and then the event is always interpreted as evil from the surrounding context (for example, a reporter using vivid pictures from the Holocaust to inform an audience of the moral evil of Hitler).
2. The Bible accurately depicts evil with enough detail to make the point but is not gratuitous or excessive in details; nor does it fixate on human depravity to the exclusion of the potential for redemption.
3. The Bible always records evil and sinful behavior and the consequences that come with them. Slavery and death are the fruit of sin, not freedom and joy.[23]

Two things to remember: (1) good art is true to life, and (2) we live in a fallen world. In light of this, sex, violence, and profanity do not automatically prohibit a movie. We should consider *how* a particular film depicts evil, namely, as a departure from the way things ought to be. Take the movie *Juno*. It portrays a true-to-life struggle of a teenage girl's decision about what to do with her baby when she gets pregnant. It is true to teenage life, a bit edgy, has some foul language, but overall is a redemptive movie. But like all movies—and all of life—it is a mixed bag.

Evaluating a movie takes discernment and nuance, but here are some helpful questions:

> Does it *depict* evil in ways that maintain the integrity and truthfulness of the story?
>
> Does it *discourage* evil, elevating the good by revealing the nature and consequences of evil?
>
> Does it *endorse* evil, portraying it as normative and without consequence?
>
> Does it *incite* us to evil acts, as pornography might?
>
> Is the evil *gratuitous*, unconnected to the story, unnecessary except to appeal to our baser instincts?[24]

An objection might be forming in your mind: Doesn't Philippians 4:8 tell us to dwell on that which is true, noble, right, and so forth? Yes, it does. But it is noble and true to recognize that God hates sin and often vividly portrayed Israel's idolatry in the Old Testament in terms of playing the slut (or the prostitute, as we see in Jeremiah 3:2–8). Now this isn't all we are to dwell on, but it is certainly included, since "all Scripture is God-breathed and is useful for teaching, rebuking, correcting and training in righteousness, so that the servant of God may be thoroughly equipped for every good work" (2 Timothy 3:16–17). Most of all, we must pray for God's wisdom and discernment and extend each other grace as we engage with one another and our culture. It will also be helpful to develop a theology of the arts that can inform and instruct us. I now turn to that task.

WHATEVER HAPPENED TO THE ARTS?

Some Christians emphasize reason, while others emphasize imagination; but why do we have to choose? Properly understood, both are gifts of God that express various aspects of what it means to be human and an image bearer. Our God embodies infinite rationality, imagination, and creativity (Psalm 19:1–4; Romans 11:33–36). But unfortunately the arts and imagination are often viewed with skepticism and practically ignored in the church. When was the last time you heard a sermon on a biblical view of the arts? This needs to change.

"Art," writes Philip Graham Ryken, "has tremendous power to shape culture and touch the human heart. Its artifacts embody the desires of the coming generation. This means that what is happening in the arts today is prophetic of what will happen in our culture tomorrow. It also means that when Christians abandon the artistic community, we lose a significant opportunity to communicate Christ to our culture."[25] But if the arts have such potential, then why do Christians, who possess such a rich artistic tradition throughout church history, have a negative view of the arts today?[26]

First, art is full of ideas and images, which lend themselves to idolatry. According to some Christians, if we avoid the arts, we can avoid the idolatry. Second, since we live in the age of science, there is a general ignorance among Christians when it comes to the arts. Third, we have tended to prefer the *functional* rather than the *beautiful*. Finally, postmodernism has relativized aesthetics and eliminated any substantive way to distinguish between good and bad. Stuart McAllister captures the understandable source of many Christians' suspicions by observing, "Much of the energy and effort of our artists and cultural architects has gone into debunking, dismantling, or deconstructing all that is good, beautiful, and respected, to be replaced with the shallow, the ugly, the ephemeral."[27]

RECAPTURING THE CHRISTIAN IMAGINATION AND THE ARTS

Recapturing the arts requires us to recognize that they have great potential, while in the same breath affirming that they are "as fallen as any other area of human existence."[28] And then we must recover and reemphasize our calling as Creative Image Bearers—those who make something of the world for the glory of God. The arts play an important part. They are valuable in themselves, but their ultimate value is grounded in God's nature and glory. As the gulf between the sacred and secular continued to widen over the last century, Christians began to devalue the arts and other worldly business and elevate Christian ministry as the only vocation that matters. If you want to serve God, then that's where the real action is.

One of the co-creators of *VeggieTales*, the wildly popular series of children's videos that teach spiritual and moral principles, almost bought into this unbiblical approach of elevating ministry. "The implicit message I received growing up was that full-time ministry was the only valid Christian service," said Phil Vischer, cofounder of Big Idea Productions. "Young Christians were to aspire to be either ministers or missionaries ... But I wanted to make movies. And from the movies and TV shows I watched growing up and the influence they had on me, I figured God could use a filmmaker or two, regardless of what anyone else said."[29] Amen, and we could use many more!

THE ARTIST'S CALLING AND THE SPIRIT OF GOD

We serve a creative God. There is a little-known story in the Old Testament that we often speed-read in order to get to "the good stuff." But it contains a theology of the arts:

Then the LORD said to Moses, "See, I have chosen Bezalel son of Uri, the son of Hur, of the tribe of Judah, and I have filled him with the Spirit of God, with wisdom, with understanding, with knowledge and with all kinds of skills — to make artistic designs for work in gold, silver and bronze, to cut and set stones, to work in wood, and *to engage in all kinds of crafts*. Moreover, I have appointed Oholiab son of Ahisamak, of the tribe of Dan, to help him. Also *I have given ability to all the skilled workers to make everything I have commanded you.*"

Exodus 31:1 – 6, emphasis added

Philip Ryken makes four observations about the theology of the arts contained in this passage and the surrounding context: (1) the artist's call and gift come from God; (2) God loves all kinds of art; (3) God maintains high standards for goodness, truth, and beauty; and (4) art is for the glory of God.[30]

Many artists feel alone. They don't quite fit in the world because of their Christian worldview. The resonance of God's truth makes them uncomfortable in the presence of certain ideas, images, and expressions of art. But then, they are viewed by the church with skepticism. Or they are told that unless a piece of art explicitly states the gospel or is plainly evangelistic, it is not valuable or Christian. This passage gives us a biblical perspective on the arts.

HOW ART AFFECTS US ALL

Earlier this spring, I had one of the more enjoyable evenings I can remember. Along with thirty other people, my wife and I watched as a man painted his story. This was a first for me, and it was a powerful reminder that God uses many mediums to engage people's hearts and minds. This gifted sketch artist talked about his own faith journey and struggles in truthful and vulnerable ways that shimmered with God's creative grace and love. He talked about the woman at the well and painted her. But then he erased that image with a rag and painted himself into that story, expressing the tension of coming to God with full buckets that we don't want him to fill — we want God on our terms. Later in the evening, he sketched Jesus on the cross. But I was struck by the power of God's love when he added the red paint on a black-and-white picture of the wound in Christ's side. He concluded his presentation as the blood-red paint dripped down the canvas. It was a beautiful moment and a much-needed reminder of Christ's redemption that is always available to us.[31]

I am not an artist. Although I love to write, I cannot draw. In fact, I am positively horrible at art. But this artist was able to captivate me with his creative gifts from God in a way that helped me think of my own story and God's love and the intersection of the two in a fresh way. Art is powerful.

ARTISTS, BEWARE

Artists' greatest strengths can also be their Achilles' heel. They feel and see reality in ways that most people do not. The subtle temptation is to see our *feelings* as ultimate, as final, rather than *truth*. But just as a minor chord awaits resolution, art does not always have the final say. Sometimes when art tries to faithfully capture feelings, it fails to tell the truth about reality from the Christian perspective. British music journalist and poet Steve Turner says that he has seen "many people get close to a position where they seemed poised to create a little divine disturbance, and then they have been destroyed by the very values they sought out to challenge."[32] The siren's song of fame is hard to resist. And if an aspiring artist is not grounded in the truth, they will likely be conformed to the pattern of this world over time by the emotional nature of the arts.

Hollywood is a mission field. We don't need to focus solely on making our own Christian film companies and films. We need to do top-notch work informed by a robust and distinctively Christian worldview. But there are certain occupational hazards that aspiring artists need to recognize and, with the support of a healthy community, face head-on.

ARE ARTISTS WELCOME IN YOUR CHURCH?

We must give our young people permission, encouragement, and opportunities to utilize their creative gifts for the glory of God, the building up of the body of Christ, and the engagement of our world. Is your church artist friendly? Do young painters and writers see their pursuit of painting or writing as being as God-ordained as going to the mission field or into the pastorate? We need to encourage and nurture them in this pursuit—especially in the area of worldview formation.

Part of our role as Creative Image Bearers is to make something *good* of the world. We are called to create kingdom-minded culture and to generate art, literature, and film that reflect the true, the good, and the beautiful. That was the goal in the garden of Eden. Although the fall has made our work difficult, we must still cultivate the arts and the imagination. As leaders, we need to nurture, equip, and encourage young artists in our churches to dream big. Imagine the potential of the next generation of artists engaging in and creating culture that expresses the rich contours of a Christian worldview. I conclude this chapter with the fitting reflections of a lifelong Christ-follower and cultural arts critic:

> We will practice selective acculturation, allowing ourselves to experience resonance with art that connects us with the joy, pain, and realities of our fellow humans while also identifying and guarding against dissonant values, ideas, beliefs, and behavior. We can be both connoisseurs and critics of culture. At home and in church, our responsibility is to teach an appreciation for the arts, along with the skills of discovery and discernment that will allow us to enjoy, evaluate, and engage culture in ways that enrich both it and us.[33]

RESOURCES FOR ENGAGING YOUR INTERSECTION

Books

- *The Shallows: What the Internet Is Doing to Our Brains* by Nicholas Carr
- *Art for God's Sake: A Call to Recover the Arts* by Philip Graham Ryken
- *Hollywood Worldviews: Watching Films with Wisdom and Discernment* by Brian Godawa
- *Word Pictures: Knowing God through Story and Imagination* by Brian Godawa
- *The Wisdom of Pixar: An Animated Look at Virtue* by Robert Velarde
- *Plugged-In Parenting: How to Raise Media-Savvy Kids with Love, Not War* by Bob Waliszewski
- *Saving Leonardo: A Call to Resist the Secular Assault on Mind, Morals, and Meaning* by Nancy Pearcey
- *The Purple Curtain: Living Out Faith and Beauty from a Biblical Perspective* by Brian Chan
- *The Next Story: Life and Faith after the Digital Explosion* by Tim Challies

Websites and DVDs

- www.pluggedin.com – Plugged In Online (reviews of movies, games, music, etc.)
- www.hollywoodworldviews.com – Brian Godawa's website and movie blog
- www.cpyu.org – Center for Parent Youth/Understanding
- www.screenit.com – Screen It movie and video game reviews
- www.actoneprogram.com – Act One, "Hollywood Above the Line"

IMPACTING CULTURE THROUGH THE ARTS

AN INTERVIEW WITH JEREMY COWART

Jonathan Morrow: How do you see your relationship with Jesus Christ impacting and influencing your artistic expressions in photography?

Jeremy Cowart: Well, from him, all creativity flows. I'm often amazed by the way ideas are delivered. My biggest, best ideas hit me in the most random moments, and the only thing I can call them is a gift from God. I had the idea for Voices of Haiti as I was eating fries at Logan's Roadhouse with my family. In an instant, God says, "Here you go. Take this and run with it. Now." I thrive on those moments when the gifts are given. It's instant excitement, instant responsibility, and thus, instant chaos, and that's exactly what happened at Logan's. Within twenty-four hours of having the initial idea, I had a flight booked to Port-au-Prince just a week after the earthquake, during a time when it was impossible to book a flight there. I had been tired of seeing people displayed as numbers and statistics on all the cable networks. I wanted to know how the people felt. So in that moment at Logan's, God gave me an idea to go down and simply talk to the people and do a photo essay of the Haitian people holding up signs expressing their thoughts on the situation. The idea was exactly what I hoped it would be. It humanized the situation and gave them a sense of respect and dignity. Just two months after I went to Haiti, I got a call from the UN in New York City. They were having a gathering of several world leaders to discuss how to begin rebuilding Haiti. They wanted to build a "hallway exhibit" of my photos that all of these world leaders would walk through before entering the meeting room. It was to inspire them before the big pledge. Ten billion dollars was pledged in that meeting to rebuild Haiti over the next twenty years. It's amazing to see such a little idea end up in the halls of the UN on such a momentous occasion. God obviously knew what he was doing, and I was just along for the ride. This seems to be how things work most of the time. It's all about executing the vision he provides.

Jonathan: Christianity teaches that every human being is made in the image of God and possesses inherent dignity. You were part of a project called Help-Portrait. What is it and why did you feel so passionate about getting involved?

Jeremy: Help-Portrait is a worldwide movement of photographers using their time, equipment, and expertise to give back to those less fortunate. That's the official definition. To me, it's a one-day worldwide photo shoot where photographers and volunteers serve the poor. We take and print for them free portraits of them and their families; we feed them, give them clothes, do their hair and makeup, and play music for them. It's a full day of pampering for the forgotten, and it's completely life changing. December 12, 2009, was one of the greatest days of my life. It was the closest thing I've seen to what heaven must feel like. My friends were running out into the streets to grab all the homeless people they could find. My favorite musicians were onstage singing with an African children's choir. Kodak brought free printers and paper. Local restaurants were feeding everyone. My fellow photographers/competitors were at my side shooting portraits of people who had never had their picture taken. Mom and Dad were spending one-on-one time with homeless people as they came in. My makeup artists became counselors to all the women from the women's shelter. I could go on and on. I've never seen anything like it. It was the gospel through and through, and I think my favorite display of love I have ever witnessed. And this event happened in forty countries for 42,000 people on that day.

Jonathan: Many churches don't say much about the arts or Christian imagination. What would you say to Christian leaders and pastors about the need to encourage another generation of Christ-followers who are artists, filmmakers, photographers, and designers?

Jeremy: That first sentence you just mentioned kind of explains everything that's wrong. The church isn't using their imagination to spread the gospel, and thus our culture is moving away from it. It's as simple as that. The arts community is the most powerful tool the church has right now, and like you said, they're largely ignoring it. Speakers, writers, painters, photographers, and entrepreneurs have more tools available than ever before to be creative in how we spread our art. The church desperately needs to rally around them and support them. I've had this occur in my own experiences with the church, unfortunately. I've run many of my ideas past churches, and I get blank stares and half-interested maybes back. So I run off and execute them myself. There seems to be this unspoken rule that if something doesn't happen on the church campus or if it doesn't involve boosting the numbers in the church, then it's not a good idea for the church. This is terribly sad to me and probably why I'm not currently involved with any church. I mean, I attend church every Sunday, but the involvement stops there. I've learned to find my community elsewhere due to the lack of support. For this to change, pastors and Christian leaders simply need to start doing a lot more listening than talking. They need to invite these creative types into a room and brainstorm on new ways they can engage the culture. These meetings would be revolutionary for any church to do. There's a conference held in Atlanta every year called Catalyst, and it focuses on exactly what I'm talking about—new ideas to engage the culture. I highly recommend this conference to all Christian leaders.

> **Jeremy Cowart** is a professional photographer from Nashville. Beginning his photography career in 2005, Jeremy quickly became a respected artistic voice in the industry. Jeremy has photographed many people in the music and entertainment fields, including Sting, Imogen Heap, Courtney Cox, and Ryan Seacrest, just to name a few, and photographed seventeen countries with the Passion World Tour in 2008. Jeremy also spends his time on social art, developing and working on creative projects that will make a lasting impact. Jeremy has worked with multiple nonprofit organizations and traveled throughout Africa to photograph and bring awareness to the needs of those people. He is also the founder of Help-Portrait, a worldwide movement of photographers using their time, equipment, and expertise to give back to those less fortunate. After the devastating earthquake hit Haiti in January 2010, Jeremy responded with his Voices of Haiti photo essay, letting the people of Haiti express their own prayers and hopes through photography. You can visit him at www.jeremycowart.com.

chapter fifteen

GOOD NEWS ABOUT INJUSTICE

Most people know that Jesus came to bring forgiveness and grace. Less well-known is the biblical teaching that a true experience of the grace of Jesus Christ inevitably motivates a man or woman to seek justice in the world.

Tim Keller, *Generous Justice*

IT IS QUITE IMPOSSIBLE to look at our world and not see the brokenness both within us and around us. Justice most certainly does not flow down like a river. At the dawn of the twenty-first century, people are more aware than ever before of the injustices and atrocities occurring around the world. The need for justice and relief is staggering.

The United Nations estimates that 27 million people are enslaved worldwide today. HIV/AIDS ravages entire countries in Africa. Genocide is still alive and well. The poor suffer starvation, and children die daily from lack of clean drinking water and adequate nutrition. There are 143 million orphans. The sex trade is booming, with millions of children being kidnapped and sold into lives of slavery. Well over a million abortions are still legally performed each year in this country alone. As Christians, what are you and I doing? What can be done? How do we engage? What does pursuing biblical compassion and justice look like? I will confess on the front end that I don't have all the answers. There are times when I am simply overwhelmed.

But as I argued earlier, Christians are called by God to be a community of radical love. And this radical love is both rooted in and flows from the gospel. Today, however, there is growing confusion over the relationship between being a Christian, being true to the gospel, and doing good works. Terms like *social justice* are invoked or criticized by everyone from talk-show hosts like Glenn Beck to members of Congress. It's important for Christians to both proclaim and practice what God's good news has to do with injustice; people are in need, and the world is watching.

THE GOOD NEWS OF THE KINGDOM OF GOD

Christians have good news to share and a mission to live out. Unfortunately, you wouldn't always know it by looking at us. To make matters worse, sometimes we confuse people about the salvation that God offers to all and calls us to practice as Christians. But we have to get this clear before we can talk about anything else. The good news of the kingdom of God was Jesus' central message. What does this mean for things like evangelism and social action? And is there a difference?

If you ask many evangelicals to define the gospel, they would probably come up with something like "Jesus came to earth to forgive us of our sins so that we can go to heaven when we die." There is certainly a lot of truth in this answer. But the belief that Christianity is all about heaven someday does not naturally lead to a life of personal discipleship to Jesus—learning from him how to live as we participate in the eternal kind of life now (John 17:3). A life of discipleship is thus often seen as an add-on for the superspiritual among us. Reducing the gospel to "death for sin" minimizes the comprehensive scope of the redemption and restoration Jesus Christ came to accomplish, and as a result, we respond less vigorously. Several Bible passages make this clear.

First, notice how Jesus inaugurated his ministry: "The Spirit of the Lord is on me, because he has anointed me to proclaim good news to the poor. He has sent me to proclaim freedom for the prisoners and recovery of sight for the blind, to set the oppressed free, to proclaim the year of the Lord's favor" (Luke 4:18–19; cf. Isaiah 61:1–2). This is his mission statement, and he is drawing on imagery from Isaiah 52:6–7:

> "Therefore my people will know my name;
>   therefore in that day they will know
> that it is I who foretold it.
>   Yes, it is I."
>
> How beautiful on the mountains
>   are the feet of those who bring good news,
> who proclaim peace,
>   who bring good tidings,
>   who proclaim salvation,
> who say to Zion,
>   "Your God reigns!"

Mark records that "Jesus went into Galilee, proclaiming the good news of God. 'The time has come,' he said. 'The kingdom of God has come near. Repent and believe the good news!'" (1:14–15). The kingdom of God is about the comprehensive reign of God and the restoration of *all* things. Individual salvation fits within this broader context. The apostle Paul summarizes: "For God was pleased to have all his fullness dwell in him, and through him to reconcile to himself *all* things, whether things on earth or things in heaven, by making peace through his blood, shed on the cross" (Colossians 1:19–20, emphasis added). Again, notice the scope of the cross. Steve Corbett and Brian Fikkert tie this theme together: "The curse is cosmic in scope, bringing decay and brokenness and death to every speck of the universe. But as King of kings and Lord of lords, Jesus is making all things new! This is the good news of the gospel."[1]

Conservative evangelicalism has tended to emphasize "death for sin" as the heart of the gospel. Theological liberalism tends to detach the work of the cross and the need for personal salvation from the good works of political and social action. The two positions need mutual correction. You can't have good news without the cross, but neither is the point of the cross simply "death for sin." The point of the cross is the restoration of a relationship with the living God through the Holy Spirit by grace alone through faith alone (Ephesians 2:8–9).

The relationship between justification by faith and our participation in the kingdom of God can be confusing. J. P. Moreland offers a helpful distinction:

> The gospel of justification by faith is to the gospel of the kingdom of God as a part is to its whole or as the beginning of a journey is to the rest of the journey. The gospel of the kingdom includes justification as an essential ingredient. And it specifies the purpose of justification, namely, to be the start of a journey. The point or *telos* of becoming justified is that it is the way we begin a life of sanctification. The gospel is an invitation to an entirely new, rich life lived from the resources of and according to the nature of another realm. We become justified so that we can enter into and learn this new way of life, a life that will be ours forever.[2]

Sin was the barrier that needed to be removed, the disease that needed to be cured. But relationship with God is and always has been God's desire for humanity. Or, to put it another way, God did not create us so that he could forgive us; he created us so that he could be with us. In our fallen world, forgiveness in Christ is the exclusive means to this relationship. New Testament scholar Darrell Bock, in *Recovering the Real Lost Gospel*, summarizes:

> Two thousand years of the church's telling the story can dull the sense of wonder the gospel should bring. Here is the Creator God reaching down to touch a rebellious people's heart through a sacrifice that He Himself brings, so

that those He created may experience the life they were originally designed to live — a life in harmony with creation because it is in accord with the Creator. The gospel is not about a death but about a death that leads many into life. It is not about avoiding something but gaining someone precious, a new vibrant relationship with the gracious and self-sacrificing God who created us to know and follow Him.[3]

Once we have entered into this new relationship with God by being born again to a living hope, a new question emerges: "Now that I am a child of God, how shall I live?" The mission of God is for the people of God. Bock reminds us that as Christians we are "part of a people who manifest the kingdom of God on earth, a kingdom that ultimately transcends national groupings or concerns. The church is ultimately a cross-cultural agent of transformation that is to serve all its neighbors."[4]

Thankfully, Christians (especially those under thirty) are becoming more involved in doing good works — this is wonderful, and we need more of it. But we also must not forget that of the 6.75 billion individuals on the planet, 2.8 billion are unreached with the message of life with God in Jesus Christ.[5] My primary aim in this chapter is to clarify the relationship of the gospel to the good works of compassion and justice. But we must not exchange the emphasis on *incarnating* the good news with the task of *proclaiming* the good news. To do so would be a grave error; we can and must pursue both (Matthew 28:19–20).

GOD CARES ABOUT INJUSTICE AND WE SHOULD TOO

Justice both reflects the heart of God and connects us to his heart. Numerous Old Testament passages speak to this idea (Psalm 11:7; 33:5; Isaiah 10:1–4; 56:1; Jeremiah 5:26–29; 9:24; 22:13–19; Amos 2:6–7; 4:1–3; 5:10–15, 24; Micah 6:8). Perhaps the two clearest examples are found in the Prophets:

> Wash and make yourselves clean.
>> Take your evil deeds out of my sight;
>> stop doing wrong.
> Learn to do right; seek justice.
>> Defend the oppressed.
> Take up the cause of the fatherless;
>> plead the case of the widow.
>
> Isaiah 1:16–17

In Jeremiah 22:16, the prophet tells of how Josiah the king pleaded the cause of the afflicted and needy, and then the prophet asks, "Is that not what it means to know me?" The implication — as convicting as it is obvious — is that those who know God are those who plead the cause of the poor and the afflicted.

With that settled, we now have a few philosophical questions that must be decided. Is the justice and equality we seek for ensuring equal *outcomes* or equal *opportunities*? There is a big difference. Should the playing field be leveled on the front end or after the fact? Moreover, and related, will a largely centralized government or decentralized government best accomplish this? These are matters for wisdom and prudence to discuss and decide in humility. But even a cursory reading of Proverbs will reveal the difference between the sluggard and the wise person who worked diligently. Do fairness and justice mean equal outcomes for both or only that each person has the same opportunity? Perhaps there are social structures or programs that make equal opportunity impossible in certain cases or actually perpetuate poverty. Justice means reform in these areas.

In light of the good news of the kingdom of God, it is important to distinguish between *evangelism* and *social action*. Ronald Sider helps us here:

> Evangelism is that set of activities whose primary intention is inviting non-Christians to embrace the gospel of the kingdom, to believe in Jesus Christ as personal Savior and Lord, and join his new redeemed community ... Social action is that set of activities whose primary goal is improving the physical, socioeconomic, and political well-being of people through relief, development, and structural change.[6]

Evangelism emphasizes the new life and relationship that God offers to all people. Social action flows from this new relationship with God because we are joining in the mission of God as he makes all things new (Matthew 5:16; Ephesians 2:10; Titus 2:14; 1 Peter 2:12). Good news leads to good works.

One of the major themes of this book is that Christianity is not just private, requiring our attention for only two hours on a Sunday morning; it is public truth and should affect the totality of life (that is, our emphasis on thinking Christianly). Unfortunately, many Christians have withdrawn from ethical, social, political, educational, and cultural issues and institutions. As Christians, we must enter into dialogue in the public square and become part of the solution, not just heralds of the problem. Throughout the history of Christianity, followers of Jesus have understood their responsibility to share the fruit of a "Christian way of life."[7] We need to follow their lead. As the preamble of the 2009 Manhattan Declaration powerfully reminds us:

> Christians are heirs of a 2,000-year tradition of proclaiming God's word, seeking justice in our societies, resisting tyranny, and reaching out with compassion to the poor, oppressed and suffering.
>
> While fully acknowledging the imperfections and shortcomings of Christian institutions and communities in all ages, we claim the heritage of those Christians who defended innocent life by rescuing discarded babies from trash heaps in Roman cities and publicly denouncing the empire's sanction-

ing of infanticide. We remember with reverence those believers who sacrificed their lives by remaining in Roman cities to tend the sick and dying during the plagues, and who died bravely in the coliseums rather than deny their Lord.

After the barbarian tribes overran Europe, Christian monasteries preserved not only the Bible but also the literature and art of Western culture. It was Christians who combated the evil of slavery: Papal edicts in the 16th and 17th centuries decried the practice of slavery and first excommunicated any-one involved in the slave trade; evangelical Christians in England, led by John Wesley and William Wilberforce, put an end to the slave trade in that country. Christians under Wilberforce's leadership also formed hundreds of societies for helping the poor, the imprisoned, and child laborers chained to machines.

In Europe, Christians challenged the divine claims of kings and success-fully fought to establish the rule of law and balance of governmental powers, which made modern democracy possible. And in America, Christian women stood at the vanguard of the suffrage movement. The great civil rights crusades of the 1950s and 60s were led by Christians claiming the Scriptures and assert-ing the glory of the image of God in every human being regardless of race, religion, age or class.

This same devotion to human dignity has led Christians in the last decade to work to end the dehumanizing scourge of human trafficking and sexual slavery, bring compassionate care to AIDS sufferers in Africa, and assist in a myriad of other human rights causes—from providing clean water in develop-ing nations to providing homes for tens of thousands of children orphaned by war, disease and gender discrimination.

Like those who have gone before us in the faith, Christians today are called to proclaim the Gospel of costly grace, to protect the intrinsic dignity of the human person and to stand for the common good.[8]

Fleshing out what is for the common good can be difficult in our society. I will discuss more about that in the next chapter. But this declaration vividly illustrates that we need to move beyond an understanding of our relationship with God as *only* an individual experience. Francis Schaeffer hit the nail on the head when he wrote, "True spirituality—the Christian life—flows on into the total culture."[9]

THE HEART OF GOD, THE ORPHAN, AND THE LOCAL CHURCH

Earlier I mentioned that there are 143 million orphans in the world today. There are numerous reasons that children don't have permanent, loving families: war, poverty, disease, drugs, alcohol, physical and mental challenges of both children and parents, abuse, neglect—it's quite a list. And to be honest, as middle-class Americans, we have difficulty wrapping our minds and hearts around these issues. I am thankful to be a part of a church that wants to do something about this number because we are convinced that God has a heart for the orphan. The prophet Hosea tells us that in God, the orphan finds mercy (Hosea 14:3). James tells us that "religion that God our Father accepts as pure and faultless is this: to look after orphans and widows in their distress" (1:27).

The teaching pastors in our church speak about this on a regular basis, and several people began a ministry called Mercy Found. Through their hard work and prayer, our congregation has become more aware of the problem and how we can play a role in the solution. Several families have adopted, many have given financially, and many more have prayed. Your church, too, can get involved in some of the following ways: child sponsorship, foster care, support for adoptive and foster families, long-term adoption, prayer support, or development of a new ministry.[10] For more on what a new ministry could look like and on the theology of adoption, see the excellent book *Adopted for Life: The Priority of Adoption for Christian Families and Churches* by Russell Moore.

ECONOMICS: A MORAL ISSUE

Every Christian who has read the Bible knows that we are called to help the poor. The critical and more controversial question is: How *best* can we go about helping the poor? Christians can and do disagree over how best to do this. But whatever one's approach, to truly help the poor, we must not only *feel* compassion but also *think* clearly and carefully. You cannot discuss poverty without discussing economics. In their helpful book *The Virtues of Capitalism*, Austin Hill and Scott Rae make the point that economics is a moral issue primarily because "every facet of our earthly lives is impacted on some level by both economic activity and economic conditions," and that everyone must answer the fundamental question: "How shall we order our lives together."[11]

Right out of the gate, *everyone* needs to recognize that there is no perfect economic system. In a fallen world, there is no system of economics that will usher in Utopia or the kingdom of God. None. With that myth debunked, we are after the *best* available system. This means we must be realistic and prudent. Second, the Bible doesn't teach a particular economic system. Orthodoxy does not require capitalism or socialism. The economic world of biblical times was very different from today's world, but the principles revealed in Scripture do still apply (though it takes greater care to faithfully apply them).

If you remember nothing else from this section, remember this: Good intentions for the poor do not necessarily translate to good outcomes for the poor. Sound economic principles must be utilized (for example, sending billions of dollars in foreign aid to foreign governments does not guarantee that the poor will be any better off). Christians must understand and care about economics precisely *because* we care for the poor and care about justice.

After studying the issue, I have become convinced that some form of free market capitalism is *the best available* system for the most number of people (if you have never read a book on capitalism that takes virtue and the Bible seriously, then I would encourage you to start by reading *The Virtues of Capitalism*). Contrary to what we often hear, capitalism does not cause poverty. In fact, the opposite is true! Hill and Rae observe:

> Capitalism provides the best means for the most people to achieve self-support and lift themselves out of poverty. To be sure, there are other conditions necessary for the market system to flourish such as an established system for the rule of law. And there is no doubt that there still remain substantial numbers of people in grinding poverty—roughly three billion of the world's population of 6.8 billion.
>
> But you have to ask, What happened to the *nearly four billion* who are no longer in poverty? They have lifted themselves out of poverty by participation in the economic activity that capitalism generates. Even though globalization has certainly not been all positive, it is largely responsible for lifting millions out of poverty in the developing world.[12]

Just since 1970, it is estimated that 1.6 billion people have emerged from poverty due to free market economics. Are there problems? Yes. Abuses? Yes. Things to be corrected? Yes. Prudent regulations and checks and balances that need to be put in place? Yes. Corruption to be rooted out? Yes. But capitalism is not the great enemy of the poor. On the contrary—given the proper social circumstances and the cultivation of virtues such as creativity, initiative, cooperation, civility, and responsibility—it is a much-needed ally.

To drive home the point that things like property rights and stable governments really make a big difference for the poor, consider the difficulty of purchasing a home in Haiti. Jay Richards, in his excellent book *Money, Greed, and God*, summarizes the obstacles many people in the developing world face:

> In Haiti, you have to jump through 65 bureaucratic hoops just to lease land from the government. Buying the land? Another 111 hoops. It would take a diligent Haitian nineteen years to pull this off, assuming he could get the time off from work, if he has work. And the fact that he's acquired property legally doesn't necessarily mean that his situation won't change tomorrow, since the country itself frequently changes owners.[13]

A NEW PARADIGM FOR HELPING THE POOR

As we continue thinking smarter about helping the poor, I want to highlight an approach from Steve Corbett and Brian Fikkert's important book *When Helping Hurts*. Again, what *feels good* to do is not necessarily what actually *does good*. Not all poverty is created equal. Therefore, we need a situation- and person-specific approach that uses appropriate resources and goals (this approach will especially help churches that are considering short- and long-term mission trips). In working to alleviate poverty from a Christian perspective, we should focus on three goals: relief, rehabilitation, and development.[14]

Relief is "the urgent and temporary provision of emergency aid to reduce immediate suffering from a natural or man-made crisis."[15] Examples include the tsunami in Indonesia, hurricane Katrina, and the devastating earthquakes in Haiti and Japan. Relief tries to "stop the bleeding" and utilizes a "provider-receiver" dynamic, which assumes that people are largely incapable of helping themselves.

Rehabilitation seeks to "restore people and their communities to the positive elements of their pre-crisis conditions."[16] This process, which begins when the "bleeding stops," utilizes a "working with" dynamic, so that those affected participate in their own recovery.

Development is the process of ongoing change so that "as the materially poor develop, they are better able to fulfill their calling to glorify God by working and supporting themselves and their families with the fruit of that work."[17] The key dynamic here is that development is done not *to* or *for* people but *with* people so that everyone involved—both helpers and helped—become more of what God intends them to be.[18]

Corbett and Fikkert found that "one of the biggest mistakes that North American churches make—by far—is in applying relief in situations in which rehabilitation or development is the appropriate intervention."[19] If we truly want to help the poor, then we must work smarter, and these three categories, along with sound economic principles, will equip us to better accomplish the good we intend to do.

GOOD WORKS OPEN HEARTS

If we engage our hurting world with compassion and good works, we will find the soil of people's hearts more ready for the gospel. Living as a community of radical love that is becoming increasingly like Jesus will help reverse some of the stereotypes applied to Christians. Ronald Sider is correct in noting that "when we care for people in Jesus' name, our acts of mercy open hearts to the gospel. When we stand with the poor to challenge the way they are treated, they are more likely to accept our invitation to turn to Christ."[20] The Bible clearly teaches that Christians are to care for the oppressed and seek justice while proclaiming the good news. The body of Christ is to be a redemptive force for good in this world.

HOW LONG, LORD?

There is a postscript to this chapter. The honesty of the psalmist when he sang, "How long, LORD?" (79:5), resonates with even the most devout believer. Why does evil persist?[21] Why hasn't God dealt with injustice? What is he waiting for? The first part of this answer is that he has—finally and comprehensively—defeated evil and injustice on the cross. But we live in the meantime, in which sin still wanders freely. Peter gives us insight into these questions:

> Do not let this one thing escape your notice, that a single day is like a thousand years with the Lord and a thousand years are like a single day. The Lord is not slow concerning his promise, as some regard slowness, but is being patient toward you, because he does not wish for any to perish but for all to come to repentance. But the day of the Lord will come like a thief; when it comes, the heavens will disappear with a horrific noise, and the celestial bodies will melt away in a blaze, and the earth and every deed done on it will be laid bare.
>
> 2 Peter 3:8 – 10 NET

God, being good, patiently waits for all who would turn to him in faith. However, pain and suffering, whatever else may be said of them, awaken us to the brevity and frailty of life and the universal need for redemption and wholeness. C. S. Lewis observes, "God whispers to us in our pleasures, speaks in our conscience, but shouts in our pain: it is His megaphone to rouse a deaf world."[22] As much as we would like to believe otherwise, our greatest good is not the absence of pain or the satisfaction of all of our desires; it is to know God. And God waits patiently for people to know him. The passage in 2 Peter, however, shows us that the patience of God will run out someday as the time of salvation passes and the time of reckoning for evil will commence. Justice will be done.

RESOURCES FOR ENGAGING YOUR INTERSECTION

Books

- *Recovering the Real Lost Gospel: Reclaiming the Gospel as Good News* by Darrell Bock
- *Generous Justice: How God's Grace Makes Us Just* by Tim Keller
- *Good News about Injustice: A Witness of Courage in a Hurting World* by Gary Haugen
- *When Helping Hurts: How to Alleviate Poverty without Hurting the Poor ... And Yourself* by Steve Corbett and Brian Fikkert
- *Churches That Make a Difference: Reaching Your Community with Good News and Good Works* by Ronald Sider, Philip Olson, and Heidi Unruh
- *Money, Greed, and God: Why Capitalism Is the Solution and Not the Problem* by Jay Richards
- *If God Is Good: Faith in the Midst of Suffering and Evil* by Randy Alcorn

Websites and DVDs

- www.ijm.org – International Justice Mission
- www.compassion.com – Compassion International
- www.mocha.com – The Mocha Club
- *Becoming a Good Samaritan*, DVD
- *Gospel in Life* by Tim Keller, DVD

JOINING TOGETHER TO LOVE THE WORLD

AN INTERVIEW WITH BARRETT WARD

Jonathan Morrow: What is the Mocha Club, how does it work, and what is the vision behind it?

Barrett Ward: Mocha Club is an online community of people giving up the cost of two mochas a month—or $7—to fund relief and development projects in Africa. We work in five main project areas: Clean Water, Education, Child Mothers + Women at Risk, Orphan Care + Vulnerable Children, and HIV/AIDS + Health Care.

Our vision is to provide a way for people who don't have hundreds or thousands of dollars to make a difference in Africa. Our community-based website allows members to start a team and invite friends to join them in giving up the cost of two mochas a month to support their chosen project. We know that today's tech-savvy generation can have a huge impact by using the viral nature of the Web. So we decided to equip Mocha Club members to spread awareness and support for Africa by inviting friends.

We're aware of people's general lack of trust that their money is being effective, and we address this by providing regular updates. Each month, through videos and blogs of the specific projects they are supporting, we update our Mocha Club members on how their $7 is helping the people of Africa.

Jonathan: How do you see your relationship with Jesus Christ impacting what you do with Mocha Club?

Barrett: Well, there wouldn't be a Mocha Club had God not intervened in my comfortable life. In my twenties, I had been making good money and doing my best to play with it. When I was twenty-nine, I started going to church because of a girl, and there I saw an opportunity to go on a trip to Peru. We arrived, and I walked into my first slum, full of tin shacks, boxes that were no more than 6' x 6' x 6'. Out of one of those shacks walked a girl—beautiful, about five years old. I was stunned and mesmerized; in that overwhelming moment, I felt that nothing made sense. I just stared at her. She caused me to come face-to-face with reality about my life pursuits to that point.

I realized how ridiculously self-absorbed I was. I started tearing through the Bible looking for answers and began with Matthew. And he kept telling me that my rewards are paid in full on earth when I seek the approval of mankind, but that what I did in private to please God would gain my rewards in heaven.

I returned home from that trip and left my job ten months later. I headed to Africa for two months. As I spent time in Africa, I found my spiritual home, and in this service I was most alive — and settled.

I joined up with African Leadership, and a year later God planted a vision for Mocha Club, and we pursued it. I continue to do this because I believe it is where God wants me to be. I love it most of the time — I don't sometimes — but I always know that I am home, in my spiritual home.

Jonathan: What has the response been from young people who have become involved with Mocha Club?

Barrett: When people are in college or in their twenties, they start to establish their pursuits and habits. That's not to say that God won't yank you out of self-absorption when he wants to, like he did me. But this is the age when your pursuits in life can become defined.

Every day, we interact with young people who prioritize giving and prioritize other people. We have students at different colleges, called campus reps, and they are talking with their friends every day about the important things that $7 can do in Africa. We host trips every summer to different projects in Africa, and these trips fill up with young adults. Really any opportunity we extend to our members, whether it's a trip to Uganda or volunteering to work the Mocha Club table at a concert, gets a great response.

We have seen in our volunteers, in our interns, in our members, that young people right now are desperate to be involved in organizations that are making a difference in the world. They don't mind spending money and time on pursuits that are important. Especially with our donation cost being so low — $7 — we find that even college students who do not have a steady income are able to give and be part of something bigger than themselves.

Jonathan: How can Mocha Club come alongside Christian leaders, pastors, and local churches in a strategic way and help them get involved?

Barrett: We provide the opportunity for people to get involved in three ways:

1. *In solidarity, give.* Sacrifice $7 a month. The website is easy to navigate, and the projects are fully explained there. It is an easy place for leaders to send their people to for more information about where the $7 goes each month.

2. *Multiply awareness.* Through the website, start your profile and invite people to join your efforts. We find this to be a great way to equip leaders to mobilize those whom they are leading. A pastor joins Mocha Club, picks a project he is passionate about, and then creates a team supporting that project. He invites his congregation and friends to join his team, thus multiplying the impact in Africa.

3. *Go, see, and serve.* We offer trips every summer to Africa so that members can see what God is doing through African Leadership and Mocha Club. We will happily partner with churches or ministries that are looking to plan a trip for their congregation.

There are other ways to partner with churches and organizations. We work with over thirty different musicians and are able to help plan and implement benefit concerts for large audiences. We also have many materials, videos, and merchandise available for leaders. We are happy to talk to and plan with any church or organization that contacts us.

> **Barrett Ward** is the executive director of the Mocha Club (www.mochaclub.org). Mocha Club is an online community of people giving up the cost of two mochas a month — $7 — to fund relief and development projects in Africa.

chapter sixteen

CHRISTIANITY AND THE PUBLIC SQUARE

Citizens of the City of God, we are resident aliens in the Earthly City. Called by Jesus to be "in" the world but "not of" the world, we are fully engaged in public affairs, but never completely equated with any party, partisan ideology, economic system, class, tribe, or national identity.

"An Evangelical Manifesto"

MUCH CONFUSION SURROUNDS the legitimacy of Christian involvement in the public square. Should Christians engage in politics? And if so, what does this look like, given the so-called "separation of church and state"? Can Christians engage on the basis of their religious beliefs, or must they present only "secular" arguments? We must address these critical questions. And to help set the stage, I take you back to a speech that Ron Reagan Jr. gave at the 2004 Democratic National Convention regarding the federal funding of embryonic stem cell research:

> Now, there are those who would stand in the way of this remarkable future, who would deny the federal funding so crucial to basic research. They argue that interfering with the development of even the earliest stage embryo, even one that will never be implanted in a womb and will never develop into an actual fetus, is tantamount to *murder*. A few of these folks, needless to say, are just grinding a political axe and they should be ashamed of themselves. But many are well-meaning and sincere. Their belief is just that, an article of faith, and they are entitled to it. But it does not follow that the "theology of a few" should be allowed to forestall "the health and well-being of the many."[1]

Well, there you have it. If you are a Christian—bless your heart—you have just been dissed. Also, did you notice how theology and well-being are framed as opposites? (This is a textbook example of the fact/value split.) Reagan is not alone in this sentiment. Most of the media express this same viewpoint. The big idea is crystal clear: people are entitled to *private religious beliefs* just as long as they don't become *public*. Is this true? Just? Good? In this chapter I'll address several common questions that will allow us to more effectively and faithfully engage in the public square.

WHAT THE BIBLE SAYS ABOUT GOVERNMENT AND POLITICAL ENGAGEMENT

The biblical purpose of government is threefold: maintain public order, restrain human evil, and promote the common good (Romans 13:1–7; Titus 3:1; 1 Peter 2:13–17). Christ-followers are to pray for their leaders (1 Timothy 2:1–2) and obey them—unless they command the people to act unjustly or to explicitly disobey God (cf. Acts 5:28–29).[2]

In Acts 16:35–38, we see the apostle Paul wielding his rights as a Roman citizen for the good of the gospel. After being beaten and imprisoned with Silas for preaching the gospel, Paul navigates the politics of his situation. Christian political philosopher Francis Beckwith makes four instructive observations:

1. Paul used his political status as a Roman citizen "to ensure that the gospel could be preached freely."
2. He was "not afraid to exercise the rights that this political status accorded him as an act of community leadership, even if it struck fear in the hearts of the magistrates."
3. "He directly cited a violation of his rights as a citizen—lack of due process ('we ... have not been tried')—against those in the government that committed the act."
4. Paul "employed political leverage to correct an injustice done to him and a fellow Christian."[3]

Christians in America enjoy far more rights as citizens than Paul ever did, and so we should courageously follow Paul's example to avail ourselves of its power in the appropriate circumstances for the good of our neighbors and the furthering of the gospel.

While some are calling for Christians to abandon the political arena due to perceptions that we are "too political," this would ultimately be unwise and a net loss for everyone because of the moral vacuum it would create. "The alternative isn't to *not* do politics," observes Michael Gerson. "The alternative is to do it better."[4]

BUT ISN'T THERE A "WALL OF SEPARATION" BETWEEN CHURCH AND STATE?

Several years ago, Larry King invited James Dobson to appear on his talk show to discuss the involvement of Christians in politics. When Dobson made a point, King challenged him, saying it would violate the separation of church and state. Dobson responded that there is no such language in the Constitution. King said he would have to look that up.

Though we frequently hear the language of the "wall of separation" thrown around in public discourse, Dobson is correct. J. Budziszewski, professor of government at the University of Texas, speaks to this myth:

> Even when you include the amendments, the Constitution says only three things about religion ...
>
> Article VI: "No religious test shall ever be required as a Qualification to any Office or public Trust under the United States."
>
> Amendment I: "Congress shall make no law respecting the establishment of religion, or prohibiting the free exercise thereof."
>
> In other words: (1) The government is not allowed to make people take a religious test in order to qualify for holding federal office; (2) Congress is not allowed to set up an official national church; and (3) Congress is not allowed to stop people from practicing their religions.
>
> These three rules are meant to protect your liberty to follow God, not to abolish it. That famous slogan about a "wall of separation" just isn't there ...
>
> Christians are free to act according to their convictions in politics, just as atheists are free to act according to theirs.[5]

The "wall of separation" actually comes from a letter that Thomas Jefferson wrote to the Danbury Baptists in 1802 and has no legal or constitutional authority in and of itself (though it was cited later in a Supreme Court case).[6] The First Amendment's Establishment Clause only addresses the government, requiring it to restrain its power regarding religion. So it is more accurate to say that we have freedom *for* religion, not freedom *from* religion, as some secularists argue. This is consistent with Jesus' statement to "give back to Caesar what is Caesar's, and to God what is God's," which affirms that the church and the state are distinct institutions with different spheres of authority, but that both exist for the common good of all people made in the image of God (Matthew 22:17–22).[7]

ON LEGISLATING MORALITY

Another common myth is that people shouldn't legislate their morality — especially Christians. But this is self-evidently false. Michael Bauman explains:

All laws, whether prescriptive or prohibitive, legislate morality. All laws, regardless of their content or their intent, arise from a system of values, from a belief that some things are right and others wrong, that some things are good and others bad, that some things are better and others worse. In the formulation and enforcement of law, the question is never whether or not morality will be legislated but which one.[8]

The law is undergirded by moral and value judgments. This is inescapable. Laws bind us to the authority of whoever issues them (for example, God and the government). But how do we know these particular laws are good and others are bad? The answer doesn't lie in the laws themselves but exists prior to the laws. What precisely is the basis for our laws? In the Declaration of Independence, the founders appealed to the "Laws of Nature and of Nature's God."[9] Secularism, which excludes any appeal to religious or spiritual arguments, has no basis from which to objectively define the public good and resorts to relativism and pragmatism, both of which seriously undermine moral discourse in America and diminish our common humanity.

THE MYTH OF STATE NEUTRALITY AND THE NOTION OF THE COMMON GOOD

Contrary to public opinion, the state is not morally neutral, because it establishes the law of the land. Furthermore, the law is a teacher, and class is in session every day. The fact of the matter is that people conform to what is enforced in a given society over time. The obvious question that must be answered is this: What lessons are being taught? Are they good lessons? What do our laws teach concerning human nature and justice? If an alien observer were to visit our country, what conclusions would they draw about what we really value?

There are two competing visions today for what human life is for and what should be included in the notion of the common good. One vision of humanity is the satisfaction of personal desires. The other is a perfectionist view that maintains "human beings share the same nature by which we can know what sorts of goods, institutions, habits, and actions help the human being fulfill his proper end or perfection."[10]

We can apply the differences between these two visions to the issue of pornography and the common good. Pornography does satisfy certain desires and appetites (in a sense), but does it contribute to the flourishing of men, women, and children as a whole? Should it be legal? Or think of the food we consume and other personal habits. When you go to the doctor for a physical, there are certain standards for health. In my case, there is a standard weight for a person who is 6 feet 2 inches tall, and the further I deviate from it, the less healthy I am. Is this a personal issue or one for the government to control? Unless we have a general idea of what a good human being is and what the role of society is, we will continue on the merry-go-round of relativism, power plays, and pragmatism.

RECOVERING PRUDENCE IN POLITICS

Compromise. It isn't one of our favorite words, especially when it comes to politics. Unfortunately, this has limited the public good that Christians have been able to accomplish in the public square. Evangelicals who hold high moral standards typically view politics as an all-or-nothing affair. There is no middle ground. This is unfortunate. When a person is unwilling to budge or compromise, they think they are being virtuous (and sometimes they are). It's a matter of principle, and they are standing up for the truth, right?

I am sympathetic to this way of thinking, but if we want to actually achieve the good we seek, then our approach needs to be more tactical. And we do this by developing a robust idea of *prudence* in politics.

The word *prudence* isn't used much anymore. Nonetheless, the idea has a rich history. Aristotle, Augustine, Thomas Aquinas, Immanuel Kant, William Wilberforce, Thomas Jefferson, John Adams, and Abraham Lincoln — just to name a few — have fruitfully reflected on and applied it over the centuries. In his excellent book *Politics for the Greatest Good*, Clarke Forsythe discusses the cardinal virtue of prudence. "Prudence is concerned with right action and requires deliberation, judgment, decision making, and execution. Wisdom understands what is right; prudence involves making the right decision and implementing it well."[11] Notice the important connection to wisdom. "Prudence," Forsythe continues, "takes account of limitations in a world of constraints and strives to achieve the greatest measure of justice — the greatest good possible — under the particular circumstances."[12] It is important to distinguish *prudence* from *pragmatism*. Prudence is a virtue because it aims at what is good. By contrast, pragmatism is simply what may work or be useful right now — not what is good in and of itself. Pragmatism is situational; prudence is teleological in that it has a particular good and wise end in mind. So what would a prudent political strategy look like?[13]

- It will *focus* on worthy goals (clarifying the specific "public good" we are aiming at).
- It will *identify* effective means to achieve these ends and the wise use of limited resources (being realistic and logical about all of the moving parts and sets priorities).
- It will *recognize* the limitations of a fallen world and its constraints on political action (Utopia and the kingdom of God are not possible this side of heaven).
- It will *seek to preserve* the possibility of future progress when all of the good cannot be immediately achieved (this is where prudent compromise occurs in the process).

Evangelicals need a prudent approach that "balances zeal with knowledge, especially knowledge of current obstacles and of effective ways to overcome them."[14] Political change comes slowly and with compromise. We need to have realistic expectations of what can be accomplished. We don't compromise on what the Bible says is right or wrong, but the nature of politics is such that concessions have to be made. "Compromise leading to incremental good is still good."[15] When speaking biblically, we want to hit a grand slam; in the political and social arena, it would be beneficial if we hit a single! To use a hot-button issue as an example: when laws were being challenged and legislation was being written regarding abortion, if Christian voters and conservative politicians would have been prudent and conceded to allow abortion in the limited cases of rape, incest, and imminent threat to the mother's life, then perhaps we would have saved millions of innocent lives. Not all, but some.

SECULARISM, PLURALISM, AND A CIVIL PUBLIC SQUARE

The best prospect for humanity living together agreeably despite deep differences lies in recovering a robust sense of tolerance, or, as Os Guinness has put it, civility.[16] The American experiment was able to accomplish something remarkable in the history of Western civilization—freedom *of* religion. Much to the chagrin of secular liberals, the language does not read freedom *from* religion. Vigorous discussion and thoughtful interaction are needed in the public square, and then we let the best ideas win.

From the Christian perspective, the goal isn't a *sacred* public square in which only the ideas rooted in Christianity (or any single religion) are preferred. Nor is the goal a *naked* public square in which no ideas from various religious traditions are even entertained. The goal, as Os Guinness describes it, is a *civil* public square:

> The vision of a civic public square is one in which everyone—people of all faiths, whether religious or naturalistic—are equally free to enter and engage public life on the basis of their faiths, as a matter of "free exercise" and as dictated by their own reason and conscience; but always within the double framework, first, of the Constitution, and second, of a freely and mutually agreed covenant, or common vision for the common good, of what each person understands to be just and free for everyone else, and therefore of the duties involved in living with the deep differences of others.[17]

Hunter Baker contends in his important work *The End of Secularism*:

> Pluralism is better than secularism because it is not artificial. In a pluralistic environment, we simply enter the public square and say who we are and what we believe. We make arguments that advert to religion or other sources of values, and

they are more or less convincing on a case-by-case basis ... Secularists ask that individuals with religious reasons pretend to think and act on some other basis.[18]

Until the tide of secularism changes and as a matter of prudence, we must continue developing and presenting arguments based on natural law and common ground (that is, "secular arguments"). We need to build as big a tent as possible and speak the language of the audience we are trying to persuade. If the Christian worldview is true, then there will be many confirmations of it in nature and reason. We should highlight these connections as *starting points* to a larger conversation as we continue to point out the failure and inadequacy of secularism. As we will see, we can make arguments based on economics that when it comes to traditional marriage, money talks. If natural marriage is continually devalued, then the number of productive, tax-paying citizens decreases because the birthrate will continue to fall. In addition, the breakdown of the family is costly both in terms of dealing with social and behavioral problems as well as legal issues (for example, custody disputes). You don't need a Bible verse for that. And when it comes to abortion choice, make it a human rights issue, not a biblical issue. There is no scientific doubt as to when a genetically distinct human life begins.

MAKING THE CASE FOR NATURAL MARRIAGE IN THE PUBLIC SQUARE

"Is There Hope for the American Marriage?" This is the title of Caitlin Flanagan's July 2, 2009, cover story for *Time* magazine. Flanagan writes, "There is no other single force causing as much measurable hardship and human misery in this country as the collapse of marriage." After laying out sociological data (including a feminist who has had her mind changed by the data that fathers really are important after all) and noting that failure of marriage "hurts children, it reduces mothers' financial security, and it has landed with particular devastation on those who can bear it least: the nation's underclass,"[19] she comes to the critical issue:

> The fundamental question we must ask ourselves at the beginning of the century is this: What is the purpose of marriage? Is it—given the game-changing realities of birth control, female equality, and the fact that motherhood outside of marriage is no longer stigmatized—simply an institution that has the capacity to increase the pleasure of the adults who enter into it? If so, we might as well hold the wake now ...
>
> Or is marriage an institution that still hews to its old intention and function—to raise the next generation, to protect and teach it, to instill in it the habits of conduct and character that will ensure the generation's own safe passage into adulthood? ...
>
> What we teach about the true meaning of marriage will determine a great deal about our fate.[20]

This isn't from a theology textbook; this is *Time* magazine. Our society is asking the fundamental question: What is the true meaning and purpose of marriage as a social institution? The basic social purpose of marriage, which exists logically prior to the state, is that it attaches mothers and fathers to their children and to each other.[21] Moreover, basic justice to the children requires they be cared for and connected in relationship with their parents, who naturally and biologically brought them into being.[22] The state has a vested interest in this taking place for the good of society as a whole because "long-term, monogamous, heterosexual unions as a rule, as a group, and by nature produce the next generation."[23] The natural institution of marriage is foundational for civilization to flourish. This is why same-sex marriage would adversely affect everyone in the end — including homosexuals.

Natural marriage has been significantly weakened in the last fifty years. And while books could be written on this, I want to highlight three factors that Jennifer Roback Morse of the Ruth Institute has pointed out before I discuss the further diminishing of marriage that will occur by the legalization of same-sex unions.

First, *no-fault divorce was introduced in 1968 in California*, making it easier and cheaper to end a loveless marriage. Removing the fault basis undermined the idea that marriage is a permanent and exclusive bond. You can now get divorced for any reason or no reason at all, and our 50 percent divorce rate reflects the implications of that decision. Simultaneously, unwed pregnancies have skyrocketed. A groundbreaking 2008 report on the costs of divorce and unwed childbearing revealed that these two factors alone cost American taxpayers $112 billion each year.[24]

Second, *the cultural impact of contraception has weakened natural marriage.* Leaving aside moral questions, the effect on marriage has been profound in that sex is now seen as a sterile, recreational activity with reproduction understood as a lifestyle choice rather than as the natural expression of oneness in marriage.

Finally, *our culture has lost any sense that men and women are different.* Gender, it is argued, is a social construction, whereas a person's sex is a biological function. A growing chorus is arguing that men and women are interchangeable — even when it comes to parenting. This is simply false. As Rutgers sociologist David Popenoe points out, "We should disavow the notion that 'mommies can make good daddies,' just as we should disavow the popular notion of radical feminists that 'daddies can make good mommies' . . . The two sexes are different to the core, and each is necessary — culturally and biologically — for the optimal development of a human being."[25] Dr. Bill Maier sums it up this way: "A just, compassionate society should always come to the aid of motherless or fatherless families. But a just, compassionate society should never, ever intentionally create motherless and fatherless families. And that's exactly what same-sex marriage does."[26]

The ship of marriage is already taking on a lot of water, but legalizing same-sex marriage could send the ship straight to the bottom. Now, to avoid misunderstanding, let me be as clear as I can: This discussion is about being *for* natural marriage and the public good, not *against* gay people. But even as I say this, we also should have realistic expectations because, "in a profoundly secular culture, which has decided that the freedom to choose is of ultimate significance, any critique of homosexuality is seen as homophobic."[27] If Christians are being hateful, then shame on them. But making the case for strengthening marriage for the good of the society is not hate speech. We can be opposed to same-sex marriage while at the same time treating people with dignity and respect and laboring to protect all people from any form of physical, emotional, or psychological abuse and bullying. These are not mutually exclusive.

While I don't have space to address the many popular slogans and arguments for gay marriage (for example, equal rights, loving relationships, and the like), they are clearly addressed and responded to in Frank Turek's short book *Correct, Not Politically Correct: How Same-Sex Marriage Hurts Everyone*. Let me cite a study mentioned in a *New York Times* article regarding monogamy and same-sex marriage:

> A study to be released next month is offering a rare glimpse inside gay relationships and reveals that monogamy is not a central feature for many. Some gay men and lesbians argue that, as a result, they have stronger, longer-lasting and more honest relationships. And while that may sound counterintuitive, some experts say boundary-challenging gay relationships represent an evolution in marriage — one that might point the way for the survival of the institution.[28]

It seems that many gay men and lesbians are not interested in stable monogamous relationships.[29] It also needs to be pointed out that "once we redefine marriage to include same-sex couples, we have no justification for denying other forms of marriage like incestuous, polygamous, or group marriage."[30]

Dr. Jennifer Roback Morse, who regularly lectures and debates on the topic and who has also served as a witness in the Proposition 8 trial in California, highlights four fundamental principles about marriage that will be undermined by same-sex unions:

1. the biological basis for parenting
2. the fact that children are ordinarily entitled to a relationship with *both* of their biological parents
3. the fact that the state *registers* parenthood; it does not *determine* parenthood (for example, the state records and registers a biological and natural fact [the birth of a child in the hospital]; now it seems that the state is getting involved [in lesbian custody cases] in determining who qualifies as a parent)[31]
4. the fact that mothers and fathers are not interchangeable; they each make distinct, unique, and important contributions to parenthood (what's

more, men will increasingly be marginalized from the family as father-hood is being reduced to the donation of sperm)[32]

These are significant reasons to be concerned about attempts at redefining marriage. Christians who bring up these issues care about the good of society and are not being bigoted and homophobic in doing so. Civility and passionate conviction can coexist.

THE LAW OF INFLUENCE

One thing is certain—someone will influence our society. Someone will make laws. Someone will raise the topics for national, judicial, and constitutional debate. So why not labor as faithfully and prudently as we can for the greatest good of others and thus fulfill our role to be salt and light? As Christians, this is one way in which we can love our neighbor as ourselves.

We must also prepare to live faithfully as a minority in an increasingly post-Christian society. If this is indeed what happens (I think the jury is still out on this one), then we have the example of millions of Christians throughout church history to learn from.

Regardless of the spirit of the age, we are to use whatever tools and opportunities are arranged for us by God for his glory and for the proclaiming of the good news of the kingdom.

RESOURCES FOR ENGAGING YOUR INTERSECTION

Books

- *The End of Secularism* by Hunter Baker
- *Politics for Christians: Statecraft as Soulcraft* by Francis Beckwith
- *Politics for the Greatest Good: The Case for Prudence in the Public Square* by Clarke D. Forsythe
- *City of Man: Religion and Politics in a New Era* by Michael Gerson and Peter Wehner
- *Politics — According to the Bible: A Comprehensive Resource for Understanding Modern Political Issues in Light of Scripture* by Wayne Grudem
- *Correct, Not Politically Correct: How Same-Sex Marriage Hurts Everyone* by Frank Turek
- *The Clash of Orthodoxies: Law, Religion, and Morality in Crisis* by Robert George

Websites and DVDs

- www.manhattandeclaration.org – The Manhattan Declaration
- www.anevangelicalmanifesto.com – An Evangelical Manifesto
- www.ruthinstitute.org – The Ruth Institute (see especially the booklet "77 Non-Religious Reasons to Support Man/Woman Marriage")
- www.familylife.com – Family Life
- *Chuck Colson on Politics and the Christian Faith*, DVD
- *The Birth of Freedom*, Acton Institute, DVD
- *Doing the Right Thing: A Six-Part Exploration of Ethics*, DVD
- *Same-Sex Marriage Affects Everyone*, The Ruth Institute, DVD

GOD AND ECONOMICS

AN INTERVIEW WITH JAY WESLEY RICHARDS

Jonathan Morrow: Christians are commanded to care for the poor, but our good intentions don't always translate into the effects we desire. Can you talk a little about the relationship between justice and economics?

Jay Richards: It's right that we ask moral questions of economics. For instance, as Christians, we should want an economic system that helps alleviate poverty and that allows people to exercise virtue. But it's important to distinguish equality before the law, which justice requires, from economic equality, which justice does not require. In fact, the twentieth century taught us that societies that try to make everyone economic equals are profoundly unjust.

We also need to be realistic. This side of God's kingdom, whenever we talk about a just society, we always have to ask: Just *compared to what*? It doesn't do anyone any good to tear down a society that is "unjust" compared to the kingdom of God if that society is *more* just than any of the ones that will replace it. And if you compare capitalism with the live alternatives, capitalism wins, hands down. It allows the most wealth to be produced and lifts by far the most people out of poverty while avoiding the grave injustices that are intrinsic to socialist economies.

Finally, it's important that we distinguish the outcomes of economic policies from our intentions for those policies. God cares about both what we do and why we do it. But, economically, only what we *do* is important. Rent control, for example, will have exactly the same effect—a shortage of lower income rental housing—whether it is implemented to help or to hurt the poor. When we focus on our good intentions rather than on the intended and unintended consequences of policies, we fall for what I call "the piety myth."

Jonathan: Is there such a thing as a distinctively biblical or Christian view of economics? If so (or if not), how do we go about integrating economics into a Christian worldview?

Jay: The Bible isn't an economics textbook, of course. But I do think that free market capitalism is, on balance, the economic system most consistent with Scripture and the Christian worldview. It presupposes the right to private property (as does Scripture); it allows fallen people to pursue their legitimate self-interest while channeling selfishness into socially beneficial outcomes. In a free market, for instance, even a greedy baker can satisfy his greed (legally) only by providing something for others that they will freely buy. Of the live options, capitalism best allows us to exercise our creative freedom to create new wealth. And it is the only known way to lift large numbers of people out of poverty. Over time, the greater economic freedom a society has, the more prosperous it is.

Jonathan: In such a politically charged environment, how would you advise Christian leaders and pastors to talk about issues like economics within the local church context and better equip Christians to engage in these areas?

Jay: We should be careful to distinguish fundamental theological truths, like the incarnation and the Trinity, from economic ideas, which are really prudential judgments. A person can have a deep, well-informed faith and still be mixed-up about economics.

Nevertheless, our faith applies to every aspect of life, which means it also applies to economics. But Christian leaders, pastors, and laypeople who want to engage in economic issues and apply their faith in the public square ought first to learn some of the basic facts of economics. For instance, we are commanded to care for the poor. But if we know nothing about economics, we won't know what policies are most likely to actually help the poor.

A bit like physics and chemistry, there are economic realities that we simply have to learn. We can't wish them away. And we can't just trust our moral intuitions. Economics is often highly counterintuitive. Just because it seems like, say, raising the federal minimum wage to $1,000 an hour would eradicate poverty, this doesn't mean that such a policy will actually do that.

And just because it seems like one person can get rich only at someone else's expense, we know that isn't true. A free exchange, by definition, is win-win, since it's free on both sides. So when I pay my barber to cut my hair, we both see ourselves as better-off as a result. Moreover, it's possible for someone to get wealthy by creating new wealth for himself and for others. A free-market economy, then, is not a zero-sum game.

Once we learn the basic, nonnegotiable realities of economics, we'll be much more capable of applying eternal theological truths to particular economic problems.

> **Jay W. Richards** is senior fellow of the Discovery Institute (www. discovery.org). He is the author of multiple books, including *The Privileged Planet* and *Money, Greed, and God: Why Capitalism Is the Solution and Not the Problem*.

chapter seventeen

QUESTIONS OF FAITH AND SCIENCE

Science ... knows a great deal. That is its strongest point. Understanding and admitting its limitations is not one of its strong points.

James Franklin, *What Science Knows: And How It Knows It*

MODERN SCIENCE regularly and triumphantly claims that it has removed the need for God. It essentially states, "In days of old, we had to rely on superstition, but *now* we can actually arrive at knowledge. Humanity has outgrown the naive invocation of God for everything we don't understand."

"Religion has run out of justifications," writes new atheist Christopher Hitchens. "Thanks to the telescope and the microscope, it no longer offers an explanation of anything important."[1] People used to genuflect when they entered a cathedral; now modern society bows at the altar of science.

Enter Christianity and the Bible. Does it really fit into our scientific world? Is the Bible hopelessly at odds with science? Although we might picture Galileo or the Scopes Monkey Trial in Dayton, Tennessee, what we hear about them is more myth than fact.[2]

Let me avoid a potential misunderstanding right from the outset: My intention is not to bash or denigrate science. Far from it! We simply need to arrive at a healthier and more accurate view of it. Christians should engage in and applaud the efforts of ethically practiced science. It is beneficial, and we have learned wonderful things from it. But it can't tell us everything, nor is it designed to.

The most helpful thing we can do when talking about faith and science is to carefully define our terms (understanding) and get a clear view of the big picture of this discussion (perspective). In our media-rich environment of slogans and sound bites, confusion abounds in our culture and in the church. Many are fearful about what science will explain away next.

IS FAITH INHERENTLY AT ODDS WITH SCIENCE?

Mark Twain once quipped, "Faith is believing what you know ain't so." This isn't Christianity. The fact that some Christians may have blind faith is not the same as Christianity itself championing blind faith and irrationality. Mainstream Christianity has always emphasized the fact that faith and reason go together. In everyday terms, faith is simply trusting in what you have good reason to believe is true. Faith in the Christian life is trust that God is who he claims to be and will do all that he has promised to do. This is reasonable because God has shown himself to be reliable and trustworthy. So faith is not belief *in spite of* the evidence, but belief *in light of* the evidence.

Further evidence for the compatibility of science and faith comes from the history of science itself. Over the past five hundred years, the vast majority of the fathers of modern science recognized no inherent conflict. Kepler, Pascal, Boyle, Newton, Faraday, Babbage, Mendel, Pasteur, and Kelvin all believed in God, and most were Christians. In fact, many viewed their belief in God as a primary motivation for their scientific inquiry. For example, Johannes Kepler, who discovered the laws of planetary motion, wrote, "The chief aim of all investigations of the external world should be to discover the rational order which has been imposed on it by God, and which he revealed to us in the language of mathematics."[3] So if some of the most intelligent scientists in the modern era did not see a conflict, why has there been such a drastic change in thinking? As we will see, the answer lies in certain philosophical, not scientific, commitments.

THE DIFFICULTY OF DEFINING SCIENCE

Now comes the hard part—defining science with precision. Although it may surprise you, any philosopher or historian of science will acknowledge that it is very difficult (and often controversial) to distinguish between a scientific explanation and a nonscientific one. This difficulty has become known as the "demarcation problem" (that is, finding the line or criterion that separates the two). For example, noted historian of science Ian Barbour concluded that "at the outset it should be stated that there is no 'scientific method,' no formula with five easy steps guaranteed to lead to discoveries. There are many methods, used at different stages of inquiry, and in widely varying circumstances."[4]

Broadly speaking, it is accurate to affirm that science is aiming at truth by utilizing a "systematic way of studying nature involving observation, experimentation, and/or reasoning about physical phenomena."[5] A geologist will use different field-specific "scientific methods" than cosmologists, geneticists, and chemists do, yet they are all pursuing scientific explanations.

Some fields and methods yield more certain results than others. So, generally speaking, historical sciences (which investigate how nature operated in the past) offer *less* certainty than operational sciences (which investigate how nature is currently operating). A chemical reaction measured and repeated in controlled experiments in the laboratory offers more certainty than explanations for why nature may have selected for the "long necked" giraffe. This doesn't mean that the historical sciences have not provided reliable knowledge, only that there is a commonsense difference that must be factored in as we evaluate scientific explanations and conclusions.

ARE THERE LIMITS TO WHAT SCIENCE CAN TELL US?

Yes. As useful as science is, its explanatory scope is not universal. Only a little reflection shows that other areas of knowledge are available to us — philosophy, ethics, history, religion, literature, economics, poetry, art, and music (just to name a few). In chapter 6, we already explored why science is not our only source of knowledge.

Because science deals with physical phenomena, it will be limited *by definition* in the same way that history is limited to dealing with the past. And that is OK. It is possible to hold both that science is not all there is *and* that it is helpful.

Ethics and purpose are two compelling examples of limits. As David Hume pointed out, you can't get an "ought to" from an "is." "What is — in the sense of science — does not determine what ought to be."[6] The classic example is that Darwinian evolution cannot account for morality and ethics. The fundamental point that Darwinist explanations miss is that "morality is not about how we do act but about how we should act."[7]

Another limitation of science concerns purpose (the fancy word is *teleology*). Oxford philosopher of science John Lennox offers a helpful thought experiment having to do with Aunt Matilda's cake:

> Why are we here? What is the purpose of our existence? It is this question above all that exercises the human heart. Scientific analysis of the universe cannot give us the answer, any more than scientific analysis of Aunt Matilda's cake could tell us why she made it. Scientific probing of the cake may tell us that it is good for humans; even that it is highly likely to have been designed specifically with humans in mind, since it is fine-tuned to their nutritional requirements. In other words, science may be able to point to the conclusion that there is a

purpose behind the cake; but precisely what that purpose is, science cannot tell us. It would be absurd to look for it within the cake. Only Aunt Matilda can reveal it to us. True science is not embarrassed by its inability at this point — it simply recognizes that it is not equipped to answer such questions.[8]

THE REAL SOURCE OF CONFLICT

Pure science is a myth; science always carries the residue of philosophical assumptions and comments. Recognizing this doesn't render scientific knowledge impossible; it just points out that people need to be aware of their precommitments when practicing science and interpreting the available evidence. One would be hard-pressed to find a clearer illustration of a philosophical commitment constraining the scientific enterprise than Harvard biologist Richard Lewontin's candid admission:

> Our willingness to accept scientific claims that are against common sense is the key to an understanding of the real struggle between science and the supernatural. We take the side of science *in spite* of the patent absurdity of some of its constructs ... *in spite* of the tolerance of the scientific community for unsubstantiated just-so stories, because we have a prior commitment, a commitment to materialism. It is not that the methods and institutions of science somehow compel us to accept a material explanation of the phenomenal world, but, on the contrary, that we are forced by our *a priori* adherence to material causes to create an apparatus of investigation and a set of concepts that produce material explanations, no matter how counter-intuitive, no matter how mystifying to the uninitiated. Moreover, that materialism is absolute, for we cannot allow a Divine Foot in the door. To appeal to an omnipotent deity is to allow that at any moment the regularities of nature may be ruptured, that miracles may happen.[9]

This passage reveals the real conflict — naturalism versus theism. As we noted earlier, *naturalism* is a scientifically oriented worldview that denies the existence of God and reduces everything to physics and chemistry. Richard Dawkins put it this way: "An atheist in this sense of philosophical naturalist is somebody who believes there is nothing beyond the natural, physical world, no *super*natural creative intelligence lurking behind the observable universe, no soul that outlasts the body and no miracles — except in the sense of natural phenomena that we don't understand yet."[10] In an interview with *WIRED* magazine, Dawkins admits the real source of conflict: "The big war is not between evolution and creationism, but between naturalism and supernaturalism."[11]

Theism holds that there is a personal creator and sustainer of the universe who is omnipotent, omniscient, essentially good, omnipresent, and eternal. Christianity believes that the Creator has revealed himself to mankind in the person of Jesus Christ, a member of the Trinity, who was resurrected from the dead in confirmation of his deity (see Romans 1:4). Therefore, Christians are committed to a supernatural world, including God, the soul, angels, and miracles.[12]

Here is the critical point for Christians to see: There is no inherent conflict between Christianity and science. Defining these two worldviews shows us the root problem: naturalism and theism are at odds, not science and Christianity. Naturalism is intrinsically atheistic because it sees nothing outside the natural or material world.

HAS SCIENCE DISPROVED GOD?

Science can no more prove or disprove God than it can tell you how much "love" or "justice" weighs. This is known as a category fallacy. To admit that science does not *require* either a theistic or atheistic interpretation is not the same thing as concluding that science cannot provide evidence for either position. And when we look at this evidence, good reasons emerge that point to a Creator. This could be a book in itself.[13] But I want to highlight a recent development that illustrates the power of the scientific evidence for God.

Antony Flew was arguably the most influential atheistic philosopher of the twentieth century. Remarkably, after a lifetime of study, writing, and teaching as an atheist, Flew rejected his atheism and now believes in God:[14] In his autobiography, *There Is a God*, Flew writes, "I now believe that the universe was brought into existence by an infinite Intelligence. I believe that this universe's intricate laws manifest what scientists have called the Mind of God. I believe that life and reproduction originate in a divine Source."[15] He states in his book that he arrived at this conclusion according to the Socratic principle that has guided him his whole career: *Follow the evidence wherever it leads.*

What is some of this evidence? Here are Flew's own words:

> Why do I believe this, given that I expounded and defended atheism for more than a half century? The short answer is this: this is the world picture, as I see it, that has emerged from modern science. Science spotlights three dimensions of nature that point to God. The first is the fact that nature obeys laws. The second is the dimension of life, intelligently organized and purpose-driven beings which arose from matter. The third is the very existence of nature.[16]

This "conversion" sent the prolific Antony Flew from the intellectual penthouse to the outhouse in the eyes of his former atheistic colleagues. A champion one day, an embarrassment the next. Some have even implied that his rejection of atheism was due to the onset of senility. Speaking of these former colleagues, Dinesh D'Souza comments, "Too closed-minded to consider Flew's arguments, these fellows would much rather belittle the intellectual capacity of the man they once revered. Hell hath no fury like an atheist scorned."[17]

COMING TO TERMS WITH EVOLUTION, CREATION, AND INTELLIGENT DESIGN

Few topics are more contentious than the creation-evolution debate. Yet while many Christians say they are against evolution, relatively few can offer an accurate definition of precisely what they are against. Not good. Especially if we are sending young Christians into the university armed with little more than "Genesis is true, and evolution [whatever that is] is false." And things really get interesting when you throw Intelligent Design into the mix.

So, how should Christians think about evolution? One of the first things we have to do when approaching a topic like this is to clearly define our terms. Doing so will allow us to distinguish between real and perceived sources of conflict.

Defining Evolution

The word *evolution* can mean several things. The word literally just means "change over time." Another definition is "an organism's adaptation to changing environments." For example, thirteen subspecies of finches live in the Galapagos Islands, and beak sizes of the finches have been found to vary as the environment goes through different seasons. This is small-scale evolutionary change taking place within an existing species that we can observe (sometimes referred to as "microevolution"). Environmental pressures along with genetic modifications drive the change occurring here, which in turn helps an organism survive and reproduce. This process is known as "natural selection," or "survival of the fittest." No Christian I know of denies that evolution occurs in either of these senses.

What is controversial, however, is *Darwinian evolution*. This is the grand story of evolution, or Richard Dawkins's "blind watchmaker thesis" that seeks to explain *everything* from molecules to man.[18] Darwinian evolution makes two central claims: (1) *All* organisms can ultimately trace their lineage back to a single-celled common ancestor (universal common descent—a much larger claim than the fact that descent with modification occurs within existing species), and (2) natural selection acting on random mutation is sufficient to explain the diversity and complexity of *all* life. These sweeping claims of Darwinian evolution (sometimes referred to as "macroevolution") seem to make the creative activity of God unnecessary. I will address this implication below.

Again, no one denies microevolution—change over time or adaptation within species over time (for example, bacteria, finch beaks, etc.). This is simply what we observe and can measure. However, evidence for microevolution is not necessarily evidence for macroevolution.[19] Just because we can observe finch beaks that change in size does not mean that these changes can produce completely new species. But if naturalism is true, then this must have happened because Darwinian evolution becomes the only game in town.[20] Incidentally, it is at this point that you need to be on the lookout for people equivocating on the meaning of evolution. Evidence for evolution in the sense of change over time is not the same thing as evidence supporting Darwin's grand theory. Natural selection may be able to explain the *survival* of the fittest, but what remains to be seen is whether it can account for the *arrival* of the fittest in the first place.

Understanding Intelligent Design

Enter the challenge of Intelligent Design (ID) to the reigning paradigm of Darwinian evolution. The main claim of Intelligent Design is that "there exist natural systems that cannot be adequately explained in terms of undirected natural causes and that exhibit features which in any other circumstance we would attribute to design."[21] By way of example, think of how we recognize and infer that Mount Rushmore is not the end result of random wind and erosion but rather the work of intelligence.

Surprisingly, many Darwinian evolutionists admit that the world looks designed. In *Why Evolution Is True*, Jerry Coyne says, "If anything is true about nature, it is that plants and animals seem intricately and almost perfectly designed for living their lives."[22] According to Richard Dawkins, "Biology is the study of complex things that appear to have been designed for a purpose."[23] In *The Greatest Show on Earth*, Dawkins says organisms look as if they were "meticulously planned."[24] Of course, Dawkins insists that the appearance of design is illusory. In contrast, Intelligent Design proponents claim that the world looks designed because it *was* designed.

The theory of Intelligent Design does challenge the Darwinian claim that all of life's complexity and diversity can emerge through a blind, undirected process. Intelligent Design — finding design in the natural world — leads to philosophical and theological questions about who the designer could be, which has further implications for the value and purpose of life. This is the controversial aspect of Intelligent Design. Rather than addressing their arguments, many Darwinists seek to dismiss Intelligent Design as religious dogma masquerading as science. But Intelligent Design is not creationism in a cheap tuxedo, because it does not begin with a religious text or a doctrinal presupposition. It is critical to understand that both Darwinian evolution and Intelligent Design *start* with the publicly available evidence and then reason from this evidence back to their conclusions.

Another common objection goes like this: "There has been so much in science that people used to put 'god' as a placeholder for until a scientific explanation became available. This is just what ID does; it is the classic god-of-the-gaps argument." However, ID is not an argument from what we don't know, but an inference from what we *do* know. Information is the hallmark of design and is always the product of a mind. When we encounter sequence-specific instructions in DNA that eerily resemble computer code, we recognize that random chance does not produce this kind of specified information.

And finally, there is the old red herring of the "poor design in nature" charge.

But this actually concedes the point. Even if we grant for the sake of argument that there is poor design in nature, poor design is still design. My 1985 Toyota Tercel had some serious design flaws (like no mirror on the passenger side!), but it was still designed. This objection is only intended to distract us from the main issue at hand—actual design or the appearance of design.

What about Theistic Evolution?

To arrive at an answer, I will analyze its viability from three perspectives: philosophical, scientific, and theological. Theistic evolutionists generally accept the picture of history provided by Darwinian evolution; they just add the word *God* to it.[25]

The first question to answer is this: Is it philosophically coherent? In other words, can we take a purposeless process (no end in mind) and merge it with a purposeful creator God (a specific end in mind)? Can God intentionally create, design, and guide by means of a blind, unguided, and accidental process? When asked in this way, the conceptual problem becomes clear. Theistic evolution seems to be at the very least incoherent, if not flat-out contradictory. It would be like telling your friends that your brother Mike is a married bachelor; you end up with two mutually exclusive concepts. If, however, one means that God intentionally made the necessary genetic selections and modifications along the way, then this is a form of Intelligent Design—not Darwinism—because it is by definition unguided.

The second question to ask is this: Is there good independent scientific evidence that Darwinian evolution is actually true (that is, in addition to a prior commitment to philosophical naturalism)? I'll briefly sketch three major scientific challenges to Darwinian evolution:

1. *The origin of first life.* Where did the information come from to produce the first amino acids, proteins, and DNA? How do you get from chemistry to biology—from non-life to life? There is no naturalistic answer to this question. The improbability of first life originating by chance alone is beyond astronomical. Nicholas Wade, a science writer for *The New York Times*, summarizes the current state of affairs regarding origins of life research: "Everything about the origin of life on earth is a mystery, and it seems the more that is known, the more acute the puzzles get … The chemistry of the first life is a nightmare to explain. No one has yet devised a plausible explanation to show how the earliest chemicals of life—thought to be RNA, or ribonucleic acid, a close relative of DNA— might have constructed themselves from the inorganic chemicals likely to have been around on the early earth. The spontaneous assembly of small RNA molecules on the primitive earth 'would have been a near miracle,' two experts in the subject helpfully declared last year."[26]

2. *The fossil record.* Rather than the fossil record revealing the gradual branch-

ing out of life forms and body plans from simple to complex organisms, the evidence reveals just the opposite. During the Cambrian explosion—sometimes called the biological "big bang"—we observe virtually all major body plans showing up in the fossil record *at the same time* in the geological blink of an eye without an evolutionary history. The organisms that were supposed to gradually evolve into one another show up suddenly, at the same time, and remain static over time. Darwin was aware of this challenge when he wrote *On the Origin of the Species* in 1859 but was hopeful the discovery of fossils would resolve this objection by yielding the necessary transitional forms to prove his theory. But the exact opposite has happened, and his famous tree of life has been turned upside down. The more fossils that are discovered, the more pronounced the problem becomes.

Moreover, Darwinian evolution has a serious "information" problem. Just as the first life would have required a breathtaking amount of specified information, so, too, the diversity of body plans that arose during the Cambrian explosion would have required a staggering infusion of new information (for example, think of how new and specific computer code must be written for various platforms, software, and web applications to function and interact). Our uniform and repeated experience is that information is always the product of a mind, not a blind random process.[27]

3. *The edge of evolution.* Darwinian evolution rises or falls on its ability to demonstrate how one species can gradually evolve into an entirely new and distinct species. But the observational evidence seems to suggest there are limits to evolvability. Charles Darwin, whose theory of natural selection was inspired in part by his own experience with "artificial selection" as he bred pigeons, realized that various traits could be altered through this process. So if he could do it, then why not nature, given long periods of time? But our experience with artificial selection, which is always intentional and aimed at a particular end result, reveals that "for essentially every trait ... there has always been a limit. Whether the organisms or selected traits are roses, dogs, pigeons, horses, cattle, protein content in corn, or the sugar content of beets, selection certainly has an effect. But all selected qualities eventually fizzle out ... There are limits to change."[28] If this is the case with an intelligently directed process, then how much more so for the blind process of natural selection that operates at the mercy of whatever variations happen to come along.[29] Moreover, by studying malaria and HIV, biochemist Michael Behe offers good evidence for an edge to evolution; there are limits to what natural selection and mutation can do.[30]

This evidence, along with other scientific challenges I don't have room to explore, casts doubt on the viability of Darwinian evolution and explains the growing list of more than seven hundred scientists from such institutions as Oxford, Cambridge, Harvard, Dartmouth, Rutgers, University of Chicago, Stanford, and University of California at Berkeley who are "skeptical of claims for the ability of random mutation and natural selection to account for the complexity of life. Careful examination of the evidence for Darwinian theory should be encouraged."[31]

The final question to answer is this: Is theistic evolution compatible with core Christian doctrine? In *Saving Darwin*, theistic evolutionist Karl Giberson dispenses with the historical Adam and Eve: "I began to wonder how an old story about a guy named 'Man' in a magical garden who had a mate named 'Woman' made from one of his ribs could ever be mistaken for actual history."[32] But Adam is not a trivial issue that can just be set aside. In fact, the historical reality of both Adam and Jesus are foundational to Christian theology. The New Testament clearly teaches that "for since death came through a man, the resurrection of the dead comes also through a man. For as in Adam all die, so in Christ all will be made alive" (1 Corinthians 15:21–22; cf. Romans 5:12–21). Again, this is not a minor issue; it is essential to understanding the nature of salvation. Even if we only considered this one issue, theistic evolution seems theologically unacceptable to someone who embraces historic Christianity.

So is theistic evolution a viable option for the Christian? Let's answer this question with another question: Why would we want to try to combine Christianity with a concept that seems philosophically unintelligible, that faces serious scientific challenges, that is compelling only if one is already committed to philosophical naturalism, and that is theologically at odds with core Christian doctrine? In my view, here's the bottom line: Darwinian evolution (in the specific sense defined above) and purposeful creation are like oil and water; they just don't mix.

Where Does Creationism Fit in This Discussion?

Creationism begins not with the observable evidence discovered from creation but with the biblical text of Genesis that affirms that in the beginning God created (Genesis 1:1). Creationism affirms the truthfulness of a literal (that is, historical-grammatical-literary) interpretation of Genesis[33] and the existence of the biblical God. It certainly is consistent with what we discover about the universe, but creationism is, first and foremost, a *theological* doctrine, and it reasons outward from that starting point.

The progression goes something like this: A Christian accepts the teachings and worldview of Jesus, who affirmed the doctrine of creation recorded in Genesis. The Christian then compares the biblical text and the physical universe and sees confirmation of this worldview (Psalm 19:1–4; Romans 1:19–20). For this reason, I suggest that it is most prudent for Christians to have the public discussion of origins at the level of naturalism versus theism and not creationism versus evolution, because one's worldview commitments will shape which interpretations of the available evidence will be allowed. Furthermore, I think the debate going on between Intelligent Design and Darwinian evolution is healthy for science and profitable because it is clarifying the nature and extent of the available evidence and the role that worldview plays in the cultural and institutional discussion.

A FINAL PLEA

Once Christians recognize that the battle exists between theism and naturalism, we can put the current debate about origins into perspective. I have two suggestions that may help us better navigate these issues. First, Christians need to present a united front opposing naturalism in the public square while also standing up for academic freedom so that questions of origins can be rigorously discussed without fear of censorship, denial of tenure, or the loss of research money.[34]

Second, and closely related, Christians must be charitable toward other Christians who disagree about which particular interpretation of Genesis is the most accurate (for example, the young earth-old earth debate). This is especially true when we discuss this topic on the Internet, on TV or radio, or in print. All the watching world sees are angry Christians not loving one another and bickering over which view of the flat-earth theory is correct. But in the same breath, we can and should develop careful exegetical and theological views on creation. All Christians who take the Bible seriously should be able to agree that God purposefully created, even if they disagree concerning the *how* and the *when*.[35]

I suggest we carry out this cultural conversation according to the following priorities:

1. In the public square, make a positive scientific and philosophical case for theism and argue against naturalism.
2. At the public level and in our churches and youth groups, have conversations about the significant scientific evidence that undermines the plausibility of Darwinian evolution and points toward Intelligent Design.
3. Only after spending significant energy on the first two priorities, turn to the in-house discussion concerning the various interpretive options of Genesis 1–2 and the age of the earth question (Intelligent Design is a big-tent approach that is compatible with various understandings of biblical creationism). Moreover, students entering the university need to know that there is more than one plausible and biblically faithful interpretation of Genesis available for them to consider.

In our age of science, these issues aren't going away anytime soon. Christians must prepare themselves to speak intelligently to the questions of faith and science raised by our culture.

RESOURCES FOR ENGAGING YOUR INTERSECTION

Books

- *Science and Faith: Friends or Foes?* by C. John Collins
- *God's Undertaker: Has Science Buried God?* by John Lennox
- *Understanding Intelligent Design: Everything You Need to Know in Plain Language* by William Dembski and Sean McDowell
- *Understanding Creation: A Biblical and Scientific Overview* by Mark Whorton and Hill Roberts
- *God and Evolution: Protestants, Catholics, and Jews Explore Darwin's Challenge to Faith* edited by Jay Richards
- *Signature in the Cell: DNA and the Evidence for Intelligent Design* by Stephen C. Meyer
- *Did Adam and Eve Really Exist? Who They Were and Why You Should Care* by C. John Collins
- *The Soul of Science: Christian Faith and Natural Philosophy* by Nancy Pearcey and Charles B. Thaxton

Websites and DVDs

- www.intelligentdesign.org – Intelligent Design
- www.faithandevolution.org – Faith and Evolution
- www.johnlennox.org – John Lennox
- *Unlocking the Mystery of Life*, DVD
- *Expelled: No Intelligence Allowed*, DVD
- *Darwin's Dilemma*, DVD
- *The Privileged Planet*, DVD
- *The Case for the Creator*, DVD
- *Metamorphosis*, DVD

SCIENCE AND THE BIBLE

AN INTERVIEW WITH C. JOHN "JACK" COLLINS

Jonathan Morrow: Your background is pretty unusual, including experience in the sciences (with two degrees from MIT) and in biblical scholarship. From this vantage point, do you think science and faith are at odds?

Collins: Well, in my own experience, they are not at odds. This is because I find the world that God made to be endlessly fascinating and worthy of study. Even more, if we want our science to be good, it takes sound critical thinking; but good critical thinking is also crucial if our faith is to be strong and well-formed.

And this makes good sense. Much of what we know as modern science was developed by Christian people, who thought they were living out their faith responsibly.

At the same time, there are people who *want* us to believe that faith and science are incompatible with each other. But when they say this, they are usually confusing "faith" with blind belief, and "science" with naturalistic reasoning (that is, everything happens by purely natural processes). These are confusions: Christian faith, at least, is not blind belief, but confidence in a person, Jesus. And science that is just naturalistic reasoning has no special claim on us. We have the right to ask why we should allow naturalism any place at all. Of course, naturalism and Christian faith are incompatible, but that's something else altogether.

Jonathan: It seems there is a great deal of confusion and contention surrounding Genesis 1 – 3 in local churches. People seem to think either we must insist on a purely "literal" reading of these chapters, or else we must simply avoid their bearing on the sciences. Do you think this is an accurate description? Why do you suppose it is so? How can we get better at having the discussion about origins from a distinctively Christian perspective in the church and in the public square?

Collins: The opening chapters of Genesis are vital for Christians, since they claim to tell us how the story of the world got under way. So it's not surprising that we care about how to read them properly. But as soon as you raise questions about what is the "proper" way to read these chapters, you sound like you are taking away from their reality. How can we tell the true story of the world except by history?

God gave us his word in the language and literary forms of their first audiences, and we should accept that we have more tools for understanding these today. I think we can show that these chapters do mean to convey "history," and that the clear presence of what we might call "figurative" or "symbolic" elements does not take away from this.

In our wider culture, we need to show that the story that explains the world we all experience — with its pleasures and sorrows, **its sin** and guilt, its yearning for God, things shared by all kinds of human beings everywhere — must have something very much like Genesis 1 – 3 as its front end. If we can see that this is the front end, then we probably will not much care just how long ago it happened. But we can also see what is even more important, namely, how we need God to forgive and help us.

Jonathan: What are your thoughts on Intelligent Design, and how it may impact the discussion of faith and science in the public square?

Collins: What you think about Intelligent Design depends on how you define it. And the best way to discuss a controversial idea fairly is to define it the way its advocates do. The Discovery Institute in Seattle houses the leading think tank for Intelligent Design today, and here is how they define their idea: *The theory of intelligent design holds that certain features of the universe and of living things are best explained by an intelligent cause, not an undirected process such as natural selection.*

This definition is simple, clear, and testable. In order to explain how the things we observe now came about, we have to work backward, like a detective: What sequence of events is the "best explanation"? Do we have good reason to believe that "an undirected process" actually has the power to bring about life, the universe, everything? We would have no reason to believe it unless we decided beforehand that this is the only kind of answer we will allow — but what gives us the right to make that decision? Well, nothing does. And if "an intelligent cause" is involved, then of course the sane person wants to know more about that intelligence. In other words, we can return to discussing deeper questions about life, morals, and meaning as part of public truth.

> **C. John Collins** (PhD, University of Liverpool) is professor of Old Testament at Covenant Theological Seminary in St Louis. With degrees from MIT and Faith Evangelical Lutheran Seminary, he pursues such research interests as Hebrew and Greek grammar, science and faith, and biblical theology. He was Old Testament chairman for the English Standard Version, and Old Testament editor for the *English Standard*

Version Study Bible. He is the author of *The God of Miracles: An Exegetical Examination of God's Action in the World* (Crossway, 2000); *Science and Faith: Friends or Foes?* (Crossway, 2003); *Genesis 1–4: A Linguistic, Literary, and Theological Commentary* (P&R, 2006); *Did Adam and Eve Really Exist? Who They Were and Why You Should Care* (Crossway, 2011).

chapter eighteen

BIOETHICS IN THE TWENTY-FIRST CENTURY

Will the future see the cure of genetically linked diseases or the redesign of human life? Will we see the dignity of every human person protected in our genetic future, or will we see human beings reduced to mere biological information? Will our genetic identities point toward something transcendent in us, or will they be used to discriminate against us? Will our children be valued because they are unique and "given," or will they be valued because they are designed and "chosen"? These are only a few of the questions presented to us in this new century.

C. Ben Mitchell, "The New Genetics and the Dignity of Humankind"

LET'S PLAY THE WORD ASSOCIATION GAME: xenotransplantation, somatic cell nuclear transfer, transgenics, nanotechnology, zygote intrafallopian transfer, pharmacogenomics, and cybernetics.[1] Anything come to mind? If you understood any of these terms, consider this: to what extent should people in general and Christians in particular utilize these forms of biotechnology? If the nineteenth century was the age of industry, and the twentieth century the information age, then ours will be the biotech century. Our generation will face moral decisions and challenges that were once the realm of sci-fi movies. Is the church ready to engage? Probably not, but it could be.

But shouldn't we just preach the Bible and let everyone else sort this stuff out?

Aside from pointing to our less-than-stellar track record with the abortion debate and embryonic stem cell research (ESCR), I want to suggest three important reasons this is an unwise response. First, if Christianity is true, then it speaks to all of life. G. K. Chesterton said it best: "If Christianity should happen to be true—that is to say, if its God is the real God of the universe—then defending it may mean talking about anything and everything. Things can be irrelevant to the proposition that Christianity is false, but nothing can be irrelevant to the proposition that Christianity is true."[2]

Second, the notion of what it means to be human is in danger of being radically redefined in our lifetime. Therefore, we have a moral imperative to engage our culture with a voice that affirms the value of all of life and grants unique dignity to humanity—regardless of age, level of development, health, disability, or status. This is a critical area of social justice.

Finally, the vast majority of Christians will encounter these questions and challenges, and some will even find themselves in a position to influence them in a redemptive way. What's more, Christian leaders and pastors will be called on to counsel those in their churches seeking wisdom about whether they can and should pursue this or that biomedical technology or end-of-life decision.

This chapter aims to arrive at some awareness and understanding of the main issues and then to acquire some moral clarity with which to proceed in a God-honoring way. Bioethics deals with what we "should or shouldn't pursue in matters of life and health."[3] But we begin with the most prevalent conversation—abortion and embryonic stem cell research (ESCR).

ENGAGING THE ABORTION-CHOICE AND EMBRYONIC STEM CELL RESEARCH DEBATES

Since the *Roe v. Wade* decision in 1973, over 50 million abortions have been performed in the United States. Few issues are more divisive in our culture. "The abortion controversy," writes Scott Klusendorf, "is not a debate between those who are pro-choice and those who are anti-choice. It's not about privacy. It's not about trusting women to decide. It's not about forcing one's morality. It's about one question that trumps all others." Klusendorf continues, "Is the unborn a member of the human family? If so, killing him or her to benefit others is a serious wrong," but if not, then "elective abortion requires no more justification than having a tooth pulled."[4] We live in a complex world. But whether or not elective abortion takes the life of an innocent human being is not complex. When it comes to *that* question, there is only one issue that matters: *What is the unborn?* Every other complex personal, emotional, and social implication of the abortion debate should be addressed *after* this primary question has been answered.

Scientifically, there is no debate about *when* human life begins or whether it is a *distinct* genetic entity. Dr. Hymie Gordon, professor of medical genetics and physician at the Mayo Clinic, states clearly: "I think we can now also say that the question of the beginning of life—when life begins—is no longer a question for theological or philosophical dispute. Theologians and philosophers may go on to debate the meaning of life or purpose of life, but it is an established fact that all life, including human life, begins at the moment of conception."[5]

Philosophically, there is no relevant difference between an *unborn, newborn,* or *adult* human person. Using the S.L.E.D. acrostic,[6] we can clearly see the four differences between the unborn, newborn, and adult:

Size: We protect the basic rights of small people just the same as bigger people. Seven foot seven basketball player Yao Ming is not more valuable than someone who is four feet tall.

Level of development: An elderly human is human; an adult human is human; a child human is human; a newborn human is human; an unborn human is human. We protect human rights independent of their stage of development.

Environment: Our human rights are unaffected by our changes of location. *Where* one is is irrelevant to *who* one is (that is, inside the womb versus outside the womb). This exposes the horrendous logic people use for the barbaric practice of partial birth abortion.

Dependency: Toddlers, the elderly in nursing homes, people with pacemakers or artificial organs, people in need of blood transfusions to stay alive— *they are all dependent on something or someone else for life.* Human beings are intrinsically valuable—regardless of their level of dependency. Viability does not determine value.

There is no *morally significant* difference between newborn, unborn, and adult human persons.[7]

It is important to underscore that the first two lines of argument are not religiously motivated or based on faith. But biblically speaking, every human being is valuable, has dignity, and was created with the capacity for relationship with God for his glory (Genesis 1:26–27; 2:7; 9:6; Exodus 20:13; Psalm 139; Isaiah 43:7; Acts 17:28). Therefore, Christians should be pro-life. Now most of us, when we hear this word, think *only* of the unborn or the issue of abortion. But this principle is much broader (as we saw in chapter 15). We are called to care for, respect, and protect *all* human life for *all* of life. This includes the elderly, those with special needs, the homeless, the hungry, the orphans, the abused, and the forgotten—as well as the defenseless unborn. They are all precious in God's eyes, and we are to be their advocate (Jeremiah 22:15–16; James 1:27). Also, it can't be repeated enough that Christians' reasons for being "pro-all-of-life" are not attached to a particular political platform or ideology; they are grounded in solid philosophical, scientific, and biblical evidence.

This reasoning applies to the embryonic stem cell research (ESCR) debate as well. A human embryo deserves the protected status of a full-fledged member of the human community. As Robert George and Patrick Lee make clear, "In the case of the human embryo, he or she already has the potential to actively develop himself or herself to the further stages of maturity of the same kind of organism he or she already is."[8] The unborn are distinct, living, and whole human beings.[9]

There is only one issue when it comes to the abortion and stem cell research: *What is the unborn?* If the unborn are full-fledged members of the human community, then they have all the rights you and I have. If the unborn are not human, then abortion and ESCR are simply the removal or destruction of bodily tissue. This is fundamentally a human rights question, not a religious question. There is no such thing as being "potentially a human." One either is or isn't. As Dr. Seuss once put it, "A person is a person no matter how small."

MAKING SENSE OF REPRODUCTIVE TECHNOLOGIES

There are 6.1 million infertile couples in America (defined as those who have been unable to conceive after a year of trying). These couples carry emotional pain, frustration, and disillusionment, which we need to be aware of and minister to.[10] But aside from the pain and desperation, should Christians do anything and everything to have a baby? Are there certain options — of the thirty-eight available technologies — that they should not ethically pursue? How should they proceed in good conscience?

Once you start talking about reproductive technologies (for example, IVF [in vitro fertilization]), it won't be long until the charge of "playing God" will be brought up. When we initially encounter the deeply mysterious, we may understandably conclude that we should not mess with it. But a thousand years ago, people would have had the same reaction to the idea of flying through the air on purpose in a large metal object. Been on an airplane recently? We need to recognize that technology is a gift of God and, broadly speaking, part of his common grace (James 1:17). We use it to *intervene* or *change outcomes* all of the time in medicine. And those are good things because we live in a fallen world.

A Christian understanding of technology means that we take each example on a case-by-case basis. For example, just because we can clone a human being for spare parts (that is, organ donation) doesn't mean we should. Humans are not commodities to be owned or sold. Exercising caution and discernment regarding biotechnology does not make us Luddites (people afraid of new technology). It is wise to ask to what extent we should use technology to try to make "better" human beings. We should resist the popular assumption that "if we *can* do it, we *should* do it."

You will search the Bible in vain for the phrase *in vitro fertilization*. Bioethicist Scott Rae offers some help here: "Scripture does give us broad general principles that we can apply—I like to think of it as Scripture giving us a set of fence-posts that provide the boundaries, outside of which one cannot go without violating an important virtue or value."[11]

Christians should begin by affirming that God's design for the family is that children are conceived and raised in the context of a lifelong union between a husband and wife. This is the ideal. Given both this principle and the protected status of human embryos and the unborn, here are specific applications of some available technologies:

> Thus, intrauterine insemination (formerly known as artificial insemination) with the husband's sperm would be acceptable (unless done in conjunction with high powered fertility drugs that leave the couple at risk for major multiple pregnancies). In vitro fertilization (IVF) would also be acceptable with the genetic materials of husband and wife, as long as no embryos are discarded (the moral equivalent of abortion) and selective termination of excess pregnancies is not practiced. The principle involved here is that every embryo created in the lab is owed an opportunity to mature in the womb ... Surrogacy is problematic for other reasons beside the employment of a third party in procreation: it may be baby-selling, and it encourages surrogates to detach from the children they are carrying—not a practice to be encouraged.[12]

God certainly can and does use reproductive technologies to give children to infertile couples. But this is an expensive route. And if these couples affirm the value of life, they often decide to use methods that can reduce the probability of conception (for example, not creating/implanting more embryos than you are willing to bring to full term). Adoption, both of embryos and children, is another consideration that couples should be encouraged to prayerfully consider.[13]

NAVIGATING THE GENETICS REVOLUTION

In February 1953, James Watson and Francis Crick discovered DNA. Fifty years later (2003), the entire human genome was mapped when the Human Genome Project was completed.[14] The more we understand about the information contained in our DNA the more carefully we need to proceed. There are both curative promises and unpredictable perils associated with our genetic futures.

First, we must guard against the temptation to reduce humans to their genetic information or to a human equation that reads thus: "Person A has Gene X and will therefore do Y." In reality, our genetic information and how environments affect us are far more complex. Dr. Francis Collins, who headed the Human Genome Project, reflects wisely on what to make of future genetic link discoveries and the implications of those discoveries for certain behaviors and diseases:

> There is an inescapable component of heritability to many human behavioral traits. For virtually none of them is heredity ever close to predictive. Environ-

ment, particularly childhood experiences, and the prominent role of individual free choices have a profound effect on us. Scientists will discover an increasing level of molecular detail about the inherited factors that undergird our personalities, but that should not lead us to overestimate their quantitative contribution. Yes, we have all been dealt a particular set of genetic cards, and the cards will eventually be revealed. But how we play the hand is up to us.[15]

In short, DNA is not destiny. This is important to underscore as we learn more about our own genetic makeup. Since researchers are in the early stages of discovering, decoding, and correlating various genes with certain traits, predispositions, or diseases, we must be increasingly mindful of the "Diagnosis/Therapy Gap." Generally speaking, it is now possible to diagnose ourselves with a disease that has not yet manifested itself or may never manifest itself. This knowledge can lead to substantial and unnecessary psychological turmoil for individuals and families as they fear what has not yet happened or may never happen. Moreover, genetic preconditions may lead to discrimination against people in the workplace, disqualify and make them less attractive than other applicants, or even make them uninsurable.

Other challenges arise from genetic screening. For example, a handful of embryos are created and screened to see if certain genetic links to diseases are present before implantation is done (IVF). The genetically "inferior" human embryos are destroyed. This subtle form of eugenics (think Nazi Germany superrace at the genetic-engineering level) selects and enhances certain traits while rejecting and terminating others in an attempt to improve humanity. But who gets to decide the ideal IQ? And which traits are indeed superior? We could produce a society of genetic haves and have-nots — genetic second-class citizens.

One kind of genetic engineering is "germ line" engineering. This process affects the eggs and sperm at a genetic level and can literally alter all future generations. The goal is to remove certain hereditary diseases from future generations. But with so many unknown environmental variables and complex genetic combinations, we should not pursue this. It's simply imprudent. To put it bluntly, *no one knows* what would happen.

Furthermore, 20 percent of human genes have been patented (40,000 gene patents already exist), a fact few people know.[16] As a society, we are going to have to answer the question of who owns our genes. With lawsuits already taking place, this issue will only grow more complex if it is left at the biotech and commercial levels that are driven by economics. We must insist that we proceed from a basis of sound bioethics grounded in the inherent dignity of humanity.

QUESTIONS WE MUST BE ASKING OF BIOTECHNOLOGY

We could go on, but you get the point. Christians have some serious thinking and influencing to do. As we wrap up this discussion, here are two questions and a principle from a group of bioethicists that must become common knowledge in our churches. They will help guide us as we face an ever-expanding buffet of biotechnologies.

The first question: "Does the technology facilitate healing or restoration from disease or disability, or is it for reengineering (so-called enhancement)?"[17] Christians need to say clearly that *we are for* therapeutic uses of biotechnology. The second question: "Does the technology require or promote the commodification or destruction of human life? Does the technology demean, debase, or degrade individuals?"[18] Christians must stand up for all of humanity—especially the weak, impoverished, and defenseless.

Finally, as technological progress is made at a dizzying pace, we must not forget that the "fundamental human problem of humankind is not physical or mental inadequacy, but sin."[19] Whether it is in economics or genetics, we are tempted to seek a Utopia where technology can save us. It can't. It can alleviate much suffering, but it cannot save us. We are broken, and only God can heal our deepest wounds through Jesus Christ. The pride that exists as we develop biotechnologies will be expressed in the way these technologies are used in the future.

God is not surprised. He knows the end from the beginning and will be with us in the midst of the unknown challenges and opportunities (Isaiah 46:10). May God give us the grace and wisdom to be good stewards of the technology we have been entrusted with for the good of humanity.

RESOURCES FOR ENGAGING YOUR INTERSECTION

Books

- *Does God Need Our Help? Cloning, Assisted Suicide, and Other Challenges* by John F. Kilner and C. Ben Mitchell
- *Human Dignity in the Biotech Century: A Christian Vision for Public Policy* edited by Charles W. Colson and Nigel M. de S. Cameron
- *The Case for Life: Equipping Christians to Engage the Culture* by Scott Klusendorf
- *Biotechnology and the Human Good* by C. Ben Mitchell et al.
- *Medical Ethics and the Faith Factor: A Handbook for Clergy and Health Care Professionals* by Robert D. Orr
- *Defending Life: A Moral and Legal Case against Abortion Choice* by Francis Beckwith
- *What Is a Person? Rethinking Humanity, Social Life, and the Moral Good from the Person Up* by Christian Smith
- *Outside the Womb: Moral Guidance for Assisted Reproduction* by Scott Rae and D. Joy Riley

Websites and DVDs

- www.cbhd.org – Center for Bioethics and Human Dignity
- www.bioethics.com – Latest bioethics news and issues
- www.caseforlife.com – The Case for Life
- www.prolifetraining.com – Life Training Institute
- www.str.org – Stand to Reason
- *Doing the Right Thing*, Colson Center, DVD
- *Making Abortion Unthinkable: The Art of Pro-Life Persuasion*, Greg Koukl and Scott Klusendorf, DVD
- *Lines That Divide*, Brian Godawa, DVD

ENGAGING BIOETHICS

AN INTERVIEW WITH SCOTT RAE

Jonathan Morrow: As a bioethicist, you are aware of challenges that most Christians have never even thought about. What are the key bioethical issues just around the corner that Christians need to be prepared to engage?

Scott Rae: Bioethics came in phases: phase 1 — taking life (abortion and euthanasia); phase 2 — making life (assisted reproduction, cloning); and phase 3 — remaking life (biotechnology). This is the phase we're currently in, and the most pressing issues have to do with the efforts of biotechnology to refashion humanity. Many biotechnological advances that are providing cures for various diseases also can be used to enhance otherwise normal traits. For example, drugs to slow memory loss in Alzheimer's patients are also being used to prevent memory loss in people who are fifty or older. "Steroids for the mind" are being used to enhance mental performance. These raise issues about access to medical resources and concerns about exacerbating the gap between the medical haves and have-nots. They illustrate the poverty of our cultural emphasis on personal autonomy alone for helping us make moral assessments of these biotechnologies.

Jonathan: It seems like the issues of cloning and genetics research frequently come up in conversations at work or in the news but are rarely addressed in the local church setting. What suggestions would you to help Christian leaders and pastors begin talking about these kinds of issues?

Scott: Pastors simply have to begin talking about these issues with their churches. They need to become a bit more educated on the subjects, and there are a lot of good accessible books and Web resources out there to do that. If they start talking about these issues, people will get the message that they are important. People in the church largely assume that if their pastor addresses something, it's important, and if he or she doesn't, it's not that important. I'd start with a basic reading of some of the main bioethics issues — summaries in a book like my *Moral Choices*. Then I would connect with one of the many websites, such as the Center for Bioethics and Human Dignity (cbhd. org), that can easily keep pastors up-to-date with news and developments in the field.

Jonathan: What is the latest on the embryonic stem cell versus adult stem cell debate? Can you share a few brief guidelines on how Christians should approach this topic?

Scott: Most of the action, medically speaking, is still with the use of adult stem cells. Most of the available treatments are with stem cells derived from *non*-embryonic sources. We should be very careful to distinguish between embryonic and adult sources of stem cells when talking about this, since there is nothing morally problematic about using adult stem cells. We should also be careful about the argument that embryos left over from infertility treatments will just be thrown away and thus we should use them. There are still major issues with donor-recipient compatibility with these stem cells. But the real issue is over the moral status of human embryos. If embryos are people too, then the benefit that comes from ending their lives is irrelevant. We would never suggest that we ought to end the lives of newborns just because there is so much benefit to other children that could come from taking their very scarce organs. Embryos are persons with the potential to mature into fetuses, newborns, toddlers, and so on. I'm encouraged at some of the progress being made in reverse differentiation of adult cells to give researchers embryonic stem cells without creating human embryos.

> **Scott B. Rae** is currently professor of Christian ethics at Talbot School of Theology, Biola University in La Mirada, California. He has a PhD in social ethics from the University of Southern California, Los Angeles, and is the author of eight books on ethics. He serves as a consultant on ethics for several southern California hospitals.

chapter nineteen

STEWARDING GOD'S CREATION

In the total expanse of human life there is not a single square inch of which the Christ, who alone is sovereign, does not declare, "That is mine!"

Abraham Kuyper

PEOPLE ARE MORE AWARE OF THE ENVIRONMENT than ever before. In fact, as I write this chapter, Earth Day is almost upon us. TV shows like *Planet Earth* and *Life* invite us to view our world in HD; it's like having a backstage pass to God's creation. Recently I watched a fascinating history of the National Parks on PBS called "America's Best Idea." I admire the men and women from generations ago who labored to preserve natural wonders like Yellowstone, Grand Teton, Yosemite, and the Grand Canyon. As a Christian, I care about the environment. Naturally, I enjoy the beauty around us, but there are deeper reasons, theological reasons, that ground my concern for what has been made.

Unfortunately, many today assume (erroneously, as I will argue) that Christians are inherently against the environment and exploit it for theological reasons. This misconception crystallized in Princeton professor Lynn White's 1967 essay "The Historical Roots of Our Ecologic Crisis," and many environmental studies students perpetuate it. Here is White's summary: "Hence we shall continue to have a worsening ecological crisis until we reject the Christian axiom that nature has no reason for existence save to serve man."[1] Is this an accurate portrayal of the biblical position? What would it mean to think Christianly about the environment?

You would be hard-pressed to find a more explosive issue these days. So, in writing this chapter, I am confident of one thing. No one will agree with everything I say on this topic (and that is OK). Some will wish I had said some things more strongly, while others will think I overstepped my bounds, so I'll confess my sins in advance. What we cannot afford to do is to *say nothing* about environmental stewardship when our culture — including millions of Christians across America — is talking about it on a regular basis (in addition to the increasing press coverage of the climate change discussions and the Gulf oil spill of 2010).[2] We need to examine the issues and allow our perspective to be shaped by what God has revealed on the topic. Just as issues related to poverty and justice are complex in terms of what solutions may actually help and not harm, so, too, are issues related to the environment.

SETTING THE RECORD STRAIGHT ON THE BIBLE AND THE ENVIRONMENT

Is God green? It depends on what *green* means. Let's start by putting some categories in place. When it comes to the environment, there are three general views:

1. *Biocentrism* maintains that the environment should be protected because it has intrinsic value. One prominent weakness of this view is that it has no natural way of adjudicating when human priorities conflict with environmental ones.

2. *Anthropocentrism* rejects the intrinsic value of nature but measures its value only insofar as it is valuable to human beings. However, if there are no checks and balances on humanity's use, then there is no natural way of preventing environmental irresponsibility. White's influential essay cited above understood Christian theology to require anthropocentrism. But this is incorrect.

3. Ethicist Scott Rae summarizes a distinctly Christian understanding of the environment as a *theocentric* view, which "gives the environment intrinsic value because it is God's good creation but places it under human dominion and trusteeship for human beings to use responsibly for their benefit."[3]

Here are several relevant biblical principles that inform a theocentric view of the environment.

First, God owns *all* of creation. "The earth is the LORD's, and everything in it, the world, and all who live in it" (Psalm 24:1). If God exists and he created all there is, then the logic is straightforward: the earth belongs to God.

Second, creation exists for and displays God's glory. Paul declares that "in [Jesus] all things were created: things in heaven and on earth, visible and invisible, whether thrones or powers or rulers or authorities; all things have been created through him and for him" (Colossians 1:16). The psalmist says, "The heavens declare the glory of God" (Psalm 19:1; cf. Romans 1:20).

Third, humans have a unique and privileged status among all of creation. Scripture teaches that men and women *alone* bear God's image (Genesis 1:27). In the Sermon on the Mount, Jesus put words to something we all intuitively know: "Look at the birds of the air; they do not sow or reap or store away in barns, and yet your heavenly Father feeds them. Are you not much more valuable than they?" (Matthew 6:26). You may come across the idea of *biological egalitarianism*, which means no species is worth more than any other species, including humans. But this is incorrect. Humans are more valuable and precious to God than plants and animals. At the same time, we affirm that God cares very much about his creation. Note the specific care and concern expressed for both animals and land in these passages:

> God saw all that he had made, and it was very good.
>
> Genesis 1:31

> The righteous care for the needs of their animals.
>
> Proverbs 12:10

> When you lay siege to a city for a long time, fighting against it to capture it, do not destroy its trees by putting an ax to them, because you can eat their fruit. Do not cut them down. Are the trees people, that you should besiege them?
>
> Deuteronomy 20:19

> For six years you are to sow your fields and harvest the crops, but during the seventh year let the land lie unplowed and unused. Then the poor among your people may get food from it, and the wild animals may eat what is left. Do the same with your vineyard and your olive grove. Six days do your work, but on the seventh day do not work, so that your ox and your donkey may rest.
>
> Exodus 23:10–12

Scripture clearly teaches that creation has intrinsic value because God created it "very good." But as Christians we must operate with the uniqueness of humanity in mind as we make personal, social, economic, or environmental decisions. Consequently, Christians must reject any proposals for human population control and reject the notion that the earth would be much better-off if there were fewer humans around to consume resources.

Fourth, humans possess a unique calling. As rational and moral beings created in God's own image, humans are commanded by God to cultivate, steward, protect, and care for the earth (Genesis 1:26–28; 2:15; Psalm 8:4–8). A steward manages the property and possessions of another. God calls Christians to be stewards of what has been made. Management and cultivation are very different from exploitation and indiscriminate consumption. Christians are called to be creative image bearers who make something of the world for the glory of God.

Finally, all of creation has been affected by the fall (Genesis 3:17–18; Romans 8:19–22). Things are not the way they are supposed to be. The effects of sin are not just individual and personal; they reverberate throughout the earth and are felt socially and globally as well. Our own fallenness, coupled with the fallenness of the world, makes our stewardship difficult and complicated. Moreover, our misuse of the environment God has created for us actually intensifies the effects of the fall in some cases, leading to increased human misery (for example, pollution).

Philosopher Jay Richards offers a crisp summary of a distinctly Christian environmental ethic:

> The biblical picture is that human beings, as image bearers of God, are placed as stewards over the created order. We bear a responsibility for how we treat and use it. We are part of the creation as well as its crowning achievement. God intends for us to use and transform the natural world around us for good purposes. Proper use is not misuse. But as fallen creatures, we can mess things up.[4]

IS GREEN THE NEW RELIGION?

This should go without saying, but the earth is not our mother, and nature is not God (cf. the movie *Avatar*). "Mother Nature" is an illusion and no more exists than does the tooth fairy. For people living under a cold Darwinian worldview, the language of "Mother Nature" helps people feel better about living without ultimate purpose and meaning. Occasions like Earth Day can serve as a helpful reminder to take seriously our calling as stewards of the environment. But nature is not God—that's pantheism and pop New Age (where all is one and all is god). Rather, Christianity teaches that one of the ways in which God is experienced and revealed is through creation. This is a really important distinction. When I experience God in a sunset, I am experiencing the God who dreamed it up in the first place. One of the oldest theological errors humans have made, and continue to make today, is to confuse the creation with the Creator (Romans 1:25). The word for this is *idolatry*. While not a popular conclusion, it is accurate. So we need to be mindful of this temptation as we speak of and advocate for creation care.[5]

HOW TO THINK CLEARLY AND CHRISTIANLY ABOUT THE ENVIRONMENT

So how do we apply all this? What does this look like when we engage such issues as recycling, personal transportation choices, water conservation, endangered species, and climate change?

Christians who agree on our common theological calling to be good stewards of the environment can and will disagree about how best to do this in the real world. Theological principles need to be distinguished from prudent efforts. Just because some Christians don't think a particular policy will be effective (that is, actually do some good), it does not mean they are being unbiblical or are shirking their responsibility to care about the environment. To be prudent simply means to give careful thought and concern to the future. Jay Richards is again helpful: "Prudential judgments ... require careful analysis of the relevant scientific, economic, and political aspects of the issue. They require us to weigh costs and benefits, and to discern where facts leave off and fashion begins."[6] Caring for the environment does not mean that every endangered species must be saved at all costs or that any family who owns an SUV must trade it in for a hybrid Prius. It is more complicated than this.

ENGAGING THE CONFUSING AND CONTROVERSIAL ISSUE OF CLIMATE CHANGE

Our society runs on sound bites and emotive images. There are some benefits to this, but when it comes to complicated issues, you can't say what needs to be said in only thirty seconds. Who can argue with a picture of a polar bear stranded on melting ice? Not only is the climate change discussion emotionally charged; it's also extremely complicated. We have already established our God-given responsibility to be good stewards of the earth. So Christians *should* care about this issue (which actually is a large web of issues).

I suggest that slogans, scare tactics, denial, censorship, vilifying the opposition, and cute pictures of polar bears are not the way to have this public discussion, because they do not provide the general public with the *understanding* to move forward in any sort of intellectually responsible way. Everyone on TV seems to want to do X, Y, and Z, and it "feels" like the right thing to do (remember the pictures of the polar bears?). As a result, we end up with vastly oversimplified questions: "Are you for or against global warming?" and "Would you like to do something to stop environmental Armageddon [check yes or no])?" We could be asking more helpful questions in the context of a civil and reasoned discussion:[7]

1. Is the planet warming?
2. If the planet is warming, is human activity (like carbon dioxide emissions) causing it?
3. If the planet is warming and we're causing it, is that bad overall?
4. If the planet is warming and we're causing it and this is bad, would the policies commonly advocated (for example, Kyoto Protocol, legislative restrictions on carbon dioxide emissions) make any difference?

My intention here is not to argue for "right" answers to each of these. But I do want to make you stop and think. There is no single "biblical" answer to any of them; they are all answered by a complex interdisciplinary web of astrophysics, meteorology, probability theory, geology, and economics.[8] For example, according to reports by NASA on the surface temperature in the United States, the warmest year on record was 1934, followed by 1998. Fred Singer and Dennis Avery document that "four of the top ten years on record are now from the 1930s, before human emissions could have been responsible, while only three of the top ten (1998, 2006, 1999) are from the last ten years."[9] This fact raises interesting and important questions. But what seems clear from the empirical data is that we are currently in a period of global warming of between 0.3 and 0.8 degree centigrade over the last hundred years. The debate is between those who think this warming trend is anthropogenic (man-made) and caused by the emission of greenhouse gasses from human activities versus those who attribute the warming trend to historical climate cycles driven by natural causes (for example, solar induced). If honest, reasoned debate and discussion are shut down, then everyone on the planet is the worse for it—especially those in the developing world who will be most affected by policy decisions.

Environmentalist Dr. Bjørn Lomborg thinks the current global warming is both real and man-made. He also argues that the current polices (for example, CO_2 emissions and Kyoto) will do virtually nothing to forestall global warming and be ridiculously expensive (to the tune of $180 billion annually). Is this the best use of all that money? How could the money be spent more wisely?

Consider water. It is hard to think about economic growth and infrastructure if you have no clean water to drink. Lomborg writes, "There are one billion people without access to clean drinking water and two and a half billion without sanitation. We could bring basic water and sanitation to all of these people within a decade for about $4 billion annually."[10] If these estimates are accurate, let the numbers sink in: We could spend $180 billion every year for the next ten years on a policy that will have virtually no impact, or we could spend $4 billion a year and virtually solve the water and sanitation crisis in a decade. In doing so, we would hasten economic growth so that more of the world will be able to adapt to the impact of climate change in the future. Which would be better? And I didn't even mention what could be done for HIV/AIDS, malaria, and malnutrition. In light of these pressing priorities, does global warming deserve all of the attention it gets? Some things feel good when we do them, and other things actually do some good. If we really care and really want to love our local and global neighbors, we need to champion the latter.

A FEW FINAL REFLECTIONS

I have been a Christian for fifteen years and have never heard a sermon on God's view of the environment. In fact, I came across only one when I was specifically searching for it.[11] We can do better. Dan Story makes an important observation:

The mind-set that all environmentalists are liberal radicals not only hinders real progress in identifying and formulating strategies to combat potentially serious environmental problems, but it gives Christianity an ecological black eye—and compromises what could be tremendous evangelistic opportunities … This is particularly true among young people and college students—who are generally more sensitive to environmental problems than most Americans and, at the same time, tend to be unchurched.[12]

By failing to engage this issue, we create a stumbling block to their belief in the Christian God. What a sad consequence, because creation exists to point to a Creator who is there and is not silent. Christ-followers have a tremendous opportunity to engage the environmental concerns of our day with solid biblical and prudent thinking. We must do the hard work and careful thinking necessary to have something worthwhile to say when those opportunities arise.

RESOURCES FOR ENGAGING YOUR INTERSECTION

Books

- *Environmental Stewardship in the Judeo-Christian Tradition: Jewish, Catholic and Protestant Wisdom on the Environment* by Robert Sirico et al.
- *Money, Greed, and God: Why Capitalism Is the Solution and Not the Problem* by Jay Wesley Richards
- *Green Like God: Unlocking the Divine Plan for Our Planet* by Jonathan Merritt
- *Cool It: The Skeptical Environmentalist's Guide to Global Warming* by Bjørn Lomborg
- *Unstoppable Global Warming: Every 1,500 Years* by S. Fred Singer and Dennis T. Avery
- *Pollution and the Death of Man* by Francis Schaeffer
- *The Stewardship Study Bible*

Websites and DVDs

- www.cornwallalliance.org – The Cornwall Alliance, "For the Stewardship of Creation"
- www.creationcare.org – The Evangelical Environmental Network
- www.acton.org – The Acton Institute

ON BEING TRULY HUMAN

AN INTERVIEW WITH DALE AND JONALYN FINCHER

Jonathan Morrow: You are the founders of Soulation. Can you share a little bit of the vision behind it?

Dale and Jonalyn Fincher: Our vision is that the gospel has become too narrowly focused and needs room to breathe. We're dedicated to setting a healthy pace and perspective on what it means to walk *appropriately human* with Jesus. This affects our approach to everything as leaders. We model the truth that men and women can work together as partners. We work to be accessible by replying to our own e-mails, by spending quality time with people who attend our events, and by doing private online chatting each week for *Ask! LIVE*. To borrow a line from Hans Rookmaaker, we believe Jesus came not to make us Christians but to make us human. We find Christians often need to relearn the gospel. So our message is the same to both Christians and non-Christians.

Jonathan: How has your unique ministry as a husband-and-wife speaking team allowed you to engage and speak to our culture? Has bringing both male and female perspectives on issues created the opportunity for good discussions?

Dale and Jonalyn: With the increased visibility of alternative sexual lifestyles, most men and women are confused with what *masculine* and *feminine* mean. In the host culture, you hear messages that marriages don't work. In our churches, you can hear that the ultimate proof of womanhood is marriage with kids and the proof of manhood is a steady paycheck. Audiences tell us they enjoy watching us interact as much as they enjoy listening to our words. This opens doors and offers fresh perspectives on what men and women can be together.

In speaking, my (Jonalyn's) experience of childbirth allows me to speak on the topic of "born again" from a mother's perspective. Jesus' phrase to Nicodemus leans heavily on women as expositors to share this concept of God rebirthing us spiritually. My (Dale's) understanding of manhood with a partner like Jonalyn at my side pushes men beyond a warrior-leader or CEO mentality of masculinity and into service and love. We both work hard to shatter gender myths and remind followers of Jesus that no matter what the culture says, the fruit of the Spirit is neither pink nor blue.

Jonathan: As you think about our current intersection of Christianity and culture, what do you see as the greatest challenge Christians are facing? What do you see as the greatest opportunity for meaningful engagement?

Dale and Jonalyn: We see two major challenges. The first is the "Christian" tendency to think of others as inferior to us, their pursuit of truth less earnest, and their experiences of love less authentic. This may surprise us, but think of our Christian subculture's reputation of acting superior to others—the way we disdain homosexuals, promote the Founding Fathers as following *our brand* of Christianity, assume anybody with half a mind would believe the Bible we're quoting to them.

Truth is, we are on equal ground with our Muslim, Mormon, and Wiccan neighbors, all trying to figure out the truth of this world. Can we invite them to pursue truth with us? Will they see a fellow learner in each of us? If we try to get into another's shoes—an atheist, scientist, feminist—we may discover ways the good news reaches every human heart, beyond what we ever imagined. If we return to the "Manners of Loving Discourse" (a series we discuss in our recent book, *Coffee Shop Conversations*), we will see others as equals on the same journey.

The second challenge is that we, as a church, often believe that an idea or program is more true simply because it makes us feel safe or in control. Many evangelicals desperately want to preserve unexamined and contaminated forms of our subculture because it feels safe and delivers larger numbers, more political control, and larger financial resources. We've watched Christian scholars abandoned by their less-studied donors and constituents because truth became less of a concern than power and tradition. This creates "Christians" more dedicated to a pastor, movement, denomination, or political party than to Jesus, which dehumanizes us all. In turn, we end up inviting people to our brand of church rather than to the triune God of Israel.

Our opportunity is to reform within, remembering that the child of God is always growing with the humility of a child. Sometimes it isn't new initiatives and programs that help change a culture, but believers taking a refreshing approach, releasing control, and walking humbly with our God in small, local ways.

> **Dale and Jonalyn Fincher** are the founders of Soulation (www.soulation.org), a husband-and-wife team dedicated to navigate ideas, stir imaginations, and help others be appropriately human. Their recent book on helping the church humanize our neighbors and engage in loving dialogue is *Coffee Shop Conversations: Making the Most of Spiritual Small Talk* (Zondervan, 2010).

Conclusion

IMAGINE IF ...

Now is the time for us to stop being thirty years behind the times. Now is the time for us to gather confidence and lead.

J. P. Moreland, *Kingdom Triangle*

WE HAVE COVERED QUITE A BIT OF GROUND, and even though more could be said, I think we have covered enough in one sitting. At this point, it may be helpful to summarize the main ideas into a working model for engagement. I propose a three-step model—Understand, Transform, Engage. It's not so much a formula as an intentional process or mind-set. It's also not linear or static, but rather ongoing and dynamic—as we understand, as we are being transformed, and as we engage. Each of these takes place in the context of community (see the chart on page 267).[1]

UNDERSTAND

In the spirit of the sons of Issachar, the task of the Christian who seeks to engage our world is first to understand the times so that we might know what we should do (see 1 Chronicles 12:32). Survey the pressure points, challenges, and opportunities that exist and discover the blind spots of both the culture and the church. It is here that we serve a more prophetic role, but always in humility, love, gentleness, and respect and for the purpose of building up and enriching, not sniping or tearing down.[2]

In surveying our own intersection, we have gathered important observations. Ours is a Christian culture that has lost the ability to think biblically and Christianly about life. We struggle to understand and live all of life from God's perspective. In this sense, we are not much different from the culture we are trying to engage—out there is already in here. We have adopted an unbiblical "us versus them" mentality toward our culture, an attitude that causes us to withdraw or to attack. In our attempt to be relevant, we have at times sacrificed distinctiveness. However, this is not the way things should be. This has happened, at least in part, because we have failed to properly distinguish between the culture and the world system. In this book, we also have explored a biblical approach to cultural engagement that calls us to be Kingdom Citizens, Everyday Ambassadors, and Creative Image Bearers while embodying and demonstrating the radical love of Jesus Christ in community.

We also have discovered opportunities to maximize Sunday mornings as a catalyst for cultural engagement. We cast a vision for being missional and give people a desire for more (see appendix 1 for more ideas). This is especially important as we think about handing off our faith to the next generation. We must do a better job of equipping them for the challenges and opportunities they face. We seek to be faithful at our unique cultural intersection and leave the results to God.

To sum up, we need to understand the current state of both Christianity and culture and understand our calling to engage the culture while opposing the influences of the world system.

TRANSFORM

Because we Christians have not been effective in our engagement in proportion to our numbers, our message has not always been clear and winsome. But more often than not, the transformation we talk about is not happening, and so the watching world sees no significant difference between how they are living and how we are living.

We have observed that our thinking and social patterns (influenced by the world system) are absorbed in our bodies in the form of habits and tendencies — most of which we no longer think about because we are always in a hurry and have no time. And the time we do have, outside of our daily work, we spend on various forms of media and entertainment, which in turn has desensitized and distracted us from the mission of God. We have bought into a lie that happiness means satisfying our pleasure in the moment rather than virtuously seeking first the kingdom of God. Generally speaking, we have passed on this vision of life to the upcoming generation, and the disastrous consequences include unprecedented depression rates and the dominant religious worldview of American teenagers today — moralistic therapeutic deism.

We desperately need holistic transformation. And I have proposed that the way to cooperate with God's work is to begin thinking Christianly about all of life, growing in the knowledge of God, learning from Jesus how to live, and focusing on the heart of spiritual transformation. Doing this will give us the competence, confidence, and character to engage well.

ENGAGE

Our culture is increasingly unwilling to hear anything the church has to say. Engaging today will require a change in thinking. We must move beyond Sunday morning Christianity and learn how to speak with a compassionate, winsome, and informed voice to our culture. We are to engage in radical love for hurting people and seek solutions to the problems of injustice our culture faces. As we begin to comprehend the need for a distinctly Christian and substantial response to the culture, we should engage in thoughtful interaction with the questions and issues of our day because Christianity, as total truth, speaks to all of life. Moreover, we are actively engaged in creating "good" culture as we fulfill the creation mandate to make something of the world for the glory of God. Finally, as we are engaging in these other areas, we are inviting others to embrace the good news of the kingdom of God and making apprentices to Jesus who will then join in the ongoing calling of understanding, transforming, and engaging.

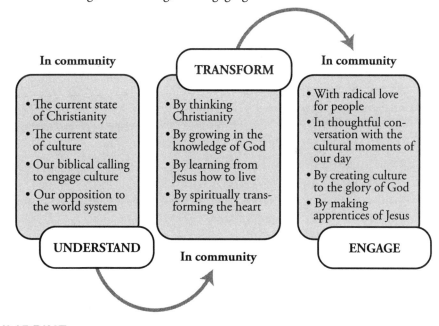

IMAGINE

Today's church is often perceived as old-fashioned, intolerant, unintelligent, and out of touch with reality. But what if the church were to once again become the place to which the world turned for answers? If we live out this God-saturated vision of life, *things* can change—*we* can change. *Imagine if ...*

> the church really became the place where our culture turned for answers again because of the radically loving community and the thoughtful faith that engages the most important questions of our day.

students caught a compelling vision for life with God that moved them to
reach this generation in new and powerful ways.

Christians were able to have meaningful conversations with believer and
nonbeliever alike about the most important questions of life and to share
the true story of Christianity.

Christians embodied a willingness to engage—not run from—challenging
ideas and were able to provide distinctly Christian answers to a confused
culture.

the next generation of Creative Image Bearers graduated from leading universities and became influential journalists, teachers, scientists, politicians,
filmmakers, entrepreneurs, and artists.

Christians became known for what we are *for* more than what we are *against*.

older Christians embraced their responsibility to personally encourage,
instruct, and mentor the next generation.

the first image that came to mind when people thought of Christianity was
radical love because of our opposition to injustice and our care of orphans,
the oppressed, and the unborn.

Christians led the way in recovering a sexual ethic that leads to human flourishing and true intimacy.

Christians seriously pursued discipleship to Jesus Christ as the one who has
the best knowledge about everything and then invited others into this
eternal way of life as well.

the marriages of Christians offered vision, hope, and life to our heartbroken
and cynical culture.

Christians led the way in defining what it means to be human in the biotech
century.

Christians embodied and announced a vision of happiness that is grounded
in the goodness and mission of God.

Now *that* is a vision worth pursuing! But it will become possible only if we
approach the task in a holistic and integrated fashion while submitting to our heavenly Father, being fueled by his grace and empowered by the Holy Spirit. If you aim
at nothing, you will hit it 100 percent of the time. We are called to be faithful to
the task God has set for us in our generation and then to leave the results to him.

My hope is that you have been both encouraged and challenged by this book.
Now comes the fun part. We must seek to apply this model to our own spheres
of influence and ministry settings. Be creative. Resist the urge to simply maintain
the status quo. There is nothing wrong with respectfully rocking the boat now and
then. Be intentionally and distinctively Christian; we don't want to change just for
the sake of change.

We can make a difference for Jesus Christ in this generation and equip those who come behind us to make a difference in the next. *It's not too late.* But the time for talking about it is coming to a close. Let's engage and look forward to the stories of God's powerful intervention in this generation—stories we will be able to tell for all eternity because we, like the sons of Issachar, understood the times and knew what we should do.

Appendix I

21 WAYS FOR YOUR CHURCH TO ENGAGE

1. Do service projects in your community in which you can join in with other churches for greater impact. Our church has participated in something called "Church Outside the Walls" — taking a Sunday morning to help repair schools, visit nursing homes, and do landscaping projects with no strings attached. It has been amazing to see walls break down. See how quickly perceptions of your church in the community will change. Pair up your children and youth ministries with older Christians so they can connect intergenerationally. This gives churches a vision for impacting the community with the good news of God. Ask the city council or mayor what needs to be done, and then do it.

2. Briefly mention current events relevant to faith and culture and include a reference to an article or blog for further exploration (for example, http://thinkchristianly.blogspot.com).

3. Sponsor a debate on the existence of God. Consider partnering with another church to sponsor a live event, or you can show a recent one on a DVD. There are a lot of debates out there to get ideas from. See www.reasonablefaith.org (William Lane Craig) and www.greatgoddebates.org (Dinesh D'Souza) for two excellent places to start. This will provide opportunities for conversations to occur.

4. As I describe in chapter 14, enlist the help of your artists and worship pastor to put on "Living Room Sessions" as a way to reach out to neighbors and friends in the warm environment of someone's home. Create environments in which artists can use their gifts to the glory of God in a winsome way.

5. Make it a goal that everyone in your church will know how to understand the gospel and effectively talk about it with others. If we don't emphasize it and train people, it won't happen. (My picks would be

the books [and DVD curriculum for] *Becoming a Contagious Christian* and *Tactics*, available at www.str.org.) In twelve weeks, you will have people who can confidently and competently engage people in spiritual conversations.

6. Create awareness for adoption and orphan care. Have an adoption Sunday and consider forming a team that leads the way in this area (www.hopefororphans.org). Highlight and interview families who have adopted and capture their stories on video to share.

7. Sponsor an art show or a short film festival at your church on an aspect of the Christian worldview. Give away scholarships ($1,000) to students at your local university (utilize campus ministries to advertise). Encourage your church to get involved and display the art. Perhaps require students to read the short book (64 pages) *Art and the Bible* by Francis Schaeffer.

8. Adopt a quarterly intersection morning during which you take a central cultural or worldview issue (for example, faith and science, the exclusivity of Jesus, or relativism) and equip your church on it.

9. Find people in your church to volunteer and teach in abstinence programs. This is a great way to impact the next generation and get adults involved. Find out about one excellent program at www.asitia.org.

10. Establish a church resource library. Stock it with the latest DVDs and books in order to equip families on their own schedule. Make a weekly display in a prominent place in your church that signals that you value engaging minds (the resources I suggest at the end of each chapter are a great place to start). For other resource lists in all areas of Christianity, see www.thinkchristianly.org.

11. Encourage people to register to vote. Work through "An Evangelical Manifesto" (www.anevangelicalmanifesto.com) or "The Manhattan Declaration" (www.manhattandeclaration.org) and provide copies for the congregation to read.

12. Take a spiritual field trip to a local Mormon temple, Buddhist temple, or Muslim mosque. In the six weeks leading up to the trip, study together what Christians believe and why and how it differs from the theology of the particular religion you are going to visit (for example, go through *Know What You Believe* by Paul Little or *World Religions and Cults 101* by Bruce Bickel and Stan Jantz). After your tour, spend an hour debriefing about what people learned and answering further questions.

13. Encourage your children and young people to partner with the Mocha Club (www.mocha.org). For the price of two mochas a month ($7), they can have a huge impact. Regularly show the video updates that the

Mocha Club provides to maintain vision and encouragement for the impact they are having through their donations.

14. As a church, adopt a school to pray for and actively seek to partner with to meet needs. Adults in your church can take advantage of opportunities to coach or tutor.

15. As a church, read and study Nancy Pearcey's *Total Truth*. This outstanding book will challenge people to love God with all of their lives, not just on Sunday mornings.

16. Have a monthly movie night accompanied by a study of Brian Godawa's book *Hollywood Worldviews*. A wonderful opportunity for outreach and worldview formation. Everyone loves a good movie!

17. Provide mentoring opportunities for the next generation. Develop a program that pairs older people in your church with high school students so they can be encouraged and prayed for on a regular basis. Consider buying a copy of *Welcome to College: A Christ-Follower's Guide for the Journey* for each student and have a mentor or parent go through it with them, a chapter a week (forty-two short chapters). This would be great to do for high school juniors and seniors or as a youth group study (www.thinkchristianly.org).

18. Increase global awareness by having a prayer night for the persecuted church (www.persecution.com) or a "prayer for the nations" night (www.joshuaproject.net).

19. Form groups that go through the Truth Project and TrueU. These are excellent DVD series that challenge and equip Christians to think about their faith and build a Christian worldview (visit www.focusonthefamily.com).

20. Bring in a speaker on end-of-life or other bioethical issues and challenges. We all will have to face these issues, but few of us are prepared (see www.cbhd.org). It is hard to think clearly in times of crisis and high emotion.

21. When Easter and Christmas roll around, prepare to engage the many "Who was Jesus?" and "Is the Bible reliable?" shows and media that pop up. A ready-made cultural moment!

Appendix 2

WHY WE THINK
THE WAY WE DO

MUCH HAS HAPPENED over the past three hundred years to shape why our generation thinks the way it does—as a culture and as the church. Understanding a little bit about how we got here will reveal some of our own blind spots and help us discover how to better speak in our culture. Here are ten significant factors:

1. *The anti-intellectual legacy of the Great Awakenings.* There were certainly many positive things that came out of these revivals, but a couple of the effects weakened the church. Perhaps the most significant were the shift to the emotional appeal in presenting the gospel and the popularization of Christian beliefs. One of the features of these movements was the anti-intellectual undercurrent. Because of this, the cultural soil of the 1800s was ripe for doctrinal confusion. During this time, the cults of Mormonism and Jehovah's Witnesses began in areas where people had been "converted" on emotions but not been grounded in the essential doctrines of Christianity. (The trend of biblical illiteracy continues today.) And as we will see with factors 2, 3, and 4, the church was unable to thoughtfully respond to the intellectual challenges.[1]

2. *Modern philosophy undermines the rationality of belief in God.* The combination of David Hume's (1711–1776) and Immanuel Kant's (1724–1804) new ideas undercut people's confidence that they could know that God exists. The writings of these philosophers argued that since God cannot be experienced by the five senses, God cannot be known (and later that the five senses themselves were not ultimately reliable). Therefore, belief in God, they reasoned, is not reasonable. Consequently, the new phenomena of prioritizing personal faith (that is, where beliefs can be true for me but not everyone else) over public knowledge began within modern Christianity (for example, think of a two-story

house where scientific facts are in the lower story of publically available truth and are what people actually know, but values, morality, and religion are taken out of the public realm of knowledge and placed in the upper story, where they must be maintained by an act of faith).[2]

3. *Higher criticism of the Bible challenges its authorship, historical accuracy, and authority.* Did Moses really write Genesis? Not according to nineteenth-century German scholarship. Moreover, the search for the historical Jesus was launched to try to recover who he was before the early church "theologized" him. Academics began to distinguish between the Jesus of history accessible to us and the Christ of faith, whom they claimed was invented later by Christians. The net result is that the word of God was seriously doubted at a time when belief in God was already under attack. Appeals to "private faith" continued in order to ward off these new intellectual challenges. This was the precursor to today's popular mentality that "you can personally believe whatever you want to, just as long as you don't think it's true."

4. *Darwinism replaces creationism as our cultural story of human origins.* In the midst of 2 and 3 above, Charles Darwin introduced his theory of evolution with the release of *On the Origin of the Species* (1859). It appeared that modern man no longer needed God to explain human origins. We are here because of natural selection — end of story. Sixty-six years later, in 1925, the Scopes Monkey Trial in Dayton, Tennessee (and the tidal wave of media coverage that the trial generated), marked the cultural shift away from creationism while galvanizing the stereotype that Christians were anti-science.

5. *Belief in God became "psychologized."* Enter Sigmund Freud and his psychology of unbelief. Since we know God doesn't exist (recall Hume and Kant), what is the best explanation for why so many people still believe in him? And since there is no evidence for God out there, something must be going on in our own minds — some neurosis or delusion. Freud's conclusion was that belief in God is the human search for a divine father figure in a scary and chaotic world; we then project the existence of God based on our neediness and inherent frailty.

6. *Science is the only intellectual game in town.* In order to purify ourselves from the uncertainties of religion and other inferior disciplines, our culture enshrined scientific knowledge. If someone on the news wants to make a point, what do they do? Trot out the scientist in the white lab coat as the authority. Philosopher J. P. Moreland sums this up well: "Scientific knowledge is taken to be so vastly superior that its claims always trump the claims made by other disciplines."[3] Science gives us

knowledge; Christianity relies on faith. The fact-value chasm continued to divide in the twentieth century, and secularism was on the rise.

7. *The rise of pluralism and relativism.* As industrialization occurred and global communication became readily accessible, the world became much smaller. Largely homogenous America was inundated with new ideas, new cultures, and new people. Today, Islam is not just something people read about; we have Muslim neighbors and coworkers. Mosques sit next to churches. What do we do with this? Surely there can't be only one way to view reality and only one way to God? Truth seems so intolerant and closed-minded. Consequently, the belief that truth is relative to individuals and cultures floods the university and broader culture. We can gain knowledge in the hard sciences, but ethics, values, and religion are relative—a matter of personal taste (like your favorite flavor of ice cream, for example). Christianity is no longer seen as unique because all religions are social constructions.

8. *The contemporary redefinition of happiness.* Happiness used to be defined as living a life of virtue (that is, human flourishing). Today it has been reduced to the satisfaction of desire (the unsavory word for this is *hedonism*), which has led to unprecedented depression in the baby boomer generation who had begun living only for themselves and their own pleasure. Psychologists have observed that this redefinition has led to the creation of "empty selves" who live only to consume. It is far easier to consume than to think or engage others. And many parents have lived out this version of happiness for their children. We see its effects with the release of every new sociological study.[4] Yet we were made to give ourselves to something much bigger than pursuing our own appetites (Matthew 6:33).

9. *Entertainment's displacement of religion as the unifying fabric of society.* Americans live to be entertained. We now organize and connect around sports events; our interest in the latest *American Idol*, *24*, *Lost*, and *CSI* episodes; and our passion for the latest movies. Everyone is on the Internet. The majority of Americans are plugged in to some form of digital technology for much of their day. For those who do go to church, the religious conversation usually ends about the time they sit down for Sunday lunch. The social media revolution is in full bloom. Cultural critic Dick Staub is right on target when he observes that "popular culture systematically teaches and preaches, informing its audience what matters most, fulfilling an educational role once occupied by schools and a spiritual role once filled by religion."[5] Neal Gabler argues that "it is not any ism but entertainment that is arguably the most pervasive, powerful, and

ineluctable force of our time—a force so overwhelming that it has finally metastasized into life."[6] And we have taken "amusement" to a whole new level! *Amuse* literally means "not thinking." Constant amusement leads to bored lives that are disengaged from the life Jesus offers and shaped according to the priorities and values of the world.[7]

10. *Progress leads to overloaded lives where busyness reigns supreme.* Well, we wanted more, and we got a lot more than we bargained for! There is an old saying (one that contains much truth) that if the devil can't make you bad, he'll make you busy. There are plenty of Christians who want to grow spiritually and engage their world, but they have no time. Correction, they have *made* no time. Consequently, we all suffer from hurry sickness at some level. Our culture worships activity and despises silence and reflection. People have scheduled out God, significant relationships, reflection, spiritual maturity, study, and serving others. It is hard to engage if all of your time is already spoken for.[8]

Life is not lived in a vacuum. Ideas have consequences. As we saw in the introduction to this book, the cumulative effect of these ten factors has led to a fragmented, confused, and largely ineffective Christianity: "The presence of evangelicals in America," notes theologian David Wells, "has barely caused a ripple."[9]

But as we have also seen, it doesn't have to be this way if we will *think Christianly.*

NOTES

Introduction: Welcome to Our Intersection

1. Richard Allen Greene, "Humanists Launch Huge 'Godless' Ad Campaign," http://religion.blogs.cnn.com/2010/11/09/humanists-launch-huge-godless-ad-campaign/ (accessed May 23, 2011).

2. Jon Meacham, "The End of Christian America," *Newsweek*, April 4, 2009, www.newsweek.com/id/192583 (accessed May 23, 2011).

3. Robert Putnam and David Campbell, *American Grace* (New York: Simon and Schuster, 2010), www.americangrace.org (accessed May 23, 2011)

4. David Kinnaman and Gabe Lyons, *unChristian: What a New Generation Really Thinks about Christianity ... and Why It Matters* (Grand Rapids: Baker, 2007), 39.

5. Christian Smith with Melinda Lundquist Denton, *Soul Searching: The Religious and Spiritual Lives of American Teenagers* (Oxford: Oxford University Press, 2005), 163.

6. *Soul Searching: A Movie about Teenagers and God*, DVD, directed by Michael Eaton and Timothy Eaton (Revelation Studios, 2007).

7. Depending on the survey, between 58 and 88 percent. "Survey: High School Seniors 'Graduating from God,'" www.christianpost.com/news/survey-high-school-seniors-graduating-from-god-31235/ (accessed February 2, 2010). See also Cathy Lynn Grossman, "Young Adults Aren't Sticking with Church," *USA Today*, August 6, 2007, www.usatoday.com/news/religion/2007-08-06-church-dropouts_N.htm (accessed February 5, 2010); "Is the Era of Age Segmentation Over?" *Christianity Today*, www.christianitytoday.com/le/communitylife/discipleship/istheeraofagesegmentationover.html, (accessed May 18, 2010); Reggie Joiner, Chuck Bomar, and Abbie Smith, *The Slow Fade: Why You Matter in the Story of Twentysomethings* (Colorado Springs: Cook, 2010), 23. However, Christian Smith puts this number at 36 percent (still a substantial number!) of teens who are abandoning their conservative Protestant (that is, evangelical) faith (see Christian Smith with Patricia Snell, *Souls in Transition: The Religious and Spiritual Lives of Emerging Adults* [Oxford: Oxford University Press, 2009], 108, 283). The category of "spiritual, but not religious" is also significantly on the rise, which makes it challenging to know what to do with some of these statistics. See John Blake, "Are There Dangers in Being 'Spiritual, but Not Religious,'" www.cnn.com/2010/LIVING/personal/06/03/spiritual.but.not.religious/index.html (accessed July 12, 2010).

8. Smith, *Soul Searching*, 89.

9. Os Guinness, *God in the Dark: The Assurance of Faith Beyond a Shadow of Doubt* (Wheaton, IL: Crossway, 1996), 82.

10. Smith, *Souls in Transition*, 294.

11. Ibid., 154–55.

12. Barna Group, "Barna Survey Examines Changes in Worldview among Christians over the Past 13 Years," www.barna.org/barna-update/article/21-transformation/252-barna-survey (accessed February 3, 2010).

13. Smith, *Souls in Transition*, 293.

14. Smith, *Soul Searching*, 170.

15. Kinnaman and Lyons, *unChristian*, 249.

16. George Barna, *The Seven Faith Tribes: Who They Are, What They Believe, and Why They Matter* (Wheaton, IL.: Tyndale House, 2009), 39.

17. Barna Group, "A Biblical Worldview Has a Radical Effect on a Person's Life," www.barna.org/barna-update/article/5-barna-update/131-a-biblical-worldview-has-a-radical-effect-on-a-persons-life (accessed February 5, 2010).

18. Ed Stetzer, Richie Stanley, and Jason Hayes, *Lost and Found: The Younger Unchurched and the Churches That Reach Them* (Nashville: Broadman, 2009), 21.

19. Pew Forum on Religion and Public Life, "U.S. Religious Landscape Survey," http://religions.pewforum.org/portraits (accessed February 5, 2010).

20. William Lane Craig, *Hard Questions, Real Answers* (Wheaton, IL: Crossway, 2003), 13.

21. Nancy Pearcey, *Total Truth: Liberating Christianity from Its Cultural Captivity* (Wheaton, IL: Crossway, 2004), 35.

22 David Kinnaman and Gabe Lyons, "Unchristian: Change the Perception," www.qideas.org/essays/unchristian-change-the-perception.aspx (accessed February 5, 2010).

23. Stetzer, Stanley, and Hayes, *Lost and Found*, 45. Yes, some of this can be chalked up to spiritual pride and self-deception — which afflicts every human — but we cannot dismiss all of these perceptions for this reason.

24. I have adapted this way of unpacking the concept of thinking Christianly from the helpful book by Josh McDowell and Sean McDowell, *The Unshakable Truth* (Eugene, Ore.: Harvest House), 17.

Chapter I: Culture Matters

1. From a Doctor of Ministry course lecture.

2. There are different senses in which *world* is used in the New Testament. I'm focusing on this particular expression of it. Other senses are seen when we understand the world as an object of God's love (John 3:16) and the propitiation of Jesus Christ (1 John 2:2).

3. For example, *world* is used in Acts 17:24 to refer to the created order; *world* in John 3:16 and 1 John 2:2 refers to all the people inhabiting the earth.

4. Barna Group, "Most American Christians Do Not Believe that Satan or the Holy Spirit Exist," www.barna.org/barna-update/article/12-faithspirituality/260-most-american-christians-do-not-believe-that-satan-or-the-holy-spirit-exist (accessed June 27, 2010).

5. Dallas Willard, *Renovation of the Heart: Putting on the Character of Christ* (Colorado Springs: NavPress, 2002), 98.

6. See Clinton E. Arnold, *3 Crucial Questions about Spiritual Warfare* (Grand Rapids: Baker, 1997); Chip Ingram, *The Invisible War: What Every Believer Needs to Know about Satan, Demons, and Spiritual Warfare* (Grand Rapids: Baker, 2006).

7. Willard, *Renovation of the Heart*, 100.

8. "Popular Culture," http://en.wikipedia.org/wiki/Pop_culture (accessed February 8, 2010).

9. "Hulu's Superbowl Commercial," http://public.youtranscript.com/zs/921.html (accessed February 8, 2010).

10. Quoted in Dick Staub, *The Culturally Savvy Christian: A Manifesto for Deepening Faith and Enriching Popular Culture in an Age of Christianity-Lite* (San Francisco: Jossey-Bass, 2007), 17.

11. Robert Velarde, "Television as the New Literature: Understanding and Evaluating the Medium," *Christian Research Journal* (2010): 46–52.

12. Francis A. Schaeffer, *The God Who Is There*, 30th anniv. ed. (Downers Grove, IL: InterVarsity, 1998), 31, emphasis added.

Chapter 2: Called to Engage

1. We are to faithfully engage politics and seek justice in our society, but we must do this as Christians and not fall into the temptation of politicizing the gospel.

2. This has been widely discussed. See the concise and helpful article by Michael Gerson and Peter Wehner, "The Success and the Failures of the Religious Right," www.huffingtonpost.com/michael-gerson/the-success-and-the-failu_b_758431.html (accessed November 22, 2010).

3. To help Christians unlock their God-authored potential, see Erik Rees, *S.H.A.P.E.: Finding and Fulfilling Your Unique Purpose for Life* (Grand Rapids: Zondervan, 2006). Greg Ogden writes, "An equipping ministry is one that assists each member of the body of Christ to function in accord with his or her God-given assigned function. This function is primarily determined by the gifts distributed by the Spirit and the shape of the call on one's life. Much of the will of God for persons is written into them. It is not so much a matter of finding something outside to give ourselves to, but to be attuned to our inner design and then find the context in which we best flourish" (Greg Ogden, *Unfinished Business: Returning the Ministry to the People of God*, rev. ed. [Grand Rapids: Zondervan, 2003], 152).

4. Tom Constable, *Tom Constable's Expository Notes on the Bible*, 2 Corinthians 5:20 (Galaxie Software, 2003).

5. See Brian Godawa, "Storytelling and Persuasion," in *Apologetics for a New Generation: A Biblical and Culturally Relevant Approach to Talking about God*, ed. Sean McDowell (Eugene, OR: Harvest House, 2009), 124.

6. See, for example, Steve Wilkens and Mark L. Sanford, *Hidden Worldviews: Eight Cultural Stories That Shape Our Lives* (Downers Grove, IL: InterVarsity, 2009).

7. Dick Staub, *The Culturally Savvy Christian: A Manifesto for Deepening Faith and Enriching Popular Culture in an Age of Christianity-Lite* (San Francisco: Jossey-Bass, 2007), 167 (the rest of his chapter is an excellent discussion of building bridges between kingdom and culture).

8. Nancy Pearcey, *Total Truth: Liberating Christianity from Its Cultural Captivity* (Wheaton, IL: Crossway, 2004), 47.

9. Ibid., 48.

10. Andy Crouch, *Culture Making: Recovering Our Creative Calling* (Downers Grove, IL: InterVarsity, 2008), 146.

11. James Davison Hunter, *To Change the World: The Irony, Tragedy, and Possibility of Christianity in the Late Modern World* (New York: Oxford University Press, 2010). Hunter argues for faithful presence, which I agree with, and speaks with great clarity about the sociology behind cultural change. But I don't think he fully represents the viewpoints of leaders like Chuck Colson, Os Guinness, and Robert George and the importance and scope of worldview formation. It is not an either-or, but a both-and. For Christians to have an impact through faithful presence, they must have a robust Christian worldview. Insofar as Hunter's work highlights and corrects the polarization and politicization of Christian engagement, it is helpful. However, we can and should love our neighbors faithfully through the political process as legitimate opportunities arise, along with making a difference in the other spheres of influence in which God has placed us.

12. Crouch, *Culture Making*, 90.

13. Ibid.

14. Ibid., 92.

15. Ibid.

Chapter 3: Equipping the Next Generation

1. Richard C. Levin, "Freshman Address: The Questions That Matter," http://opa.yale.edu/president/message.aspx?id=2 (accessed May 26, 2010).

2. Ibid., emphasis added. I am indebted to the helpful article by Paul J. Maurer, "Hollowed Halls: Confession of an Ivy League President," *Salvo* (Spring 2010).

3. See Neil Gross and Solon Simmons, "How Religious Are America's College and University Professors?", http://religion.ssrc.org/reforum/Gross_Simmons.pdf (accessed June 27, 2010).

4. Richard Rorty, "Universality and Truth," in *Rorty and His Critics*, ed. Robert B. Brandom (Oxford: Blackwell, 2000), 21–22.

5. Christian Smith with Patricia Snell, *Souls in Transition: The Religious and Spiritual Lives of Emerging Adults* (Oxford: Oxford University Press, 2009), 293.

6. Archibald D. Hart, *Thrilled to Death: How the Endless Pursuit of Pleasure Is Leaving Us Numb* (Nashville: Nelson, 2007), 73–96.

7. Institute for American Values, "Hardwired to Connect: The Scientific Case for Authoritative Communities"; see the executive summary at www.americanvalues.org/html/hardwired_-_ex_summary.html (accessed June 27, 2010).

8. Christian Smith with Melinda Lundquist Denton, *Soul Searching: The Religious and Spiritual Lives of American Teenagers* (New York: Oxford University Press, 2005), 89.

9. David Kinnaman and Gabe Lyons, *unChristian: What a New Generation Really Thinks about Christianity—and Why It Matters* (Grand Rapids: Baker, 2007), 81.

10. Smith, *Souls in Transition*, 239.

11. Steve Wilkens and Mark L. Sanford, *Hidden Worldviews: Eight Cultural Stories That Shape Our Lives* (Downers Grove, IL: InterVarsity, 2009), 25. Their summary is based

on Steven Garber, *The Fabric of Faithfulness: Weaving Together Belief and Behavior*, expanded ed. (Downers Grove, IL: InterVarsity, 2007).

12. Fuller Youth Institute, "Hurt: Inside the World of Today's Teenagers," http://fulleryouthinstitute.org/2005/08/hurt (accessed June 27, 2010).

13. Josh McDowell, "A Fresh Apologetics: Relationships That Transform," in *Apologetics for a New Generation: A Biblical and Culturally Relevant Approach to Talking about God*, ed. Sean McDowell (Eugene, OR: Harvest House, 2010), 60.

14. Andy Stanley and Stuart Hall, *The Seven Checkpoints: Seven Principles Every Teenager Needs to Know* (West Monroe, La.: Howard, 2001), 101–30. I have found this book to be very helpful.

15. See Christian Smith with Melinda Lundquist Denton, *Soul Searching: The Religious and Spiritual Lives of American Teenagers* (Oxford: Oxford University Press, 2005).

16. Sean McDowell, *Apologetics for a New Generation* (Eugene, OR: Harvest House, 2009), 20.

17. Greg Ogden, *Unfinished Business: Returning the Ministry to the People of God*, rev. ed. (Grand Rapids: Zondervan, 2003), 259.

18. Smith, *Souls in Transition*, 286.

19. Ibid., 255.

20. See "Is the Era of Age Segmentation Over: An Interview with Kara Powell," *Christianity Today*, www.christianitytoday.com/le/communitylife/discipleship/istheeraofagesegmentationover.html (accessed June 27, 2010).

21. Reggie Joiner, *Think Orange: Imagine the Impact When Church and Family Collide* (Colorado Springs: Cook, 2009), 23.

Chapter 4: Thinking Christianly about All of Life

1. James W. Sire, *The Universe Next Door: A Basic Worldview Catalog*, 5th ed. (Downers Grove, IL: InterVarsity, 2009), 20.

2. See Steve Wilkens and Mark L. Sanford, *Hidden Worldviews: Eight Cultural Stories That Shape Our Lives* (Downers Grove, IL: InterVarsity, 2009).

3. A prominent sentiment today is that language creates reality, or at least we have no direct access to reality. Rejecting this view, Darrell Bock suggests (correctly, I believe) that evangelicals adopt "critical realism," by which he means "there is a reality external to us … We have awareness and knowledge of it, so that our accounts of that reality at least roughly correspond with it, though we're not infallible or exhaustive in our understanding of it" (Darrell L. Bock, *Purpose-Directed Theology: Getting Our Priorities Right in Evangelical Controversies* [Downers Grove, IL: InterVarsity Press, 2002], 22). This concept is discussed in more detail in R. Scott Smith, *Truth and the New Kind of Christian: The Emerging Effects of Postmodernism in the Church* (Wheaton, IL: Crossway, 2005), 170–90. For a more thorough analysis of postmodernism in theology and the church, see Millard J. Erickson, Paul Kjoss Helseth, and Justin Taylor, eds., *Reclaiming the Center: Confronting Evangelical Accommodation in Postmodern Times* (Wheaton, IL: Crossway, 2004).

4. *The Unshakable Truth* by Josh and Sean McDowell does a great job of demonstrating where doctrine and life connect.

5. Islam will be an ever-increasing force to deal with in the years ahead; see Philip

Jenkins, *The Next Christendom: The Coming of Global Christianity* (Oxford: Oxford University Press, 2002).

6. James Davison Hunter, *Culture Wars: The Struggle to Define America* (New York: Basic, 1991), 211.

7. Charles W. Colson and Nancy Pearcey, *How Now Shall We Live?* (Wheaton, IL: Tyndale House, 1999), 26.

8. Bertrand Russell, *Why I Am Not a Christian* (New York: Simon and Schuster, 1957), 107, 115.

9. Richard Dawkins, *River Out of Eden: A Darwinian View of Life* (New York: Basic, 1995), 133.

10. Francis Beckwith, William Lane Craig, and J. P. Moreland, *To Everyone an Answer: A Case for the Christian Worldview* (Downers Grove, IL: InterVarsity, 2004), 373.

11. Francis Beckwith and Gregory Koukl, *Relativism: Feet Firmly Planted in Mid-Air* (Grand Rapids: Baker, 1998), 13.

12. The *Cambridge Dictionary of Philosophy* defines postmodernism as "a complex cluster concept that includes the following elements: an anti- (or post-) epistemological standpoint; anti-essentialism; anti-realism; anti-foundationalism; opposition to transcendental arguments and transcendental standpoints; rejection of the picture of knowledge as accurate representation; rejection of truth as correspondence to reality, rejection of the very idea of canonical descriptions; rejection of final vocabularies, that is, rejection of principles, distinctions, and descriptions that are thought to be unconditionally binding for all times, persons, and places; and a suspicion of grand narratives" (*The Cambridge Dictionary of Philosophy*, ed. Robert Audi [Cambridge: Cambridge University Press, 1999], 725).

13. A theme developed in Nancy Pearcey, *Total Truth: Liberating Christianity from Its Cultural Captivity* (Wheaton, IL: Crossway, 2004).

14. C. S. Lewis, *The Weight of Glory and Other Addresses* (New York: Macmillan, 1980, 92.

15. This is my way of summarizing Ronald Nash's view on how to choose a worldview (Ronald H. Nash, *Worldviews in Conflict: Choosing Christianity in a World of Ideas* [Grand Rapids: Zondervan, 1992], 54–72).

16. Pearcey, *Total Truth*, 396.

17. For a helpful introduction, see Kenneth R. Samples, *A World of Difference: Putting Christian Truth-Claims to the Worldview Test* (Grand Rapids: Baker, 2007), 39–72.

Chapter 5: Cultivating a Thoughtful Faith

1. In contrast to our subjective experience and the testimony of the Holy Spirit in our lives. Other people do not have access to our experiences. But they do have access, for example, to the historical evidence for the resurrection and scientific evidence for the beginning of the universe.

2. For more, see Sean McDowell, *Apologetics for a New Generation* (Eugene, OR: Harvest House, 2009).

3. Jude 3 (NLT).

4. Quoted in J. P. Moreland, *Love Your God with All Your Mind: The Role of Reason in the Life of the Soul* (Colorado Springs: NavPress, 1997), 85.

5. Os Guinness, *God in the Dark: The Assurance of Faith beyond a Shadow of Doubt* (Wheaton, IL: Crossway, 1996).

6. This point is driven home from information I learned from J. P. Moreland and William Lane Craig—two of my heroes of the faith. My understanding of the nature and importance of apologetics has been greatly shaped by them, and I admire their example of courageous faith. Craig expands on this and other reasons for apologetics in William Lane Craig, *On Guard: Defending Your Faith with Reason and Precision* (Colorado Springs: Cook, 2010).

7. J. Gresham Machen, *What Is Christianity?* (Grand Rapids: Eerdmans, 1951), 162.

8. Charles Malik, *The Two Tasks* (Westchester, IL: Cornerstone, 1980), 32.

9. Christopher Hitchens, *God Is Not Great: How Religion Poisons Everything* (New York: Twelve, 2007), 282.

10. Richard Dawkins, *The God Delusion* (New York: Houghton Mifflin, 2008), 5.

11. Ibid.

12. C. S. Lewis, *The Weight of Glory and Other Addresses* (New York: Macmillan, 1980), 28.

13. Tim Keller, "Preparing for the Big Issues Facing the Church," http://thegospel coalition.org/blogs/tgc/2010/03/01/preparing-for-the-big-issues-facing-the-church (accessed March 15, 2010).

14. William Lane Craig, *Reasonable Faith: Christian Truth and Apologetics*, 3rd ed. (Wheaton, IL: Crossway, 2008), 20.

15. See Quentin Smith, "The Metaphilosophy of Naturalism," *Philo* 4/2 (2001), http://www.philoonline.org/library/smith_4_2.htm (accessed May 18, 2011).

Chapter 6: Confident Engagement Flows from Knowledge

1. J. I. Packer, *Knowing God*, 20th anniv. ed. (Downers Grove, IL: InterVarsity, 1993), 14–15.

2. Regardless of one's view on the eschatology of Daniel 11, his point is clear that knowledge of God leads to resisting the corrupting influences of the world.

3. Nancy Pearcey, *Saving Leonardo: A Call to Resist the Secular Assault on Mind, Morals, and Meaning* (Nashville: Broadman, 2010), 31–32.

4. Philosophers typically define knowledge as "justified true belief." See Richard Feldman, *Epistemology* (Foundations of Philosophy Series; Upper Saddle River, NJ: Prentice Hall, 2003).

5. Dallas Willard, *Knowing Christ Today: Why We Can Trust Spiritual Knowledge* (New York: HarperOne, 2009), 15.

6. Quoted in *The Apologetics Study Bible*, eds. J. P. Moreland, Paul Copan, and Ted Cabal (Nashville: Broadman, 2007), 1766.

7. Garrett J. DeWeese and J. P. Moreland, *Philosophy Made Slightly Less Difficult: A Beginner's Guide to Life's Big Questions* (Downers Grove, IL: InterVarsity, 2005), 77. I believe that this approach, called "particularism," is the best way to solve the problem of skepticism (the problem of the criterion).

8. And valid deductive arguments. But someone can always deny a premise to escape a conclusion.

9. Timothy J. Keller, *The Reason for God: Belief in an Age of Skepticism* (New York: Dutton, 2008).

10. John Ortberg, *Faith and Doubt* (Grand Rapids: Zondervan, 2008), 175–76.

11. Bertrand Russell, *Religion and Science* (New York: Oxford University Press, 1997), 243.
12. See Sean McDowell and Jonathan Morrow, *Is God Just a Human Invention? And Seventeen Other Questions Raised by the New Atheists* (Grand Rapids: Kregel, 2010).
13. Andy Stanley, *It Came from Within!* (Sisters, OR: Multnomah, 2006), 147.
14. Ibid., 149. For more on biblical forgiveness, see Nancy Leigh DeMoss and Lawrence Kimbrough, *Choosing Forgiveness: Your Journey to Freedom* (Chicago: Moody Press, 2006).
15. Stanley, *It Came from Within!*, 151.
16. Martin Seligman, "Boomer Blues," *Psychology Today* 18 (October 1988): 50–55.
17. Paul Campos, "We're Healthy and Wealthy, But Not Happy," *Orange County Register* (July 10, 2005), 1.
18. Erik Thoennes, e-mail correspondence (Fall 2010).
19. A. W. Tozer, *The Knowledge of the Holy: The Attributes of God and Their Meaning in the Christian Life* (New York: HarperCollins, 1992), 1.
20. J. P. Moreland, *Kingdom Triangle: Recover the Christian Mind, Renovate the Soul, Restore the Spirit's Power* (Grand Rapids: Zondervan, 2007), 137.
21. I state this because of the tendency to minimize the importance and even possibility of systematic theology. I am not arguing for a reductionism, which seeks to extract all the propositions from the narratives of Scripture because they are what is really important at the end of the day, but I do want to resist the postmodern approach of reducing Christianity to a story that is true for only the Christian community. Christianity is the true story that defines reality—it is total truth.
22. David K. Clark, *To Know and Love God: Method for Theology* (Wheaton, IL: Crossway, 2003), 424.
23. I am indebted to Garry DeWeese for his explanation of this relationship.

Chapter 7: Becoming Like the Jesus the World Needs [1]

1. John Ortberg, *Love Beyond Reason: Moving God's Love from Your Head to Your Heart* (Grand Rapids: Zondervan, 1998), 79.
2. I am indebted to several people for informing and forming the ideas of this chapter—especially John Ortberg, Dallas Willard, and J. P. Moreland. I make no claim to the originality of the content here, though I have tried to organize and synthesize it in a way that seems helpful to me. I am deeply grateful. On a side note, I was encouraged to learn that John Ortberg had a similar experience when he first encountered the writings of Dallas Willard.
3. For an excellent exploration of the person and work of Christ, see Fred Sanders and Klaus Issler, *Jesus in Trinitarian Perspective: An Introductory Christology* (Nashville: Broadman, 2007).
4. A helpful phrase often used by John Ortberg in his sermons.
5. Darrell Bock, *Recovering the Real Lost Gospel: Reclaiming the Gospel as Good News* (Nashville: Broadman, 2010), 28.
6. Dallas Willard, *The Divine Conspiracy* (San Francisco: HarperSanFrancisco, 1998), 95.
7. See the excellent DVD *Faith Lessons: In the Dust of the Rabbi*, vol. 6, by Ray Vanderlaan.
8. Dallas Willard, *Renovation of the Heart: Putting on the Character of Christ* (Colorado Springs: NavPress, 2002), 242.

9. Dallas Willard, *The Spirit of the Disciplines: Understanding How God Changes Lives*, 2nd ed. (San Francisco: Harper, 1999), 7.

10. John Ortberg, *The Life You've Always Wanted: Spiritual Disciplines for Ordinary People* (Grand Rapids: Zondervan, 2002), 41–48. His insights were helpful for me to connect some dots.

11. See Bill Hull, *The Complete Book of Discipleship: On Being and Making Followers of Christ* (Colorado Springs: NavPress, 2006), 142–44.

12. Ortberg, *The Life You've Always Wanted*, 45.

13. Ibid., 46.

14. Ibid., 47. This is a common understanding of a discipline.

15. Dallas Willard, *The Great Omission: Reclaiming Jesus' Essential Teachings on Discipleship* (New York: HarperCollins, 2006), 74.

16. Dallas Willard, *The Divine Conspiracy: Rediscovering Our Hidden Life in God* (San Francisco: HarperSanFrancisco, 1997), 418.

17. Ortberg, *Love Beyond Reason*, 79.

18. Andy Stanley, *The Best Question Ever* (Sisters, OR: Multnomah, 2004), 183–85. See also his *The Principle of the Path: How to Get from Where You Are to Where You Want to Be* (Nashville: Nelson, 2008).

Chapter 8: Becoming Like the Jesus the World Needs [II]

1. Again, I want to acknowledge my great indebtedness to the work of Dallas Willard for my summary discussion of the heart, flesh, desire, will, mind, and the VIM pattern of change. He goes into much more detail in *Renovation of the Heart* (Colorado Springs: NavPress, 2002), and in *The Divine Conspiracy* (San Francisco: HarperSanFrancisco, 1997). I highly recommend studying both of these books.

2. See George Eldon Ladd and Donald Alfred Hagner, *A Theology of the New Testament*, rev. ed. (Grand Rapids: Eerdmans, 1993), 515–20.

3. Note the following passages: "For the mind set on the flesh is death, but the mind set on the Spirit is life and peace" (Romans 8:6 NASB). "For the flesh sets its desire against the Spirit" (Galatians 5:17 NASB). "Keep watching and praying that you may not enter into temptation; the spirit is willing, but the flesh is weak" (Matthew 26:41 NASB). "Abstain from fleshly lusts which wage war against the soul" (1 Peter 2:11 NASB). Compare James 4:1–3.

4. I am not advocating perfectionism here. But we tend to aim too low when it comes to the level of real spiritual transformation that can occur in our lives by the power of God (cf. 2 Peter 1:3–4).

5. C. S. Lewis, *Mere Christianity* (New York: Simon and Schuster, 1996), 119–22.

6. For more on this, see Timothy J. Keller, *Counterfeit Gods: The Empty Promises of Money, Sex, and Power, and the Only Hope That Matters* (New York: Dutton, 2009).

7. "Impulsive will must give way to reflective will. The reflective will is oriented toward what is good for the person as a whole … not merely to what is desired" (Dallas Willard, "Spiritual Formation and the Warfare between the Flesh and the Human Spirit," www.dwillard.org/articles/artview.asp?artID=132 (accessed July 6, 2010).

8. Willard, *Renovation of the Heart*, 95.

9. Dallas Willard and Jan Johnson, *Renovation of the Heart in Daily Practice: Experiments in Spiritual Transformation* (Colorado Springs: NavPress, 2006), 72.

10. Willard, *Renovation of the Heart*, 248.

11. See J. P. Moreland, *The Recalcitrant Imago Dei: Human Persons and the Failure of Naturalism* (London: SCM Press, 2009); J. P. Moreland and Scott B. Rae, *Body and Soul: Human Nature and the Crisis in Ethics* (Downers Grove, IL: InterVarsity, 2000).

12. Jeffrey Schwartz and Sharon Begley, *The Mind and the Brain: Neuroplasticity and the Power of Mental Force* (New York: Regan, 2002); William D. Backus and Marie Chapian, *Telling Yourself the Truth* (Minneapolis: Bethany House, 2000).

13. See J. P. Moreland and Klaus Issler, *The Lost Virtue of Happiness: Discovering the Disciplines of the Good Life* (Colorado Springs: NavPress, 2006), 85–106; John Ortberg, *God Is Closer Than You Think* (Grand Rapids: Zondervan, 2005), 77–94.

14. Robert S. McGee, *The Search for Significance*, rev. ed. (Nashville: Word, 2003), 141–42.

15. See Dallas Willard, "Living a Transformed Life Adequate to Our Calling," www.dwillard.org/articles/artview.asp?artID=119 (accessed July 6, 2010).

16. David G. Benner, *Sacred Companions: The Gift of Spiritual Friendship and Direction* (Downers Grove, IL: InterVarsity, 2002), 16.

17. Richard A. Swenson, *Margin: Restoring, Emotional, Physical, Financial, and Time Reserves to Overloaded Lives* (Colorado Springs: NavPress, 2002).

18. John Ortberg, *The Life You've Always Wanted: Spiritual Disciplines for Ordinary People* (Grand Rapids: Zondervan, 2002), 76–77.

19. Ibid., 77.

20. Willard, *Renovation of the Heart*, 85–91.

21. Willard puts it all together: "Nourishing our mind with good and godly ideas, images, information, and the ability to think creates our *vision* … From these, we *intend* to be formed so that God is a constant presence in our mind, crowding out false ideas, destructive images, misinformation about God, and crooked beliefs. As for means, certain tried and true disciplines aid us in the transformation … of our thought life toward the mind of Christ. We cannot transform our ideas, images, information, or thought processes into Christlikeness by direct effort, but we can adopt certain practices that indirectly have that effect" (Willard and Johnson, *Renovation of the Heart in Daily Practice*, 80).

Chapter 9: Can We Do That in Church?

1. "Trusting Christ does not take the form of merely believing things about him. Moreover, knowing the 'right answers' does not mean we truly believe them. To believe them means we are set to act as if these 'right answers' are true. Perhaps the hardest thing for sincere Christians to come to grips with is the level of real unbelief in their own lives: the unformulated skepticism about Jesus that permeates all dimensions of their being and undermines the efforts they do make toward Christlikeness" (Dallas Willard and Jan Johnson, *Renovation of the Heart in Daily Practice: Experiments in Spiritual Transformation* [Colorado Springs: NavPress, 2006], 60).

2. J. P. Moreland and Klaus Issler, *In Search of a Confident Faith: Overcoming Barriers to Trusting in God* (Downers Grove, IL: InterVarsity, 2008), 22.

3. Ibid.

4. Dallas Willard, *The Divine Conspiracy: Rediscovering Our Hidden Life in God* (San Francisco: HarperSanFrancisco, 1997), 92.

5. See Chris Beard, "Why Ida Fossil Is Not the Missing Link," www.newscientist.com/article/dn17173-why-ida-fossil-is-not-the-missing-link.html (accessed July 7, 2010); Brian Switek, "The Dangerous Link between Science and Hype," www.timesonline.co.uk/tol/comment/columnists/guest_contributors/article6360606.ece (accessed July 7, 2010); Jonathan Morrow, "Ardi, the Human Ancestor Who Wasn't," http://think christianly.blogspot.com/2010/06/ardi-human-ancestor-who-wasnt.html (accessed July 7, 2010).

6. Quoted in William A. Dembski and Jonathan Wells, *The Design of Life: Discovering Signs of Intelligence in Biological Systems* (Dallas: Foundation for Thought and Ethics, 2008), 68.

7. See the excellent DVD *Darwin's Dilemma*, directed by Lad Allen (La Habra, CA: Illustra Media, 2009).

8. Henry Gee, *In Search of Deep Time* (New York: Free Press, 1999), 23, 32, 116–117. See also Dembski and Wells, *The Design of Life*, 57–92.

Chapter 10: Jesusanity versus Christianity

1. Ben Witherington, *The Gospel Code: Novel Claims about Jesus, Mary Magdalene, and Da Vinci* (Downers Grove, IL: InterVarsity, 2004), 1.

2. Back of the box of Jesus Nodder.

3. Darrell L. Bock and Daniel B. Wallace, *Dethroning Jesus: Exposing Popular Culture's Quest to Unseat the Biblical Christ* (Nashville: Nelson, 2007), 4.

4. My intention is not to diminish childlike faith in God or his Word—this is a good thing (though as C. S. Lewis said, we must go beyond a childish faith). Not everyone has to have studied textual criticism to trust the Bible. But in the face of sophisticated charges—which are everywhere today—we must give people more than just the option of accepting the Bible by willpower alone. For more on how we know Christianity to be true as believers, see William Lane Craig, *Reasonable Faith: Christian Truth and Apologetics*, 3rd ed. (Wheaton, IL: Crossway, 2008), 29–62.

5. A prime example people in our churches (especially students) encounter is that Jesus is no different from the pagan myths of Osiris or Mithras. For case-by-case refutations of charges that Christianity borrowed from pagan mystery religions, see the excellent work of J. Ed Komoszewski, M. James Sawyer, and Daniel B. Wallace, *Reinventing Jesus: How Contemporary Skeptics Miss the Real Jesus and Mislead Popular Culture* (Grand Rapids: Kregel, 2006), 220–58; Lee Strobel, *The Case for the Real Jesus: A Journalist Investigates Current Attacks on the Identity of Christ* (Grand Rapids: Zondervan, 2007), 157–87; Ronald H. Nash, *The Gospel and the Greeks: Did the New Testament Borrow from Pagan Thought?*, 2nd ed. (Phillipsburg, N.J.: P&R, 2003).

6. I have written more fully about these questions in *Is God Just a Human Invention? And Seventeen Other Questions Raised by the New Atheists*, *The Apologetics Study Bible for Students*, and *Welcome to College: A Christ-Follower's Guide for the Journey*. For more study, see the books mentioned at the end of this chapter.

7. Coptic Gospel of Thomas, sayings 113 and 114, cited in Bart D. Ehrman, *Lost Scriptures: Books That Did Not Make It into the New Testament* (Oxford: Oxford University Press, 2003), 28.

8. Craig Evans, *Fabricating Jesus: How Modern Scholars Distort the Gospels* (Downers Grove, IL; InterVarsity, 2008).

9. Larry W. Hurtado, *How on Earth Did Jesus Become a God? Historical Questions about Earliest Devotion to Jesus* (Cambridge, UK: Eerdmans, 2005), 25. His most thorough treatment is in *Lord Jesus Christ: Devotion to Jesus in Earliest Christianity* (Cambridge, UK: Eerdmans, 2003).

10. For the best and most accessible treatment of this evidence, see Gary R. Habermas and Michael R. Licona, *The Case for the Resurrection of Jesus* (Grand Rapids: Kregel, 2004). For more on Christians having believed in Jesus' resurrection from the beginning, see Gary Habermas, "The Resurrection of Jesus Time Line," in *Contending with Christianity's Critics: Answering New Atheists and Other Objectors*, eds. Paul Copan and William Lane Craig (Nashville: Broadman, 2009), 113–25.

Chapter 11: Truth, Tolerance, and Relativism

1. See Philip Jenkins, *The Next Christendom: The Coming of Global Christianity*, rev. ed. (Oxford: Oxford University Press, 2007).

2. C. John Sommerville, *The Decline of the Secular University* (Oxford: Oxford University Press, 2006), 19.

3. "What kind of world would it be if relativism were true? It would be a world in which nothing was wrong—nothing is considered evil or good, nothing is worthy of praise or blame. It would be a world in which justice and fairness are meaningless concepts, in which there would be no accountability, no possibility of moral improvement, no moral discourse. And it would be a world in which there is no tolerance" (Francis Beckwith and Gregory Koukl, *Relativism: Feet Firmly Planted in Mid-Air* [Grand Rapids: Baker, 1998], 69).

4. C. S. Lewis, *God in the Dock: Essays on Theology and Ethics*, ed. Walter Hooper (Grand Rapids: Eerdmans, 1970), 108–9.

5. Ravi Zacharias, quoted in Norman L. Geisler and Paul K. Hoffman, *Why I Am a Christian: Leading Thinkers Explain Why They Believe* (Grand Rapids: Baker, 2001), 268.

6. Lesslie Newbigin, *The Gospel in a Pluralist Society* (Grand Rapids: Eerdmans, 1989), 9.

7. Alvin Plantinga, "Pluralism," in *The Philosophical Challenge of Religious Diversity*, eds. Philip L. Quinn and Kevin Meeker (New York: Oxford University Press, 2000), 179.

8. Ross Douthat, "Let's Talk about Faith," *New York Times*, January 10, 2010, www.nytimes.com/2010/01/11/opinion/11douthat.html (accessed April 5, 2010).

9. Brett Kunkle, "Is Jesus the Only Way," in *The Apologetics Study Bible for Students* (Nashville: Broadman, 2010), 1140.

Chapter 12: Taking the Bible Seriously

1. Here is a helpful definition of biblical inerrancy: "The Bible (in its original writings) properly interpreted in light of which culture and communication means had developed by the time of its composition will be completely true (and therefore not false) in all that it affirms, to the degree of precision intended by the author, in all matters relating to God and his creation" (David S. Dockery, *Christian Scripture: An Evangelical Perspective on Inspiration, Authority, and Interpretation* [Nashville: Broadman, 1995], 64).

2. This section is slightly modified from my appendix in Sean McDowell and Jonathan Morrow, *Is God Just a Human Invention? And Seventeen Other Questions Raised by the New Atheists* (Grand Rapids: Kregel, 2010).

3. J. Ed Komoszewski, M. James Sawyer, and Daniel B. Wallace, *Reinventing Jesus: How Contemporary Skeptics Miss the Real Jesus and Mislead Popular Culture* (Grand Rapids: Kregel, 2006), 82. Wallace provides an excellent and accessible introduction to textual criticism in this book (pp. 53–117).

4. Bart D. Ehrman, *Misquoting Jesus: The Story Behind Who Changed the Bible and Why* (New York: HarperCollins, 2005), 90.

5. Darrell L. Bock and Daniel B. Wallace, *Dethroning Jesus: Exposing Popular Culture's Quest to Unseat the Biblical Christ* (Nashville: Nelson, 2007), 55–58.

6. Ibid., 60.

7. Ibid., 70.

8. Lisa Miller, "Our Mutual Joy," *Newsweek*, December 6, 2008, www.newsweek. com/2008/12/05/our-mutual-joy.html (accessed May 27, 2010).

9. Timothy J. Keller, *The Reason for God: Belief in an Age of Skepticism* (New York: Dutton, 2008), 109–10.

10. The slavery in ancient Israel was "qualitatively vastly different from slavery in the large imperial civilizations — the contemporary ancient Near Eastern empires, and especially the latter empires of the Greeks and Romans. There the slave markets were glutted with captives of war and displaced peoples, and slaves were put to degrading and dehumanizing labour. And, of course, Israelite slavery was even more different from the ghastly commercialized and massive-scale slave trade that Arabs, Europeans, and Americans perpetrated on Africa" (Christopher J. H. Wright, *Old Testament Ethics for the People of God* [Downers Grove, IL: InterVarsity, 2004], 333).

11. I deal with the Bible and slavery issue in greater detail in McDowell and Morrow, *Is God Just a Human Invention? And Seventeen Other Questions Raised by the New Atheists.*

12. J. Scott Duvall and J. Daniel Hays, *Journey into God's Word: Your Guide to Understanding and Applying the Bible* (Grand Rapids: Zondervan, 2008), 131.

13. Gordon D. Fee and Douglas K. Stuart, *How to Read the Bible for All Its Worth*, 3rd ed. (Grand Rapids: Zondervan, 2003), 179.

14. Paul Copan, *How Do You Know You're Not Wrong? Responding to Objections That Leave Christians Speechless* (Grand Rapids: Baker, 2005), 197. Copan has a helpful discussion of the Law of Moses on pages 170–197.

15. Fee and Stuart, *How to Read the Bible for All Its Worth*, 167.

16. Miller, "Our Mutual Joy," *Newsweek*, December 6, 2008, www.newsweek. com/2008/12/05/our-mutual-joy.html (accessed May 27, 2010).

17. I relied on the helpful discussions in Joe Dallas, *The Gay Gospel? How Pro-Gay Advocates Misread the Bible* (Eugene, OR: Harvest House, 2007), 159–216; Dennis P. Hollinger, *The Meaning of Sex: Christian Ethics and the Moral Life* (Grand Rapids: Baker, 2009), 171–97; Paul Copan, *When God Goes to Starbucks: A Guide to Everyday Apologetics* (Grand Rapids: Baker, 2008), 77–118. See also Thomas E. Schmidt, *Straight and Narrow? Compassion and Clarity in the Homosexuality Debate* (Downers Grove, IL: InterVarsity, 1995); Robert A. J. Gagnon, *The Bible and Homosexual Practice: Texts and Hermeneutics* (Nashville: Abingdon, 2001) — the most thorough biblical study of homosexuality.

18. Alan Shlemon, "Homosexuality: Know the Truth and Speak It with Compassion," in *Apologetics for a New Generation: A Biblical and Culturally Relevant Approach to Talking about God*, ed. Sean McDowell (Eugene, OR: Harvest House, 2009).

Chapter 13: Recovering God's Design for Sex

1. Andy Stanley, *The Best Question Ever* (Sisters, OR: Multnomah, 2004), 107–8.
2. Jennifer Roback Morse, *Smart Sex: Finding Life-Long Love in a Hook-Up World* (Dallas: Spence, 2005), 61.
3. Dennis P. Hollinger, *The Meaning of Sex: Christian Ethics and the Moral Life* (Grand Rapids: Baker, 2009).
4. Ibid., 111.
5. For more extensive documentation and explanation, see Joe S. McIlhaney Jr. and Freda McKissic Bush, *Hooked: New Science on How Casual Sex Is Affecting Our Children* (Chicago: Northfield, 2008), 81–91.
6. "Oxytocin: Don't Sniff It If You Want to Hang On to Your Money" *The Medical News*, June 2005, www.news-medical.net/news/2005/06/01/10597.aspx (accessed January 15, 2010).
7. The neurochemical that helps men bond to their spouses and their children is vasopressin. It has not been studied as extensively as oxytocin in women.
8. McIlhaney and Bush, *Hooked*, 35–41.
9. Ibid., 38.
10. Ibid., 105.
11. Covenant Eyes, www.covenanteyes.com (accessed November 29, 2010).
12. Cited in William M. Struthers, *Wired for Intimacy: How Pornography Hijacks the Male Brain* (Downers Grove, IL.: InterVarsity, 2009), 20.
13. Naomi Wolf, "The Porn Myth," http://nymag.com/nymetro/news/trends/n_9437/ (accessed June 1, 2010).
14. Struthers, *Wired for Intimacy*, 85.
15. Ibid., 106.
16. Dallas Willard, "Beyond Pornography: Spiritual Formation Studied in a Particular Case," www.dwillard.org/articles/artview.asp?artID=133 (accessed June 1, 2010).
17. There is a time and a place to talk about this important issue. See my discussion in chapter 16.
18. Alan Chambers, *God's Grace and the Homosexual Next Door* (Eugene, OR: Harvest House, 2006), 17–18.
19. Ibid., 32.
20. If people aren't born gay, what causes homosexuality? Here are just some of the possible environmental or developmental factors that may contribute but that will look different for each individual:

    - experiences, choices, reactions, and the moral cultural climate
    - childhood trauma (for example, loneliness following divorce)
    - sexual experimentation/behavior with same sex
    - sexual abuse or molestation
    - persecution from same-sex peer group
    - poor relationship with father/mother
    - passive, detached father
    - controlling, interfering mother
    - stiflingly close relationship to an opposite-sex parent

    See Stanton L. Jones and Mark A. Yarhouse, *Homosexuality: The Use of Scientific Research in the Church's Moral Debate* (Downers Grove, Ill.: InterVarsity, 2000),

47–92. Regarding the question of whether it is possible for homosexuals to change, see Stanton L. Jones and Mark A. Yarhouse, *Ex-Gays? A Longitudinal Study of Religiously Mediated Change in Sexual Orientation* (Downers Grove, Ill.: InterVarsity, 2007). For a concise summary of both of these issues, see Paul Copan, *When God Goes to Starbucks: A Guide to Everyday Apologetics* (Grand Rapids: Baker, 2008), 94–107. For the most comprehensive and helpful resource addressing these and other questions, see Joe Dallas and Nancy Heche, *The Complete Christian Guide to Understanding Homosexuality: A Biblical and Compassionate Response to Same-Sex Attraction* (Eugene, OR: Harvest House, 2010).

21. Dallas and Heche, *Guide to Understanding Homosexuality*, 193.

22. Quoted in Dr. Warren Throckmorton, "Homosexuality Caused by Failure to Bond with Same-Sex Parent?", www.opposingviews.com/i/homosexuality-caused-by-failure-to-bond-with-same-sex-parent, accessed November 29, 2010.

23. I am indebted to Andy Stanley for his writing and practical teaching on this subject. See Stanley, *The Best Question Ever*, 107–40.

Chapter 14: Engaging Our Media-Saturated Universe

1. George Barna, "Media Exposure, Addiction," www.georgebarna.com/2010/01/media-exposure-addiction (accessed July 9, 2010).

2. Ibid.

3. Claudia Wallis, "genM: The Multitasking Generation," *Time*, March 27, 2006, www.time.com/time/magazine/article/0,9171,1174696,00.html (accessed July 9, 2010); see Amanda Lenhart et al., "Social Media and Young Adults," www.pewinternet.org/Reports/2010/Social-Media-and-Young-Adults.aspx (accessed July 9, 2010).

4. "The Net's effect on our intellectual lives will not be measured simply by average IQ scores. What the Net does is shift the emphasis of our intelligence, away from what might be called a meditative or contemplative intelligence and more toward what might be called a utilitarian intelligence. The price of zipping among lots of bits of information is a loss of depth in our thinking" (Nicholas Carr, quoted in Janna Quitney Anderson and Lee Rainie, "Does Google Make Us Stupid?", http://pewresearch.org/pubs/1499/google-does-it-make-us-stupid-experts-stakeholders-mostly-say-no [accessed July 9, 2010]; see Carr's article, "Is Google Making Us Stupid?", *The Atlantic*, July/August 2008, www.theatlantic.com/magazine/archive/2008/07/is-google-making-us-stupid/6868 [accessed July 9, 2010]).

5. Shane Hipps, *Flickering Pixels: How Technology Shapes Your Faith* (Grand Rapids: Zondervan, 2009), 42–43.

6. Ibid., 26.

7. See Barna, "Media Exposure, Addiction," www.georgebarna.com/2010/01/media-exposure-addiction (accessed July 9, 2010).

8. Ibid.

9. Dick Staub, *The Culturally Savvy Christian: A Manifesto for Deepening Faith and Enriching Popular Culture in an Age of Christianity-Lite* (San Francisco: Jossey-Bass, 2007), 8.

10. John Ortberg, *The Life You've Always Wanted: Spiritual Disciplines for Ordinary People* (Grand Rapids: Zondervan, 2002).

11. Dallas Willard, *The Divine Conspiracy: Rediscovering Our Hidden Life in God* (San Francisco: HarperSanFrancisco, 1997), 305.

12. See "Mass Mingling," http://trendwatching.com/trends/massmingling (accessed July 9, 2010).

13. See Don Tapscott, *Grown Up Digital: How the Net Generation Is Changing Your World* (New York: McGraw-Hill, 2009).

14. Check out Net Nanny (www.netnanny.com), Bsecure (www.bsecure.com), and Covenant Eyes (www.covenanteyes.com). Monitor and limit screen time.

15. For more on this, see the excellent books by psychologists Henry Cloud and John Townsend, *Boundaries with Teens: When to Say Yes, How to Say No* (Grand Rapids: Zondervan, 2006); *Boundaries with Kids: How Healthy Choices Grow Healthy Children* (Grand Rapids: Zondervan, 2001); see also Family Life, www.familylife.com.

16. Brian Godawa, *Hollywood Worldviews: Watching Films with Wisdom and Discernment* (Downers Grove, IL: InterVarsity, 2009), 28–29.

17. Being entertained is not necessarily a bad thing. It isn't wrong to have some fun and blow off some steam, to enjoy life and temporary pleasures (Ecclesiastes 8:15). But if they are all we live for, that is a problem.

18. With gratitude to John Stonestreet, I share his three-step method that he teaches students at Summit's outstanding worldview camps (visit www.summit.org).

19. For an in-depth review, see Brian Godawa's excellent article "Avatar: A Postmodern Pagan Myth," in *Christian Research Journal* (www.equip.org). I draw on some of his insights here. Also, see Patrick Zukeran, "Avatar and the Longing for Eden," a review by Probe Ministries, www.probe.org/site/c.fdKEIMNsEoG/b.6094815/k.2270/Avatar_and_the_Longing_for_Eden.htm?tr=y&auid=6589634 (accessed July 9, 2010).

20. See Todd Hertz, "Avatar," *Christianity Today*, www.christianitytoday.com/ct/movies/reviews/2009/avatar.html?start=2, accessed July 9, 2010.

21. See the helpful discussion in Staub, *The Culturally Savvy Christian*, 151–57.

22. See the full list of what the Bible includes in these areas in Brian Godawa, *Hollywood Worldviews: Watching Films with Wisdom and Discernment* (Downers Grove, IL: InterVarsity, 2009), 32–59.

23. Ibid., 49–57.

24. Staub, *The Culturally Savvy Christian*, 154.

25. Philip Graham Ryken, *Art for God's Sake: A Call to Recover the Arts* (Phillipsburg, NJ: P&R, 2006), 14.

26. Ibid., 11–15.

27. Stuart McAllister, "What Is Good and Who Says?", www.rzim.org/resources/read/asliceofinfinity/todaysslice.aspx?aid=8707 (accessed May 20, 2011).

28. Ryken, *Art for God's Sake*, 12.

29. Terry Mattingly, "Veggies Attack the Funny Gap," http://listserv.virtueonline.org/pipermail/virtueonline_listserv.virtueonline.org/2002-October/004218.html (accessed July 9, 2010); see Nancy Pearcey, *Total Truth: Liberating Christianity from Its Cultural Captivity* (Wheaton, IL: Crossway, 2004), 36–37.

30. Ryken, *Art for God's Sake*, 18.

31. Our worship pastor developed the idea of Living Room Sessions, creating an environment where this kind of creative expression can take place in a missional context in people's homes.

32. Steve Turner, *Imagine: A Vision for Christians in the Arts* (Downers Grove, IL: InterVarsity, 2001), 117.

33. Staub, *The Culturally Savvy Christian*, 156.

Chapter 15: Good News about Injustice

1. Steve Corbett and Brian Fikkert, *When Helping Hurts: How to Alleviate Poverty without Hurting the Poor — and Yourself* (Chicago: Moody Press, 2009), 33.

2. J. P. Moreland, *The God Question: An Invitation to a Life of Meaning* (Eugene, OR: Harvest House, 2009), 163.

3. Darrell Bock, *Recovering the Real Lost Gospel: Reclaiming the Gospel as Good News* (Nashville: Broadman, 2010), 17.

4. Darrell Bock, "The Politics of the People of God," *Christianity Today*, September 2005, www.christianitytoday.com/ct/2005/september/28.85.html (accessed May 20, 2011). For an excellent development of the kingdom of God *now* and *not yet*, see Darrell L. Bock, *Jesus According to Scripture: Restoring the Portrait from the Gospels* (Grand Rapids: Baker, 2002), 565–93.

5. "Great Commission Statistics," www.joshuaproject.net/great-commission-statistics.php (accessed June 5, 2010).

6. Ronald J. Sider, *Good News and Good Works: A Theology for the Whole Gospel* (Grand Rapids: Baker, 1999), 163.

7. For a wonderful summary, see Alvin J. Schmidt, *How Christianity Changed the World* (Grand Rapids: Zondervan, 2004).

8. Manhattan Declaration: A Call of Christian Conscience," http://manhattandeclaration.org/the-declaration/read.aspx (accessed June 7, 2010).

9. Francis A. Schaeffer, *True Spirituality: How to Live for Jesus Moment by Moment*, 30th anniv. ed. (Wheaton, IL: Tyndale House, 2001), 158.

10. Visit our church's website (www.fbcrc.org) for further links and information.

11. Austin Hill and Scott B. Rae, *The Virtues of Capitalism: A Moral Case for Free Markets* (Chicago: Northfield, 2010), 11.

12. Ibid., 36.

13. Jay W. Richards, *Money, Greed, and God: Why Capitalism Is the Solution and Not the Problem* (New York: Harper One, 2009), 74.

14. This discussion (with quotes) is taken from Corbett and Fikkert, *When Helping Hurts*, 103–5.

15. Ibid.

16. Ibid.

17. Ibid.

18. Ibid.

19. Ibid.

20. Sider, *Good News and Good Works*, 179.

21. When you encounter the vast literature on evil, two *intellectual* problems of evil emerge: (1) it is *logically contradictory* for the Christian God and evil to coexist, and (2) given the magnitude, duration, and intensity of evil in the world, it is *highly improbable* that God exists. It is now widely regarded among professional philosophers that the idea of God and evil are not *logically* incompatible (for example, like saying that "square circles" exist). This is largely due to Alvin Plantinga's famous Free Will Defense. All that is needed is a *possible* morally sufficient reason that God allows evil:

    A world containing creatures who are significantly free (and freely perform more good than evil actions) is more valuable, all else being equal, than a world containing no free creatures at all. Now God can create free creatures, but He can't *cause* or *determine* them to do only what is right. For if He does so, then they aren't significantly free after all; they do not do what is right freely. To create creatures capable of moral good, therefore, He must create creatures capable of moral evil; and He can't give these creatures the freedom to perform evil and at the same time prevent them from doing so. As it turned out, sadly enough, some of the free creatures God created went wrong in the exercise of their freedom; this is the source of moral evil. The fact that free creatures sometimes go wrong, however, counts neither against God's omnipotence nor against His goodness; for He could have forestalled the occurrence of moral evil only by removing the possibility of moral good." (Alvin Plantinga, *God, Freedom, and Evil* [Grand Rapids: Eerdmans, 1977], 30)

But maybe the issue is the amount and intensity of evil in the world making it *improbable* that God exists. This objection deals formally with probability theory. We must remember that whenever the probability of an event is calculated, it is always done relative to a certain amount of background information. Christians can admit that God's existence might be improbable *if only the evidence from evil is factored into the equation*. But if other evidence is factored in as well, then this second intellectual objection fails. As philosopher of religion William Lane Craig makes clear:

"[The Christian] will insist that we consider, not just the evil in the world, but all the evidence relevant to God's existence, including the ontological argument for a maximally great being, the cosmological argument for a Creator of the universe, the teleological argument for an intelligent Designer of the cosmos, the noölogical argument for an ultimate Mind, the axiological argument for an ultimate, personally embodied Good, as well as evidence concerning the person of Christ, the historicity of the resurrection, the existence of miracles, plus existential and religious experience. When we take into account the full scope of evidence, the existence of God becomes quite probable ... Indeed, if he includes the self-authenticating witness of the Holy Spirit as part of his total warrant, then he can rightly assert that he knows that God exists, even if he has no solution to the problem of evil." (William Lane Craig, *Hard Questions, Real Answers* [Wheaton, IL: Crossway, 2003], 112)

As to the extent of evil in our world, humans are simply in no position to judge how much would be necessary were we to know God's reasons for allowing it. This is not a cop-out, just an honest assessment of our limited cognitive abilities and historical perspective. Given that God is infinitely wiser than humans, we would expect his reasons for allowing evil to be beyond our grasp. For more, see my chapter in Sean McDowell and Jonathan Morrow, *Is God Just a Human Invention?* (Grand Rapids: Kregel, 2010).

22. C. S. Lewis, *The Problem of Pain* (New York: HarperCollins, 2001), 91.

Chapter 16: Christianity and the Public Square

1. "Ron Reagan Jr. Calls for Increased Stem Cell Research," www.grg.org/RReaganJr. htm (accessed June 8, 2010).

2. For a discussion of civil disobedience and what it means in our society, see the Manhattan Declaration, http://manhattandeclaration.org/the-declaration/read.aspx (accessed June 8, 2010).

3. Francis Beckwith, *Politics for Christians: Statecraft as Soulcraft* (Downers Grove, Ill.: InterVarsity, 2010), 74.

4. Quoted in Sarah Pulliam Bailey, "Faithfully and Politically Present," *Christianity Today*, November 2010, www.christianitytoday.com/ct/2010/november/5.37.html (accessed November 29, 2010).

5. J. Budziszewski, *How to Stay Christian in College* (Colorado Springs: NavPress, 2004), 116.

6. For more on the story of this slogan, see Beckwith, *Politics for Christians*, 94–98.

7. Ibid., 63–67.

8. Michael Bauman, "Legislating Morality," in *To Everyone an Answer: A Case for the Christian Worldview*, eds. Francis J. Beckwith, William Lane Craig, and J. P. Moreland (Downers Grove, IL: InterVarsity, 2004), 254–55. For a fuller treatment, see Norman L. Geisler and Frank Turek, *Legislating Morality: Is It Wise? Is It Legal? Is It Possible?* (Eugene, OR: Wipf and Stock, 2003).

9. For more on the basis and application of natural law, see J. Budziszewski, *The Line through the Heart: Natural Law as Fact, Theory, and Sign of Contradiction* (Wilmington, DE: ISI, 2009).

10. Beckwith, *Politics for Christians*, 125.

11. Clarke D. Forsythe, *Politics for the Greatest Good: The Case for Prudence in the Public Square* (Downers Grove, IL: InterVarsity, 2009), 17.

12. Ibid.

13 Ibid.

14. Ibid.

15. Stephen Monsma and Mark Rodgers, "Practical Issues in Concrete Political Engagement," in *Toward an Evangelical Public Policy: Political Strategies for the Health of the Nation*, ed. Ronald J. Sider and Diane Knippers (Grand Rapids: Baker, 2005), 333.

16. Os Guinness, *The Case for Civility: And Why Our Future Depends on It* (New York: HarperOne, 2008).

17. Ibid., 135–37. For more on this topic, see Brendan Sweetman, *Why Politics Needs Religion: The Place of Religious Arguments in the Public Square* (Downers Grove, IL: InterVarsity, 2006).

18. Hunter Baker, *The End of Secularism* (Wheaton, IL: Crossway, 2009), 194. For an argument against the three primary reasons given for a secular public square, see Beckwith, *Politics for Christians*, 119–43.

19. Flanagan summarizes: "On every single significant outcome related to short-term well-being and long-term success, children from intact, two-parent families outperform those from single-parent households. Longevity, drug abuse, school performance and dropout rates, teen pregnancy, criminal behavior and incarceration—if you can measure it, a sociologist has; and in all cases, the kids living with both parents drastically outperform the others" (Caitlin Flanagan, "Is There Hope for the American Marriage?", *Time*, July 2, 2009, www.time.com/time/nation/article/0,8599,1908243–2,00.html (accessed November 29, 2010).

20. Ibid.

21. I am indebted to Jennifer Roback Morse of the Ruth Institute for helping me gain understanding about this topic. The audio of her outstanding lecture "The Institution Formerly Known as Marriage" can be accessed at http://ruthinstitute.libsyn.com/index.php?post_id=614311. Especially helpful, too, is Alan Shlemon, "Extreme Home Makeover: How Same-Sex Marriage Affects Our Families and Our Futures"; CD/MP3 available at www.str.org.

22. This is the normative vision. There will always be legitimate and understandable exceptions, but they are still exceptions. This does not imply second-class citizenship or devalue other extenuating circumstances. The point is to recognize a normative principle for the good of society as a whole.

23. See Shlemon, "Extreme Home Makeover."

24. See Benjamin Scafidi, "The Taxpayer Costs of Divorce and Unwed Childbearing," www.marriagedebate.com/pdf/ec_div.pdf (accessed June 11, 2010).

25. David Popenoe, *Life without Father: Compelling New Evidence That Fatherhood and Marriage are Indispensable for the Good of Children and Society* (New York: Free Press, 1996), 197.

26. Bill Maier, "Same-Sex Marriage," in Joe Dallas and Nancy Heche, *The Complete Christian Guide to Understanding Homosexuality: A Biblical and Compassionate Response to Same-Sex Attraction* (Eugene, OR: Harvest House, 2010), 373.

27. Michael W. Goheen and Craig G. Bartholomew, *Living at the Crossroads: An Introduction to Christian Worldview* (Grand Rapids: Baker, 2008), 121.

28. Scott James, "Many Successful Gay Marriages Share an Open Secret," *New York Times,* January 28, 2010, www.nytimes.com/2010/01/29/us/29sfmetro.html (accessed June 11, 2010).

29. See Mollie Ziegler Hemingway, "Same Sex, Different Marriage," *Christianity Today,* May 2010, www.christianitytoday.com/ct/2010/may/11.52.html (accessed June 11, 2010).

30. See Shlemon, "Extreme Home Makeover."

31. See Jennifer Roback Morse, "More Disputed Lesbian Custody Cases, www.ruthblog.org/2010/05/24/more-disputed-lesbian-custody-cases (accessed July 15, 2010).

Chapter 17: Questions of Faith and Science

1. Christopher Hitchens, *God Is Not Great: How Religion Poisons Everything* (New York: Twelve, 2007), 282.

2. See, for example, John C. Lennox, *God's Undertaker: Has Science Buried God?* updated ed. (Oxford: Lion, 2009), 23–26.

3. Quoted in John Lennox, "Challenges from Science," in *Beyond Opinion: Living the Faith We Defend*, ed. Ravi Zacharias (Nashville: Nelson, 2007), 110.

4. Quoted in J. P. Moreland, *Christianity and the Nature of Science: A Philosophical Explanation* (Grand Rapids: Baker, 1989), 59.

5. Stephen C. Meyer, *Signature in the Cell: DNA and the Evidence for Intelligent Design* (New York: HarperOne, 2009), 402.

6. Quoted in James Franklin, *What Science Knows: And How It Knows It* (New York: Encounter, 2009), 243.

7. Dinesh D'Souza, *Life after Death: The Evidence* (Washington, D.C.: Regnery, 2009), 221.

8. John C. Lennox, *God's Undertaker: Has Science Buried God?* (Oxford: Lion, 2007), 176–77.

9. Richard Lewontin, "Billions and Billions of Demons," *The New York Review of Books*, January 9, 1997, http://www.drjbloom.com/Public%20files/Lewontin_Review.htm (accessed May 20, 2011).

10. Richard Dawkins, *The God Delusion* (New York: Houghton Mifflin, 2008), 35 (emphasis in original).

11. Quoted in R. Albert Mohler, "The New Atheism," http://richarddawkins.net/articles/369-the-new-atheism (accessed January 24, 2011).

12. For a helpful exploration of miracles, see C. John Collins, *The God of Miracles: An Exegetical Examination of God's Action in the World* (Wheaton, IL: Crossway, 2000); R. Douglas Geivett and Gary R. Habermas, *In Defense of Miracles: A Comprehensive Case for God's Action in History* (Downers Grove, IL: InterVarsity, 1997).

13. I explore this evidence in my book *Is God Just a Human Invention?*

14. He is not so much a Christian as a Deist.

15. Antony Flew and Roy Abraham Varghese, *There Is a God: How the World's Most Notorious Atheist Changed His Mind* (San Francisco: HarperOne, 2007), 88.

16. Ibid., 89.

17. "More on Anthony Flew's Conversion to Theism," http://theconstructivecurmudgeon.blogspot.com/2007/11/more-on-anthony-flews-conversion-to.html (accessed May 20, 2011).

18. Richard Dawkins, *The Blind Watchmaker: Why the Evidence of Evolution Reveals a World Without Design* (New York: Norton, 1986).

19. See William A. Dembski and Jonathan Wells, *The Design of Life: Discovering Signs of Intelligence in Biological Systems* (Dallas: Foundation for Thought and Ethics, 2008).

20. See the interview with Sean McDowell in chapter 9.

21. William A. Dembski, *The Design Revolution: Answering the Toughest Questions About Intelligent Design* (Downers Grove, IL: InterVarsity, 2004), 45.

22. Jerry Coyne, *Why Evolution Is True* (New York: Viking, 2009), 1.

23. Dawkins, *The Blind Watchmaker*, 1.

24. Richard Dawkins, *The Greatest Show on Earth: The Evidence for Evolution* (New York: Free Press, 2009), 216.

25. For more on those who advocate forms of theistic evolution, go to www.biologos.com; for critiques of this approach, go to www.faithandevolution.com.

26. Nicholas Wade, "Life's Origins Get Murkier and Messier; Genetic Analysis Yields Intimations of a Primordial Commune," *New York Times*, June 13, 2000, www.nytimes.com/2000/06/13/science/life-s-origins-get-murkier-messier-genetic-analysis-yields-intimations.html?pagewanted=all (accessed October 20, 2010).

27. For more on this evidence, see Stephen C. Meyer, *Signature in the Cell: DNA and the Evidence for Intelligent Design/Darwin's Dilemma*, book and DVD set (San Francisco: HarperOne, 2009; La Habra, CA: Illustra Media, 2009).

28. Ray Bohlin, "Limits to Evolvability," in William A. Dembski and Mike Licona, *Evidence for God: 50 Arguments for Faith from the Bible, History, Philosophy, and Science* (Grand Rapids: Baker, 2010), 86–87.

29. Ibid.

30. See Michael J. Behe, *The Edge of Evolution: The Search for the Limits of Darwinism* (New York: Free Press, 2007). For more on the powerful objection that Darwinian evolution is not able to account for the existence of irreducibly complex organisms and systems (for example, the bacterial flagellum), see Michael J. Behe, *Darwin's Black Box: The Biochemical Challenge to Evolution* (New York: Simon and Schuster, 1996).

31. For more on the signers of the "Scientific Dissent from Darwinism" document, see www.dissentfromdarwin.org/faq.php (accessed December 2, 2010).

32. Karl Giberson, *Saving Darwin: How to Be a Christian and Believe in Evolution* (San Francisco: HarperOne, 2008), 8.

33. For three interpretations on the days of Genesis 1, see David G. Hagopian, ed., *The Genesis Debate: Three Views on the Days of Creation* (Mission Viejo, CA: Crux, 2001). The interpretation most compelling for me is C. John Collins, *Science and Faith: Friends or Foes?* (Wheaton, IL: Crossway, 2003; see also his *Genesis 1–4: A Linguistic, Literary, and Theological Commentary* [Phillipsburg, NJ: P&R, 2006]).

34. Jonathan Wells, *The Politically Incorrect Guide to Darwinism and Intelligent Design* (Washington, DC: Regnery, 2006), 181–94; see also his *Expelled: No Intelligence Allowed*, DVD.

35. For a young earth perspective on Genesis, see www.answersingenesis.com; for an old earth perspective, see www.reasons.org.

Chapter 18: Bioethics in the Twenty-First Century

1. See Charles W. Colson and Nigel M. de S. Cameron, *Human Dignity in the Biotech Century: A Christian Vision for Public Policy* (Downers Grove, IL.: InterVarsity, 2004). "The church must mount a massive educational ministry to help Christians understand biotechnology from a Christian perspective. That is to say, since all truth is God's truth, and since we live in a world that faces the brave new world of biotechnology, Christians have an obligation to understand how God's revelation applies to those technologies" (C. Ben Mitchell and John F. Kilner, "Remaking Humans: The New Utopians versus a Truly Human Future," http://cbhd.org/content/remaking-humans-new-utopians-versus-truly-human-future (accessed May 23, 2011).

2. *The Daily News*, December 12, 1903.

3. John Frederic Kilner and C. Ben Mitchell, *Does God Need Our Help? Cloning, Assisted Suicide, and Other Challenges in Bioethics* (Wheaton, IL: Tyndale House, 2003), xii-xiii.

4. Scott Klusendorf, *The Case for Life: Equipping Christians to Engage the Culture* (Wheaton, IL: Crossway, 2009), 19.

5. Quoted in Francis Beckwith, *Defending Life: A Moral and Legal Case against Abortion Choice* (Cambridge: Cambridge University Press, 2007), 68.

6. Beckwith, *Defending Life*, 159–60.

7. Philosophically speaking, there are two views: the *functional* view and the *essentialist* view. An increasing number of people are arguing for a functional view of personhood that seeks to distinguish a human person from a human being. An unborn child will, of course, be a human being but *not yet* a person. Personhood is determined by satisfying certain criteria such as brain activity, consciousness, the ability to reason and think, the capacity to communicate, self-awareness, and self-motivated activity. In other words, if an entity functions in a certain way, then it is a person. One of the strongest criticisms of this view is that it understands personhood as something one can have in degrees (kind of like a barometer), and thus dignity and value are degreed properties as well. On the other hand, the essentialist view maintains that "a person functions as a person *because* she *is* a person and not because she functions as a person. That is, personhood is not something that arises when certain functions are in place, but rather something that grounds these functions whether or not they are ever actualized in the life of a human being" (Francis J. Beckwith, *Abortion and the Sanctity of Human Life* [Joplin, MO: College Press, 2000], 72). Personhood is something you either have or you don't — there aren't degrees of persons. Francis Beckwith writes, "Intrinsic value is

not a matter of degree; one either has it or does not. Intrinsic value, therefore, cannot be conditioned on the level of human capability, for if one had more capability, one would have more value" (Francis J. Beckwith, "What Does It Mean to Be Human?" *Christian Research Journal* [2003]: 19. Human life is valuable at every stage no matter how small or big, how young or old. In the essentialist view, "The unborn are not potential persons, but human persons with great potential" (Beckwith, *Abortion and the Sanctity of Human Life*, 74–75). See Jonathan Morrow, *Welcome to College: A Christ-Follower's Guide for the Journey* (Grand Rapids: Kregel, 2008), 311–12.

8. Robert George and Patrick Lee, "Reason, Science, and Stem Cells: Why Killing Embryonic Human Beings Is Wrong," *National Review*, July 20, 2001, http://old. nationalreview.com/comment/comment-george072001.shtml (accessed April 18, 2010).

9. See Klusendorf, *The Case for Life*, 76.

10. For help for couples walking through infertility, see "Stepping Stones" at www. bethany.org/step; "Hannah's Prayer" at www.hannah.org.

11. Scott B. Rae, "Bioethics and the Pastor," www2.talbot.edu/faculty/sundoulos/ archive/09_spring/secondfeature/ (accessed May 23, 2011); for a fuller treatment, see Scott B. Rae, *Moral Choices: An Introduction to Ethics*, 3rd ed. (Grand Rapids: Zondervan, 2009), 155–88.

12. Ibid.

13. For embryo adoption, see www.nightlight.org/adoption-services/snowflakes-embryo/ default.aspx; for other adoption opportunities, see www.hopefororphans.org; Russell D. Moore, *Adopted for Life: The Priority of Adoption for Christian Families and Churches* (Wheaton, IL: Crossway, 2009).

14. For a compelling look at the evidence for design in DNA, see Stephen C. Meyer, *Signature in the Cell: DNA and the Evidence for Intelligent Design* (New York: HarperOne, 2009).

15. Francis S. Collins, *The Language of God: A Scientist Presents Evidence for Belief* (New York: Free Press, 2006), 263.

16. "Court Strikes Down Patents on Two Human Genes; Biotech Industry Trembles," http://blogs.discovermagazine.com/80beats/2010/03/30/court-strikes-down-patents-on-two-human-genes-biotech-industry-trembles (accessed April 21, 2010).

17. C. Ben Mitchell et al., *Biotechnology and the Human Good* (Washington, DC: Georgetown University Press, 2007), 139.

18. Ibid.

19. Ibid., 147.

Chapter 19: Stewarding God's Creation

1. Lynn Townsend White Jr., "The Historical Roots of Our Ecologic Crisis," *Science*, 155/3767 (March 10, 1967): 1203–07, www.uvm.edu/~gflomenh/ENV-NGO-PA395/articles/Lynn-White.pdf (accessed May 23, 2011).

2. Russell Moore, "The Gulf of Mexico and the Care of Creation," www.russellmoore. com/2010/05/01/the-gulf-of-mexico-and-the-care-of-creation/ (accessed May 23, 2011).

3. Scott B. Rae, *Moral Choices: An Introduction to Ethics*, 3rd ed. (Grand Rapids: Zondervan, 2009), 352.

4. Acton Institute, *Environmental Stewardship in the Judeo-Christian Tradition: Jewish,*

Catholic, and Protestant Wisdom on the Environment (Grand Rapids: Acton Institute for the Study of Religion and Liberty, 2007), 3.

5. Albert Mohler, "NewsNote: Thinking Green: The New Religion," www.albert mohler.com/2010/01/12/newsnote-thinking-green-the-new-religion (accessed July 14, 2010). For a twelve-part documentary responding from a Christian perspective to radical environmental claims, visit www.resistingthegreendragon.com.

6. *Environmental Stewardship in the Judeo-Christian Tradition*, 3.

7. Jay Wesley Richards, *Money, Greed, and God: Why Capitalism Is the Solution and Not the Problem* (New York: HarperOne, 2009), 197.

8. For a helpful list of resources, reports, and scientists on both sides of this debate, see "Getting All Hot about Global Warming," www.arn.org/blogs/index.php/3/2007/04/06/getting_all_hot_about_global_warming (accessed January 24, 2011).

9. S. Fred Singer and Dennis Avery, *Unstoppable Global Warming: Every 1500 Years* (New York: Rowman & Littlefield, 2007), vii.

10. Bjørn Lomborg, *Cool It: The Skeptical Environmentalist's Guide to Global Warming* (New York: Vintage, 2008), 110–11.

11. John Ortberg addressed it in a sermon titled "Is God Green?", www.mppc.org/series/ripple-effect/john-ortberg/god-green (accessed May 10, 2010).

12. Dan Story, "Should Christians Be Environmentalists?" *Christian Research Journal*, 33/4 (2010), 27.

Conclusion: Imagine If...

1. I haven't had space to develop this theme in this book. But I am assuming that we are all in agreement that the biblical teaching presupposes that community is vital for understanding, transformation, and engagement.

2. Os Guinness has modeled this well in our generation.

Appendix 2: Why We Think the Way We Do

1. I am indebted to J. P. Moreland for initially connecting these dots for me, first in his book and then as his student (J. P. Moreland, *Love Your God with All Your Mind: The Role of Reason in the Life of the Soul* [Colorado Springs: NavPress, 1997]; see also Mark A. Noll, *The Scandal of the Evangelical Mind* [Grand Rapids: Eerdmans, 1994]; George M. Marsden, *Fundamentalism and American Culture*, 2nd ed. [New York: Oxford University Press, 2006]; Nancy Pearcey, *Total Truth: Liberating Christianity from Its Cultural Captivity* [Wheaton, IL: Crossway, 2004], 251–323).

2. Though it has been growing since the time of William of Ockham and Thomas Aquinas. See Pearcey, *Total Truth*, 63–121.

3. J. P. Moreland, *Kingdom Triangle: Recover the Christian Mind, Renovate the Soul, Restore the Spirit's Power* (Grand Rapids: Zondervan, 2007), 41.

4. Ibid., 21–26.

5. Dick Staub, *The Culturally Savvy Christian: A Manifesto for Deepening Faith and Enriching Popular Culture in an Age of Christianity-Lite* (San Francisco: Jossey-Bass, 2007), 16.

6. Neal Gabler, *Life: The Movie: How Entertainment Conquered Reality* (New York: Knopf, 1998).

7. See Neil Postman, *Amusing Ourselves to Death: Public Discourse in the Age of Show Business*, 20th anniv. ed. (New York: Penguin, 2006).

8. See Richard A. Swenson, *In Search of Balance: Keys to a Stable Life* (Colorado Springs: NavPress, 2010).

9. David F. Wells, *No Place for Truth: Or Whatever Happened to Evangelical Theology?* (Grand Rapids: Eerdmans, 1993), 293.

ABOUT THE AUTHOR

Jonathan Morrow is the founder of www.thinkChristianly.org. He is the author of *Is God Just a Human Invention? And Seventeen Other Questions Raised by the New Atheists* (with Sean McDowell), *Welcome to College: A Christ-Follower's Guide for the Journey* and contributed the chapter "Introducing Spiritual Formation" to *Foundations of Spiritual Formation: A Community Approach to Becoming Like Christ*. Jonathan also contributed several articles to *The Apologetics Study Bible for Students*. He graduated with an MDiv and an MA in philosophy of religion and ethics from Talbot School of Theology, where he is pursuing a DMin in engaging mind and culture. Currently, Jonathan is the equipping pastor at Fellowship Bible Church in Murfreesboro, Tennessee. His book *Welcome to College* has been featured on *Family Life Today*, *Point of View* with Kerby Anderson, *Stand to Reason*, and Apologetics.com. He and his wife, Mandi, have two children. You can visit him at www.thinkChristianly.org.

Share Your Thoughts

With the Author: Your comments will be forwarded to
the author when you send them to *zauthor@zondervan.com*.

With Zondervan: Submit your review of this book
by writing to *zreview@zondervan.com*.

Free Online Resources at
www.zondervan.com

Zondervan AuthorTracker: Be notified whenever your favorite
authors publish new books, go on tour, or post an update
about what's happening in their lives at www.zondervan.com/
authortracker.

Daily Bible Verses and Devotions: Enrich your life with daily
Bible verses or devotions that help you start every morning
focused on God. Visit www.zondervan.com/newsletters.

Free Email Publications: Sign up for newsletters on Christian
living, academic resources, church ministry, fiction, children's
resources, and more. Visit www.zondervan.com/newsletters.

Zondervan Bible Search: Find and compare Bible passages in
a variety of translations at www.zondervanbiblesearch.com.

Other Benefits: Register to receive online benefits like
coupons and special offers, or to participate in research.

ZONDERVAN®

ZONDERVAN.com/
AUTHORTRACKER
follow your favorite authors